WORLD TEXTILES

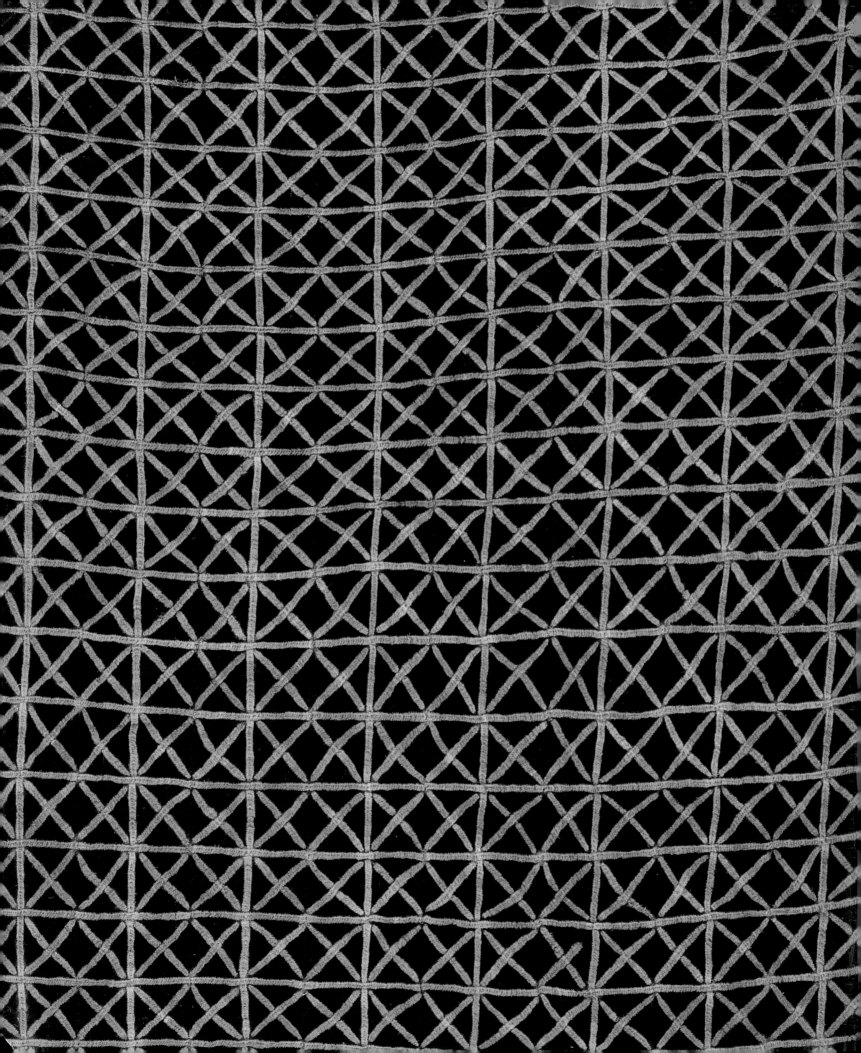

WORLD TEXTILES

A VISUAL GUIDE TO TRADITIONAL TECHNIQUES

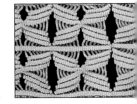

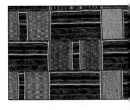

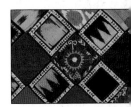

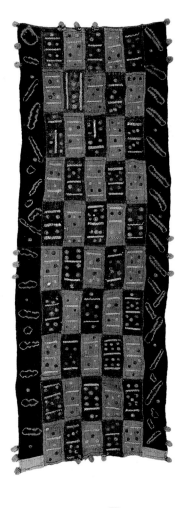

JOHN GILLOW AND BRYAN SENTANCE

WITH 778 ILLUSTRATIONS, 551 IN COLOUR

Thames & Hudson

FOR YVONNE GILLOW AND FOR POLLY

Had I the heavens' embroidered cloths
Enwrought with golden and silver light,
The blue and the dim and the dark cloths
Of night and light and the half light
I would spread the cloths under your feet:
But I, being poor, have only my dreams;
I have spread my dreams under your feet;
Tread softly because you tread on my dreams.

He Wishes for the Cloths of Heaven
W.B. Yeats

page 1, Embroidered shawl, from the Indonesian island of Sumba, worked in chain stitch; **page 2**, Indigo-dyed cloth made by the Dogon people of Mali with a pattern created by the stitched-resist technique; **page 3**, Raphia apron made by the Kuba of the Congo (formerly Zaire), employing patchwork, embroidery and stitched dye resist; **page 5**, Nineteenth-century tapestry-woven Kashmir shawl; **page 6**, **left**, Maranau woman's marriage 'malong', from Mindanao in the Philippines, with tapestry-woven silk bands; **page 6**, **top**, Black Miao girl's embroidered jacket; **page 6**, **centre**, Kano *luru* stripweave cotton blanket, Nigeria; **page 6**, **below**, Blanket, from Nagaland, India, with a central band painted with images of animals and trophy heads; **page 7**, **above**, **left**, Woman's tie and dye silk shawl from Tajikistan; **page 7**, **above**, **right**, Chauhan *rumal*, from Sind, Pakistan, sewn together from strips of cloth edged with sawtooth appliqué; **page 7**, **below**, **right**, Meghwal *choli*, from Sind, Pakistan, decorated with embroidery and mirrors.

First published in the United Kingdom in 1999 by Thames & Hudson Ltd, 181A High Holborn, London WC1V 7QX

www.thamesandhudson.com

Design by David Fordham

© 1999 Thames & Hudson Ltd, London

First paperback edition 2004

British Library Cataloguing-in-Publication Data
A catalogue record for this book is available from the British Library
ISBN 0-500-28247-1

Printed and bound in Singapore by C.S. Graphics

Man is the shuttle, to whose winding quest
And passage through these looms
God order'd motion, but ordain'd no rest.

Henry Vaughan (1622–95), *Silex Scintillans, Man*

CONTENTS

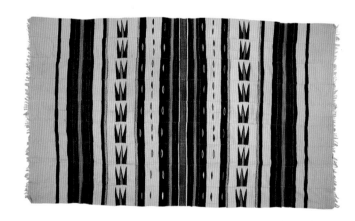

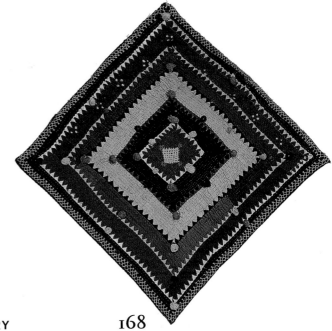

INTRODUCTION

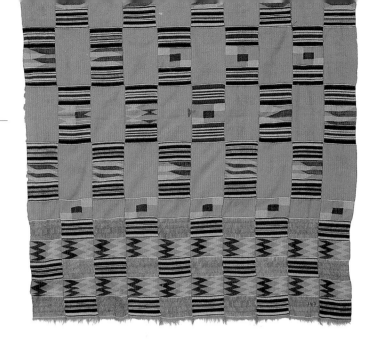

THE history of the world can be read in textiles; the rise of civilizations and the fall of empires are woven into their warp and weft along with the great adventures of conquest, religion and trade. The greatest highway ever made, the Silk Road, was not for the transportation of gold or armies, but for the trading of the most luxurious and desirable commodity of all, silk textiles.

Study of the traditional textiles of the world reveals at times an amazing diversity of techniques and styles, while at others we can only wonder at the way in which cultures separated by vast distances have developed such similar solutions to problems of design and construction. Sometimes only a limited number of solutions may be possible, but the frequency of similarities in techniques and the choice of motifs and symbols makes one wonder if this is evidence of ancient unrecorded trade routes or if it is substantiation of Jung's theory that we have a collective unconscious.

THE PURPOSE OF THIS BOOK

THERE are many valuable volumes that concentrate either on an intensive study of one specific aspect of textile construction or decoration, such as weaving, dyeing or embroidery, or are devoted to the textiles produced in one geographic region. In this book, by displaying the fabrics of many places side by side, we hope to provide a basis for comparison and thereby a greater understanding of the techniques involved and a greater awareness of the diversity of stylistic interpretation. Our main priority in the selection of illustrations has been to choose not only the most beautiful textiles from the widest possible geographical range, but also those that show the techniques most clearly.

Our rather ambitious aim has been to include as many techniques as possible, often, in the interests of space, in a generalized rather than a specific form, and to provide illustrations from as much of the world as we possibly can. Many of the textiles illustrated were collected on our own travels over the last twenty-five years, and

Opposite: This patchwork quilt from Banni Kutch in North-West India can be read like a textile compendium. Its construction involved a diverse range of techniques and it shows examples of printing, dyeing, embroidery, patchwork and appliqué.

Above: A kente cloth woven by the Ashanti of Ghana. Long strips, which have been woven by men on narrow looms, are sewn together to form a voluminous toga-like garment with a distinctive chequerboard effect.

Below: This selection of metal, plastic and wooden knitting needles demonstrates the variety of materials that have been exploited to manufacture textiles. The four needles on the left are for 'circular' knitting without a seam and the small one on the right is for knitting cables.

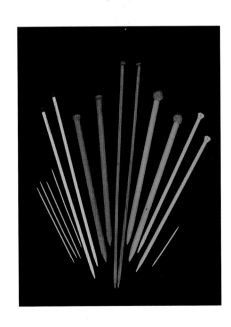

others were generously lent by travellers, collectors and enthusiasts to whom we are much indebted.

WHAT IS A TEXTILE?

THE word 'textile' comes from the Latin verb *texere*, a word which was used by the Romans to mean 'to weave', 'to braid' or 'to construct'. It is a fairly versatile word, open to interpretation, which was even used by Livy in the context of building when he wrote of '*casae ex arundine textae*' (huts built of reeds). In fact, whether it is a basket, a blanket or a wattle and daub hut, the techniques employed have much in common. Therefore, rather than confining our choice of fabrics and structures according to arbitrary, academic parameters, we have made a personal selection of what to include in this book based on our own interpretation of what is appropriate and what will bring a greater understanding of the subject as a whole.

Above, left: *Indigo-dyed textiles from the Gambia. Indigo is a unique, colourfast dye that has been in use for more than 4,000 years. The patterns have been produced by tightly sewing the cloth before dyeing which prevents the dye penetrating into the areas designated for the white patterns.*

Above, right: *'Casae ex arundine textae' (huts built of reeds). Zulus weaving a hut out of flexible branches.*

THE HISTORY OF TEXTILES

TEXTILES are made of perishable materials and only survive the millennia when preserved under exceptional circumstances such as the felts discovered buried in the permafrost of Noin Ula in Mongolia which date from around the 4th century BC, or the weavings found in the pre-Columbian tombs preserved by the dry air of the Peruvian coast. However, much has been learned from written sources and even from ancient carvings and artefacts. Egyptian tombs contain paintings of spinning and the weaving of linen while, in the *Odyssey*, the Greek poet Homer describes how Penelope, the hero's wife, evaded the attentions of her unwelcome suitors by weaving a large and delicate shroud for her father-in-law, Laertes, a scene illustrated on a 5th-century BC vase. The story of the development of textiles is therefore largely a yarn spun from deduction and conjecture rather than hard evidence. Archeological finds, though, point to a high level of skill and sophistication at an astoundingly early date.

RIGHT: PENELOPE
AT HER LOOM, FROM
A GREEK VASE, 5TH
CENTURY BC.

BELOW: AN
ANCIENT EGYPTIAN
TOMB PAINTING OF
WOMEN WEAVING
ON A SINGLE
HEDDLE LOOM.

BELOW: MEDIAEVAL
EUROPEAN PEASANT
SHEARING SHEEP,
FROM A BOOK OF
HOURS.

THE FIRST FABRICS

ONE of the most basic needs of mankind is protection from the elements. Early hunters utilized the skins of animals they had killed for food. The excavation of Neolithic sites has yielded evidence that tools were used to scrape the hides clean and that needles made from bone slivers were used to sew them together. The first prestigious garments were probably the skins of rare or dangerous animals worn by daring hunters. In many northern regions, such as amongst the Inuit of the Northern Territories of Canada, skins are still the preferred mode of dress since a satisfactory substitute for the insulation they provide against the cold and damp has never been found.

In some tropical regions, such as Fiji, Samoa and Central Africa, an alternative to leather was acquired by stripping the inner bark off certain trees and beating it until it became soft and flexible. A similar material – felt – was developed by pastoral communities who were inspired by the matted coats of sheep and goats.

As the craft of basket-making became more and more refined, it became feasible, with twining and interlacing, to employ an enormous variety of animal or plant fibres in the construction of flexible fabrics. Experimentation by succeeding generations also saw the development of techniques to make more flexible fibres and the invention of spinning which was used in different parts of the world to make yarn from wool, linen, cotton or silk.

Above: *Unyoro men, from Uganda, dressed in cloth made from the bark of ficus natalensis.*

Below, left: *Woven textiles decorated using the warp-ikat technique. Before weaving the cloth, the pattern is established by carefully tying and dyeing the warp yarn in preselected places. These examples were made in, from left to right, Bokhara, Uzbekistan; Oaxaca, Mexico; Flores, Indonesia; Aleppo, Syria; Sarawak, Malaysia.*

Below: *A Samoyed family of herdsmen from Siberia. In cold, wet weather they wear their reindeer-skin garments with the fur on the inside.*

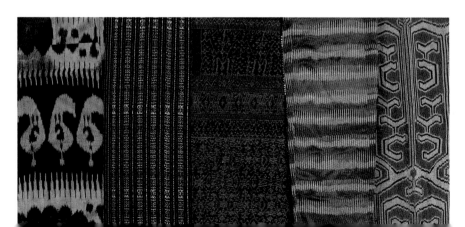

Welsh Costume   Valentines Series

The development of better-quality yarns and further experiments with their manipulation resulted in fixed structures on which warp threads could be stretched out to maintain tension, while a weft thread was painstakingly woven in and out with the fingers. The true loom was developed from this structure with the invention of the heddle, a device that made the process quicker and simpler by raising alternate warps all at once, opening a shed through which the weft could be passed.

Above, right: An old woman in traditional Welsh costume. She is using four needles to knit seamless woollen socks.

Right: A group of Aborigine men, from Australia, decorated with paint and flowers. They are about to participate in a magical ceremony to make edible snakes abundant.

Below: A shawl, from Ahmedabad, in North-West India, with a pattern printed using carved wooden blocks. The finished item has been glazed with egg-white to impart a sheen. For centuries, textiles have been produced in India specifically for export. Shawls like this are intended for the Yemeni market.

ABOVE: CLAMPED-RESIST DYED TEXTILE FROM AHMEDABAD, GUJARAT, NORTH-WEST INDIA.

THE DECORATION OF TEXTILES

THE evolution of the decoration of textiles followed several unrelated routes. One developed from the textures produced by the actual process of construction and the effect of colour variations such as stripes, bars and checks. From these humble beginnings weaving specialists ultimately explored the complexities of tapestry, brocades and supplementary warp or weft patterning.

Another route, that of decoration applied to the surface of a piece of finished cloth, was probably developed from body painting and tattooing, initially employing the same pigments and dyes, and eventually achieved the sophistication of batik, ikat and multi-coloured printing.

From the experience of tailoring cloth, patching and mending it, and the need to use every available scrap of material, the sewing skills required for the making of appliqué, quilting and patchwork were developed, while the decorative possibilities of the stitches themselves led to the refined art of embroidery.

Above: *A Pueblo Indian wearing a Navaho tapestry-woven blanket. The tribes of the south-west were the only North American peoples to develop the use of the true loom. With the introduction of sheep's wool towards the end of the 16th century, blanket weaving became an art form. The most famous exponents are the Navaho.*

Above, right: *An exquisite 19th-century ivory fan from Belgium. A painted central panel floats on an intricate ground depicting landscapes and flowers worked in Brussels needlepoint lace. Both needlepoint and bobbin lace were made in Brussels, often with parts of the process performed by different women under the aegis of a master.*

SPINNING A YARN

THROUGH the history of textiles run tales of magic, romance and industrial espionage. The very act of telling a story is known as 'spinning a yarn'.

The gods themselves are the greatest exponents of the textile arts. Athene, goddess of wisdom, was challenged to a weaving competition by the conceited Arachne. The latter, of course, lost and for her presumption was turned into a spider to spin and weave forever. In Scandinavia parents told their children that the stars we now know as Orion's belt represented the distaff with which Frigga, the wife of Odin, spun the clouds.

Penelope is not the only heroine whose fate was ravelled up in her textile skills. Vassilisa the Beautiful, a Russian peasant girl, eventually married the Tsar who was impressed by her needlework, and many a princess or lazy girl has needed the assistance of a goblin or spirit such as Tom Tit Tot or Rumplestiltskin to weave prodigious quantities of yarn or even straw into gold.

As for industrial espionage, the secret of silk, so one story tells, was smuggled out of China by a princess who hid silkworms in her elaborate coiffure, while the arcane knowledge of Flemish weavers was stolen in the 14th century by an English cat burglar who climbed on the roof of a weaving shed in Bruges.

TRADITIONAL TEXTILES

THE availability of a particular material has led to localized specialization in specific techniques. When this is combined with the dictates of social values and the influence of climate and lifestyle, a community's textiles develop distinctive traditional characteristics. A cut-pile raphia cloth from the Congo (formerly Zaire) bears little resemblance to a silk brocade sari from Benares, India, but each epitomises the culture that has produced it. Tradition is not static. It is a living thing that evolves gradually with all the influences on a community – contact with outsiders, prosperity or hardship,

WOMAN SPINNING, CHINESE STONE CARVING FROM THE HAN DYNASTY.

Left: *A bolster cover from Swat-Kohistan, Pakistan. Dense patterns are typically embroidered in satin stitch or darning stitch using red silk floss thread on a background of black cotton. Pre-Islamic motifs such as the Tree of Life and solar discs are still in use.*

Below, left: *A Spanish woman wearing a heavily fringed* manton de Manila *embroidered with flowers.*

Right: *Magigabow, a Seminole Indian from Florida. He is wearing a blanket decorated with distinctive appliqué built up in superimposed layers like the* molas *of the Kuna of Panama. By 1910, this technique had been supplanted by machined patchwork.*

climatic change. Within a community, rural or urban, a sense of identity and belonging is marked by the clothes that people wear and the textiles they make. Tradition does not exert a stranglehold, but provides a foundation on which a fertile imagination may build. Within this framework the opportunity to display one's wealth or status through the use of expensive materials such as silk and metal thread, or the construction of outfits requiring time-consuming weaving or embroidery such as the 'eight knives' robes commissioned by Yoruba men in Nigeria exists. As does the chance to show one's marital status, which is the case in the Andes where unmarried men advertise their availability to potential wives through the patterns knitted into their caps. All over the world a major part of a girl's youth has traditionally been spent sewing a trousseau or dowry for her bottom drawer in preparation for the day she begins a new life in her own home as a married woman.

In many places, whatever the religious inclination, garments are embellished with magical designs to protect the wearer from evil spirits and accidents or to attract good luck and the protection of supernatural powers.

Much time and expense is lavished on textiles for no better reason than vanity and the love of beauty. The most sublime outlet for innovation must surely be the clothing lovingly embroidered by devoted mothers for their children such as the sparkling mirrorwork jackets embroidered by women in Gujarat, India, and Sind, Pakistan.

It could be argued that the manufacture of traditional objects by hand gives a very real sense of identity and belonging, something so often lacking in the depersonalized world of mass-production. Communities grow and change. Tradition and textiles evolve. It is only when a way of life ceases to be viable and a community dies that tradition dies out. There have been many instances in the past of attempts to subjugate cultural groups by banning their traditional dress. Such was the case after the defeat of the Jacobite army at Culloden, Scotland, in 1746 when an Act of Parliament was passed banning the wearing of tartan on pain of transportation for seven years. At the beginning of the 20th century Kemal Atatürk, the first President of modern Turkey, banned the wearing of the fez as part of his plan to drag Turkey into the modern world. During the Cultural Revolution (1966–68) the Chinese government banned the wearing of traditional costume by ethnic minorities such as the Tibetans. However, even today, many communities around the world retain their traditional costume as a living symbol of their cultural identity.

CONCLUSION

THESEUS, escaping from the Labyrinth, followed the route he had marked with a ball of yarn. In the interest of clarity, on this journey through the textile maze, we have chosen to follow a sequence which we hope will give a comprehensive outline of each technique described and will generally lead on to a greater understanding of the technique that follows.

We have tried to select textiles that represent living cultures and that are still individually made using methods that have been employed for generations. Traditional textiles are a statement of identity that say, 'This is where I am from. This is what I do. This is who I am!'

Above: *A Caucasian peasant woman wearing a traditional costume of a skirt, blouse and apron enhanced with embroidery and pulled-thread work.*

Below: *A* toran, *door hanging, from Gujarat in India. The opulent encrustation of sequins and couched gold-thread embroidery is typical of the Indian love of glitter and glamour.*

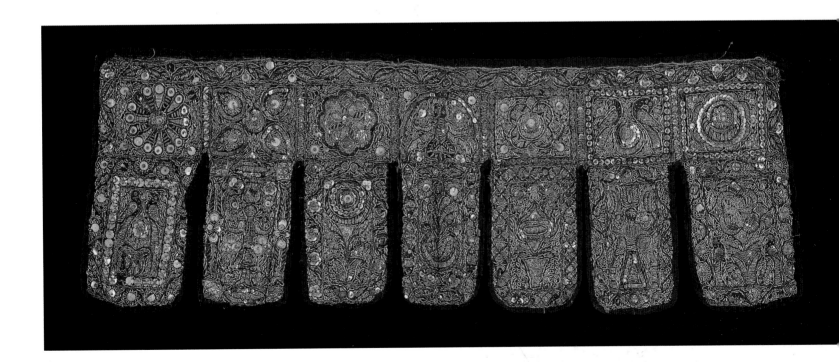

MATERIALS

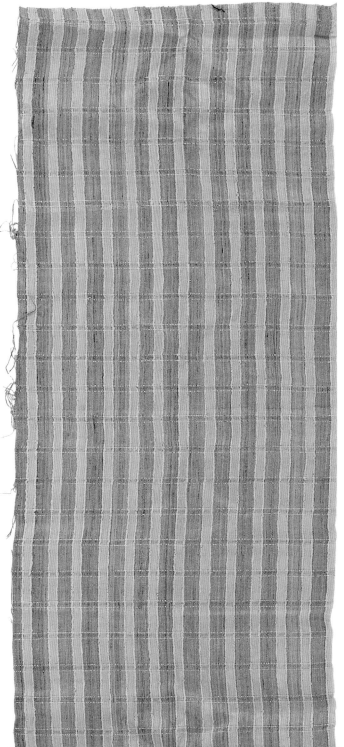

FAR LEFT: PYGMY
BARK CLOTH FROM
THE CONGO
(FORMERLY ZAIRE).

NEAR LEFT: TUSSAR,
WILD SILK, YARDAGE
FROM MADHYA
PRADESH, INDIA.

BELOW: KUBA RAPHIA
CLOTH FROM THE
CONGO (FORMERLY
ZAIRE).

MATERIALS

THE Earth has so many diverse regions, such climatic, topographic and biological variety that many different materials have been exploited and methods have evolved to process them. Different regions are home to different flora and fauna, sheep require grazing, silk worms need warmth, raphia palms only thrive in the tropics. For millennia the only materials that could be utilized were those that were locally available and specialized expertise was developed in the exploitation of specific resources. Over the centuries the evolution of the global market and the establishment of trade routes have made the same materials available at a price to everyone who inhabits this planet.

LUXURY

MATERIALS that are not easily obtained, because they are difficult to grow or must be acquired through trade, become desirable as a sign of wealth and status. Specialized, often city based, 'luxury' crafts have evolved to process these materials, frequently to a high level of sophistication.

Above: *Two Basque women, from the French Pyrenees, winding wool into a ball in preparation for knitting. Leaning against the woman on the left is a distaff used in spinning.*

Left: *An Iban woman, from Sarawak, Malaysia, using a cotton gin. The fluffy bolls of the cotton plant are crushed between the rollers of the gin, as though being squeezed in a mangle. As the cotton fibres are pulled out, seeds, burrs and impurities are extracted.*

Left: *Indian cotton workers. The large bows are held above a pile of cotton and struck with a mallet. The vibrations cause the cotton fibres to separate and fluff up.*

Right: *The cultivation of flax was once a major industry in Eastern Europe. Here, a Latvian peasant is at work breaking down the woody stems so that the linen fibres can be extracted.*

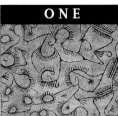

Right: *A Samoan woman preparing* tapa *cloth. Once the bark of the paper mulberry tree has been beaten out into a sheet resembling a tough, papery felt it is decorated with the juices of tropical plants.*

RELIGION

R ELIGION has been another powerful influence on the use of certain materials. In Hindu and Buddhist cultures the orthodox shun the use of leather and other by-products of the slaughter of animals, while Muslim men are traditionally forbidden to wear silk next to their skin. Paradoxically, this led to the invention of *mashru*, a silk textile woven in satin weave with a cotton weft, that lies next to the skin. *Mashru* means 'permitted' in Arabic.

The other side of the coin is that religious ceremony, particularly in the Christian church, has always been enhanced with fine embroidery and expensive materials. For all the major creeds, workshops, specializing in many of the textile crafts, have grown up to supply the market.

MODERN MATERIALS

I NDUSTRIALIZATION and new technology have led to the development of many cheap synthetic materials which have often supplemented or replaced natural fibres. Although 'synthetic' and 'traditional' are not harmonious terms, in many places man-made fibres have been adopted enthusiastically into folk textiles. In West Africa the Yoruba of Nigeria have created dazzling effects by weaving lurex into their cloth and in Pakistan it is possible to find embroidered blouses of which the main feature is couched cellophane.

Left: *Peasants, from the Czech Republic, extracting bast fibres from hemp stalks after the First World War.*

Above: *Weaving on a vertical loom in Cameroon, using fibres extracted from the fronds of the raphia palm.*

19

SKIN AND HIDE

SINCE prehistoric times the skins of small animals and the hides of large ones have provided a tough, but flexible, material suitable for making clothes and a wide range of useful equipment.

Rawhide

A FRESH skin begins to rot very quickly and must be cured by drying or salting, all the flesh having first been scraped away. This produces a strong, but inflexible, material called rawhide. When wet, rawhide can be bent and moulded and then it becomes stiff and hard when left to dry. The Plains Indians of North America, who pursued a nomadic lifestyle largely dependant on the herds of buffalo, used rawhide to make large envelopes or parfleches for transporting food and belongings, and as shields for battle and frames for saddles.

LEFT: AN ELITE AZTEC WARRIOR DRESSED IN JAGUAR SKINS, FROM THE CODEX MENDOZA.

Above: *A dyed and painted leather bag or bolster cover with patterns and colouring typical of Moroccan leatherwork.*

Far left: *This large sheet of leather was used to cover a camel's load, from Sind in Pakistan. It is decorated with leather appliqué and embroidery in thick thread.*

Below: *A pair of brain-tanned leather gauntlets embroidered with cut-glass beads, made around 1900 by Native Americans of the Plateau region.*

Leather

To produce the flexible and versatile material we call leather, a longer process called tanning is necessary. After the flesh and hair have been scraped away and the curing completed, the skin or hide is either smoked, rubbed with animal or fish oils, or immersed in a solution of vegetable matter or chemicals. In much of the world this is traditionally carried out in pits. Some solutions, such as that of oak bark, require immersion for as long as a year. Finally, the leather is rinsed, dried and oiled to make it waterproof.

Above: *A Ruthenian woman, from the Western Ukraine, wearing traditional costume. The large sheepskin waistcoat is embellished with embroidery and leather appliqué.*

Right: *A Hungarian sheepskin coat with punched leather appliqué. Sheepskin garments can still be seen in many rural areas of Eastern Europe where they have been a feature of costume since time immemorial.*

Above: *A sheepskin waistcoat with floral embroidery, from the Carpathian Mountains of the Ukraine. Similar waistcoats are also worn in the mountainous regions of Afghanistan.*

Uses

LEATHER may be dyed, tooled, cut, moulded or stitched to provide a wide range of strong, hard-wearing items including shoes, belts, bags and protective clothing. For centuries, the leather work of Morocco, using hide transported across the Sahara from Sokoto in Nigeria, has been particularly admired for its quality, suppleness and craftsmanship.

Right: *Nahraminyeri, a Ngarrindjeri woman, from South Australia, wearing a possum-skin cloak with a pouch for her child, 1880.*

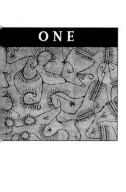

Left: *Lamo, a cheerful, but ragged, boy, from Leh in Ladakh, Northern India, wearing a woollen goncha. This is typical of the traditional costume worn by inhabitants of the Himalayas who are of Tibetan stock.*

Above: *A wool kilim, from Uzbekistan, made using mainly natural-coloured wool. The patterns have been created with a combination of soumak weaving and embroidery, also in wool. The distinctive hooked-wave motifs are often referred to as 'running dog'.*

WOOL AND HAIR

THE hairy coats of many wild animals provided our ancestors with fibres that could be manipulated in a number of ways to create textiles. Clothes made of wool were worn in Sumeria at least 4,000 years ago. In most parts of the world one species, or sometimes more, has been domesticated and bred selectively to produce high-quality wool or hair – for instance, sheep and goats in Europe, Africa and Asia, camels in Central Asia, and alpaca and vicuña in South America. The Salish people of the American North-West coast even kept packs of small, white-haired dogs, probably Pomeranians, for their wool. The most widely reared animal is the sheep and the finest wool is cashmere, which is actually made from the soft chest hairs of Himalayan goats.

Above: A sleeveless pullover knitted by a man from Hazarajat, Afghanistan.

The properties of wool and hair

ANIMALS have hair or fleece to create an insulating layer to conserve their body heat and to repel rain. Woollen textiles retain these properties and are therefore greatly valued in cold regions. Wool also keeps heat out and is widely used by desert peoples for tents and clothing. Each individual hair is covered in tiny scales which not only repel moisture, but also cause the fibres to mat together, giving greater strength and density. These scales impart a lustrous appearance. Natural oils, such as lanolin, are secreted from glands near the hair follicles. Clothing made up without losing this greasiness remains to some extent waterproof and is very practical for sailors and fishermen. The pullovers of the Aran Islands, off the West coast of Ireland, and Guernsey, one of the Channel Islands, retain a distinctive oily smell.

Finally, wool has a wavy quality called crimp which causes the fibres to wrap around each other during spinning, thus making a stronger yarn. The springiness of the crimp also means that woollen clothes keep their shape well.

Above: Natural-coloured wool products from Bolivia. On a sheep and vicuña wool poncho lie two double-weave sheep's wool belts, an alpaca hat and a sheep and alpaca wool money pouch.

Left: A shepherd's woollen coat, from the mountainous Chitral valley of North Pakistan, embroidered with multi-coloured wool. In the cold hills and mountains of the world, wool is not only the material most readily available, but it also provides the best protection against the elements.

ABOVE: SUMERIAN RULER WEARING A SKIRT OF TUFTED WOOL, 2600 BC.

FELT

Aʟᴛʜᴏᴜɢʜ the oldest known felt textiles, those discovered at the Scythian burial site of Pazyryk in Siberia, can only be dated to about 500 BC, it seems likely that felt was the first wool fabric used by mankind. Wool felts unaided – the scaly surface of the fibres ensures that damp wool quickly becomes matted and irreversibly tangled even while still on an animal's back. In spring, wild sheep moult and shed lumps of matted fleece. For our ancestors to have observed this and then to have tried to induce the effect artificially would have been but a small innovative step.

A felt bag, folded like an envelope, with wool tassels and patterns of cloth appliqué, from North Afghanistan.

Opposite, above: *A woman's apron, from Guizhou in China, made of felted silk filaments.*

Below: *A felt rug or* numdah *from Kirghizia. The pattern was laid out with dyed wool fibres before the rolling process.*

Opposite, inset: *Felt cloaks on the plains of Anatolia have been made in the same way for the last 3,000 years.*

Traditional felt making

IN Central Asia, where felt making has an ancient history, felt has been made in the same way for many generations. The sheep are washed in a river and shorn and the resulting fleece is then beaten with sticks to remove grit and burrs – spiny seed heads or any unwanted particles of vegetable matter. To separate the fibres further, the wool may then be combed or carded and if coloured felt is required, the wool may be dyed at this point. Next, the wool is spread evenly on a reed mat that has been sprinkled with soapy water and then the wool is sprinkled with hot water, rolled up inside the reed mat and tied up into a bundle. This is rolled backwards and forwards for several hours, usually under the forearms of a group of kneeling women. The result, when the bundle has been unwrapped and dried, is a densely intermeshed fabric that can be cut, stitched or moulded.

Uses

FELT, in a variety of thicknesses, is used in Europe, Asia, North Africa and South America in the construction of warm boots, hats, coats, bags, rugs and coverings for the tents, yurts or gers in which they live.

Below: *A donkey-cart cover, from Kashgaria in Chinese Turkestan, where such items are regarded as cheap and disposable. The dynamic, geometric pattern has been achieved using two different colours of natural, undyed wool.*

WOOLLEN YARN

To convert wool fibres into a form that can be manipulated more easily they must be spun into yarn. First the wool needs to be carded or combed to remove impurities, disentangle the fibres and align them in one direction.

Carding

THE Romans are credited with the invention of carding. By mounting the prickly heads of teasels on a wooden cross called a *carduus* (Latin for thistle) they were able to brush or tease the fibres into alignment. This eventually evolved into a pair of wooden blocks with rows of bent wire teeth set into a leather pad on each surface. A small amount of wool is carefully stroked between them until all the fibres are parallel. It is then removed and gathered into a loose bundle, called a rolag, ready for spinning.

Combing

BY combing wool from a longer-haired sheep with long-tined combs, longer, better-separated fibres are produced that are used to weave smooth-surfaced worsted cloth.

ABOVE: ENGLISH WOMAN AT HER SPINNING WHEEL, MID-17TH CENTURY.

Left: *A herdsman's blanket woven in Rajasthan, India, from locally produced yarn. The main ground is of undyed yarn with a pattern of supplementary weft weaving. Because Rajasthan is mostly desert, it can become extremely cold at night and a blanket is essential.*

Right: *Woollen hand-loom woven cloth, from Lhasa, Tibet, used for edging men's garments. After weaving, the cloth is decorated with rows of crosses, traditionally achieved by pressing the bunched up cloth through a wide-gauge wooden sieve into dye vats or alternatively by block printing.*

Opposite, near left: *A hand-knitted Fair Isle hat, from the Scottish Shetland Islands, with the popular 'snowflake' motif, worked in typically pale-coloured wool.*

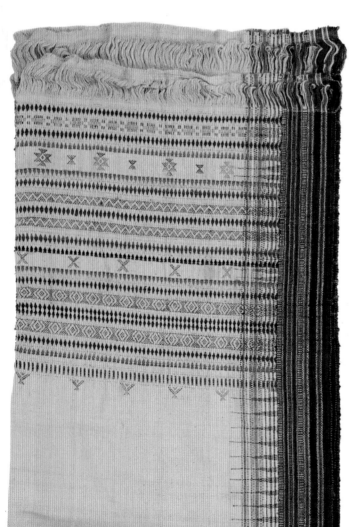

Spinning

THE simplest way to twist wool into strands is to roll it between the fingers, but a spindle is employed to achieve greater uniformity and length. The spindle is basically a stick with a weight, or whorl, at the bottom. Fibres are drawn out from the rolag, which is sometimes attached to a distaff, and fastened to the top of the spindle which is then set spinning either freely suspended in the air or with its tip on the ground. The spinning twists the fibres together into yarn. As the spun yarn gets longer it is wound around the spindle and more fibres are drawn out from the rolag. A spindle spun clockwise will produce a Z twist and spun anti-clockwise it will produce an S twist. The spinning wheel is merely a more mechanized method of achieving a consistent yarn.

Uses

As yarn, wool can easily be knotted, twined or interlaced into a diverse range of warm, flexible textiles suitable for everyday wear in cooler climates such as Northern Europe and the high altitudes of the Andes or the Atlas Mountains of North Africa.

Above: *A Romanian man at Sighetu market, with a woollen cape draped over his shoulder.*

Near right: *A chullo, from Puno in Peru, knitted in a pleasing combination of dyed and naturally coloured wools.*

Far right: *A Bolivian chullo with intricately patterned bands depicting animals and birds. Many Bolivian knitters are illiterate and mistakes often occur in the lettering.*

COTTON

COTTON is obtained from the hairy fibres surrounding the seed-head of a semi-tropical plant of the genus *Gossypium*. It can be spun into a strong, fine thread or yarn that is ideal for even weaving and so has become one of the most popular and widely used of all textile materials, although garments made from it are most suitable for warmer climates. The oldest known cotton yarn was produced in Mohenjo-Daro in Pakistan 3,000 years ago.

Processing cotton

WHEN the fluffy cotton seed-heads or bolls open they are plucked and ginned. Ginning is the removal of the seeds by rolling the bolls under an iron or wooden rod or by squeezing them through a special mangle called a cotton gin. Then the fibres are untangled and fluffed up into a loose mass by beating them with sticks or by plucking the string of a bow against them. Finally, the mass is gathered into a rolag and spun, with spindle or wheel, into yarn or thread.

Uses

BECAUSE of its strength, smoothness and fineness, cotton is excellent for making densely woven, hard-wearing rugs and cloth. Calico, for example, is a sturdy, unbleached cotton fabric named after Calicut, a town on the Indian Malabar coast, where it was originally woven. On the other hand, this strength and fineness facilitate the weaving of delicate, loosely woven fabrics such as muslin which originally came from Mosul in Iraq.

Above: *A cotton flag from Ghana. The banners of the Fante men's societies are decorated with appliqué pictures that convey allegorical messages.*

Below: *A huilpil,* woman's poncho, from Chiapas in Mexico, woven from undyed, naturally coloured cotton yarn with patterns of birds and flowers.

Opposite: *A Yoruba indigo-dyed cotton cloth. Machine stitching has been used to resist the dye and make the pattern.*

Opposite, inset: *Two small Buddhist monks, from Myanmar (Burma), dressed in cotton robes dyed with saffron or turmeric.*

RIGHT: WEAVING COTTON IN PERU, FROM A POT OF THE MOCHE PERIOD (AD 300–500).

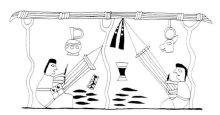

Below: *A 'hunting cloth', from Herat in Western Afghanistan, embroidered on a cotton ground with cotton thread.*

SILK

For generations, the secrets of silk manufacture, shrouded in myth and mystery, were known only to the Chinese. The desire for this most fabulous of fabrics led to the establishment of the greatest trade route the world has ever known – the Silk Road – which stretched from Lanzhou in China to Rome in Italy, where silk togas cost their weight in gold. Legends tell how in the 6th century AD two monks smuggled the cocoons of a few silk worms to Byzantium in hollowed-out walking sticks and so brought the knowledge of sericulture, the rearing of silk worms, to the West.

Sericulture

THE finest silk is made by the caterpillar of the silk moth, *Bombyx mori*, which only feeds on the leaves of the white mulberry tree, *Morus alba*. As it is a delicate creature, sensitive to noise and draughts, it is impossible to rear on a large scale and so a cottage industry grew up which carefully nurtures the greedy grubs until they reach three to four inches long and spin themselves a cocoon. The cocoon is dried in the sun to kill the pupa inside before it can become a moth and damage the filament by eating its way out.

Reeling silk thread

REELING silk is a specialist's job. The cocoons are thrown into a cauldron of boiling water to soften the gum that binds the filaments together. With great care several filaments at a time are reeled onto a bobbin to make one long, smooth thread. The more filaments that are wound together, the thicker the thread will be and therefore the heavier the cloth woven from it. The finest shawls are woven from thread made by reeling together the filaments of only four cocoons.

Floss silk and embroidery threads are spun using damaged and inferior filaments. Wild silk is collected in China, Eastern India and Africa from the cocoons of uncultivated *Antheraea* moths, but it yields a coarser thread. The Ashanti people of Ghana, among others, acquire their silk threads by unravelling silk textiles imported from Europe.

Uses

SILK is highly prized as the raw material of luxury fabrics since it is soft and has a beautiful sheen. It is easy to dye, has surprisingly good insulating properties and is strong enough to have been used in the manufacture of parachutes.

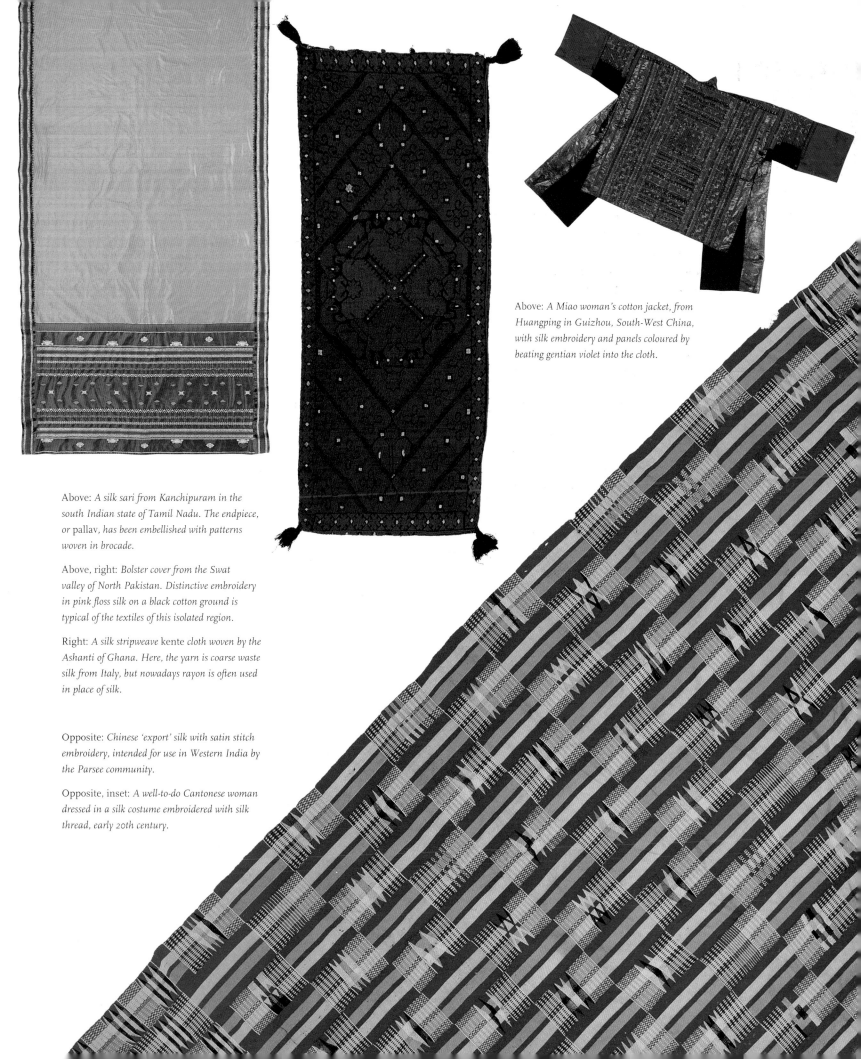

Above: *A Miao woman's cotton jacket, from Huangping in Guizhou, South-West China, with silk embroidery and panels coloured by beating gentian violet into the cloth.*

Above: A silk sari from Kanchipuram in the south Indian state of Tamil Nadu. The endpiece, or pallav, *has been embellished with patterns woven in brocade.*

Above, right: *Bolster cover from the Swat valley of North Pakistan. Distinctive embroidery in pink floss silk on a black cotton ground is typical of the textiles of this isolated region.*

Right: *A silk stripweave* kente *cloth woven by the Ashanti of Ghana. Here, the yarn is coarse waste silk from Italy, but nowadays rayon is often used in place of silk.*

Opposite: *Chinese 'export' silk with satin stitch embroidery, intended for use in Western India by the Parsee community.*

Opposite, inset: *A well-to-do Cantonese woman dressed in a silk costume embroidered with silk thread, early 20th century.*

BARK

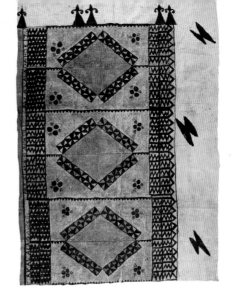

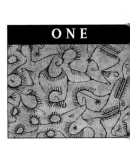

Oₙ ᴇ of the oldest methods of obtaining clothing without weaving cloth on a loom was to make it from the inner bark of certain trees. This method was fairly widespread, and is still found in well-wooded areas in Africa, South-East Asia and Polynesia.

Bark cloth

Iɴ Indonesia and Polynesia the inner bark of the paper mulberry tree, *Broussonetia papyrifera*, is used to make cloth, while in Central Africa the preferred source is a species of fig tree, *Ficus natalensis*. In Central Africa a sheet of bark is removed from the tree, steamed to soften it and then placed over a log and beaten with grooved wooden mallets until the fibres become felted together. The fibres lie longitudinally and beating causes the fabric to stretch widthways, resulting in a large sheet of cloth.

In Tonga *tapa* cloth is made by stripping a whole sapling of its outer bark, soaking it in sea-water for about two weeks and then stripping off the inner bark. This is cut into thin strips which are then beaten against a flattened log with a hardwood beater. This process felts the bark, giving it strength and flexibility, and more than doubles its width. The strips are then pasted together with arrowroot to form a very large cloth and painted or stencilled with the sap of certain trees, which stains them black or brown.

The bark of the fig tree oxidizes to the rich reddish brown typical of African bark cloth, while the *tapa* cloth made from the paper mulberry remains off white.

Bark fibre

Oɴ the American North-West coast the Tlingit and Kwakiutl wove blankets from the shredded bark of the red cedar. The Ainu of Hokkaido, Japan, traditionally wear garments woven from the thin bark of the atsui tree or of elm-bark fibre.

Uses

Bₐʀᴋ cloth was once common day-to-day wear, but its use has largely been superseded by cotton except for ritual and ceremonial use. In Fiji the creamy ground of *tapa* cloth is stencilled with bold floral and geometric shapes in brown and black.

Above, right: A large tapa *cloth, from Tonga, more than three metres long. As mulberry bark does not stretch much, large sheets are made by joining strips together with arrowroot paste.*

Right: Painted bark cloth from Astrolabe Bay, Papua New Guinea.

Below: The Kuba people of the Congo (formerly Zaire) use raphia textiles for everyday use, but prefer bark cloth for ceremonial use. This wrap-around apron is made of bark cloth with an embroidered raphia edging.

Opposite: A large tapa *cloth from Fiji. The geometric stencilling has been applied so densely that the pattern appears to be in cream on brown rather than vice versa.*

Opposite, insets, from top to bottom: *Basu Fondong, King of Cameroon in the 1920s, wearing bark cloth strikingly decorated with hand-painted flowers; a Samoan girl wearing* tapa *cloth with a typical bold, monochrome pattern; an Ainu couple, from North Japan, dressed in garments made of woven elm-bark fibre.*

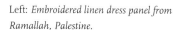

LINEN

BAST fibres are obtained from the stalks of certain dicotyledonous plants. The supreme example of a bast fibre is linen, which is made from the stems of the flax plant, *Linum usitatissimum*. A shirt-like garment (*c.* 2800 BC) from the Egyptian Early Dynastic period is the oldest surviving specimen of linen cloth.

Linum usitatissimum

ABOVE: *LINUM USITATISSIMUM*, THE FLAX PLANT.

Left: *Embroidered linen dress panel from Ramallah, Palestine.*

Below: *Turkish linen towel with silk embroidery.*

Processing flax

FIRST the seeds are removed by rippling or pulling the stems through a coarse comb. The stems are soaked in water so that the bast fibres can be separated easily from the woody parts. This is called retting. Then the stems are broken by beating or crushing them in a hinged wooden device called a brake. Finally, the stems are tapped and stroked to free the bast fibres from the unwanted woody portions and combed through a hackle with iron teeth. The end product is a fine fibre that can be spun into tough thread or yarn.

Uses

SINCE Ancient Egyptian times linen cloth has been used for making fine-quality clothing worn by the wealthy or by the general populace on special occasions. It is a popular base for needlework and to this day, although cotton has replaced it for daily use, beautifully embroidered linen shirts and blouses are the preferred costume for weddings in Eastern Europe. The terms 'bed linen' and 'table linen' are still in common usage, although most sheets and tablecloths are now made from cheaper materials.

Above: *Greek linen coverlet with cross-stitch embroidery around the border. The warps and wefts of linen cloth are easy to count which makes it an ideal base for counted-thread embroidery.*

Right: *A long linen chemise, from the Balkans, with counted-thread embroidery in wool yarn on the sleeves and hems. Red, the colour of life, is the most widely used colour in Eastern European embroidery.*

Below: *A Norwegian girl, from Hardanger, wearing a skaut, the traditional linen headgear of a married woman.*

Right: *The sleeve of a Bulgarian linen blouse embroidered with cotton and silk thread.*

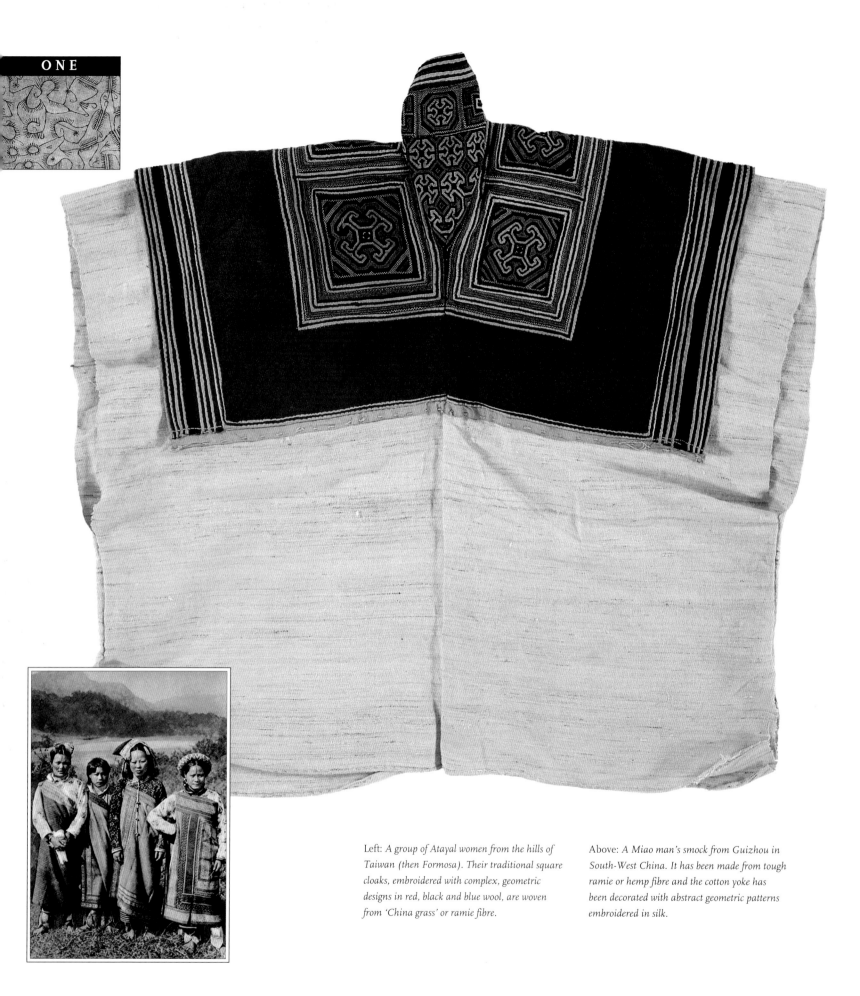

Left: *A group of Atayal women from the hills of Taiwan (then Formosa). Their traditional square cloaks, embroidered with complex, geometric designs in red, black and blue wool, are woven from 'China grass' or ramie fibre.*

Above: *A Miao man's smock from Guizhou in South-West China. It has been made from tough ramie or hemp fibre and the cotton yoke has been decorated with abstract geometric patterns embroidered in silk.*

OTHER BAST FIBRES

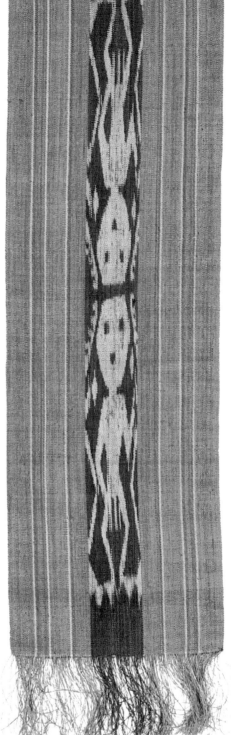

Many other plants are prepared in much the same way as linen, although the bast fibres they yield are generally much coarser and more suitable for finger weaving than loom weaving.

In West Africa a large number of plants of the genus *Hibiscus* are used, notably *Urena lobata* and *Sida rhombifolia*. In Borneo the lemba plant, *Curculigo latifolia*, which grows wild, is harvested for its fibres. The Indian province of West Bengal has an economy largely based on the processing of jute, *Corchorus capsularis* and *C. olitorius*. Various members of the nettle family, genus *Urticaceae*, have been exploited in Asia and North America including ramie, *Boehmeria nivea*, a native of China and the East Indies.

The milkweed, genus *Asclepia*, was widely used by the indigenous peoples of North America. The plant most extensively cultivated for its bast fibres must be hemp, *Cannabis indica*, which has been grown in Asia, Europe, Africa and North America.

Similar fibres

In the Philippines the abaca palm, *Musa textilis*, a small banana-like plant, provides tough, silky fibres used in the weaving of warp ikat.

Uses

Most bast fibres are used in the manufacture of matting, netting, rope and string. Strong bags, belts and burden straps constructed from bast twine are also widespread. Canvas woven from hemp and linen is a tough material that can be made up into bags, tarpaulins, tents, sailcloth and work clothes. Hemp-woven skirts are much valued in South-East Asia as they keep their pleats much longer than skirts made of cotton.

Above, left: *A Mandaya mantle, from Mindanao in the Philippines, made from abaca fibre dyed and woven using the warp-ikat technique.*

Above, centre: *A warp-ikat* selendang, *from Kalimantan, Indonesia, woven from wild-orchid fibres.*

Above, right: *A galla covers the back of the neck of Banjara women in India. It is embroidered with bast fibres.*

RAPHIA AND LEAF FIBRES

RAPHIA, or raffia, is a grassy fibre extracted from the leaves of a palm tree, *Raphia ruffia* or *R. taedigera*, that grows extensively round the fringes of the tropical forests of Central and West Africa and on the island of Madagascar. The mature leaves can grow as long as fifty feet (15.25 metres), but only the young leaflets are used.

Preparing raphia

THE leaflets are cut from the palm before they reach six feet (1.8 metres) in length. The soft tissues of the underside of the leaf are stripped away with the edge of a knife or peeled off by hand to leave behind the upper epidermis. These translucent fibres are tied in hanks and dried in the sun. Finally, each fibre is split lengthways with the fingers, a comb or a snail shell to produce a silky strand three to four feet (90 cm–120 cm) long.

Uses of raphia

RAPHIA is most familiar in Europe and North America as a grassy string used by gardeners, but in fact it is used to make some silky, even luxurious, textiles. Most raphia textiles, like those of the Congo (formerly Zaire) and the Côte d'Ivoire, are smaller than four feet by three feet (120 cm x 90 cm) as their size is limited by the length of a raphia strand, although dance skirts are made by sewing several woven

pieces into a long strip. The Kuba of the Kasai River area of the Congo (formerly Zaire) make distinctive velvety textiles using embroidery and cut pile. In Madagascar raphia fibres are twisted together to make a yarn long enough to weave on a loom, while in Nigeria lengths are sometimes simply knotted together.

Other leaf fibres

ON the Tanimbar Islands, warp-ikat cloths are woven from fibres obtained from the lontar palm, *Borassus fiabelliformis*, and in other parts of Indonesia threads are obtained from *Sago* and *Pandanus* palms. In the south-west region of North America the fibres of the yucca, *Yucca aloifolia*, were once used in the making of sandals and baskets, while another New World plant, *Agave sisalana*, was introduced to the Canary Islands by the Spanish for the manufacture of sisal and its use has since spread to many other tropical parts of the world.

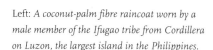

Left: *A coconut-palm fibre raincoat worn by a male member of the Ifugao tribe from Cordillera on Luzon, the largest island in the Philippines.*

Right: *A patchwork and appliqué raphia-fibre dance skirt made by the Kuba of the Congo (formerly Zaire). The most common motif in Kuba craftwork is comma-shaped, known as* shina mboa, *the tail of a dog.*

Opposite: *Kuba raphia textiles. The base cloth is woven by men and the embroidery, also in raphia, is executed by women.*

Opposite, inset above: *A Portuguese farmer protected from the rain by a raincoat made of grass.*

Opposite, inset below: *Chinese coolies wearing rice-straw raincoats.*

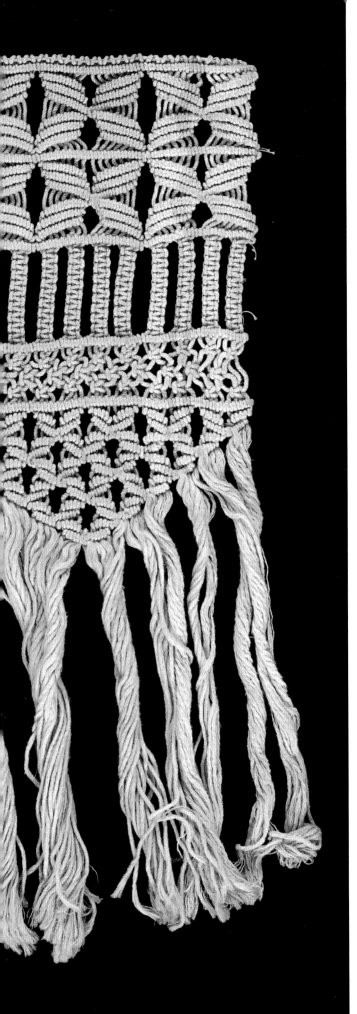

NON-LOOM TEXTILES

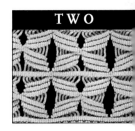
LEFT: ENGLISH 19TH-CENTURY COTTON MACRAMÉ.

BELOW: HAMMOCK OF INTERLINKED COTTON WARPS FROM MERIDA IN MEXICO (DETAIL).

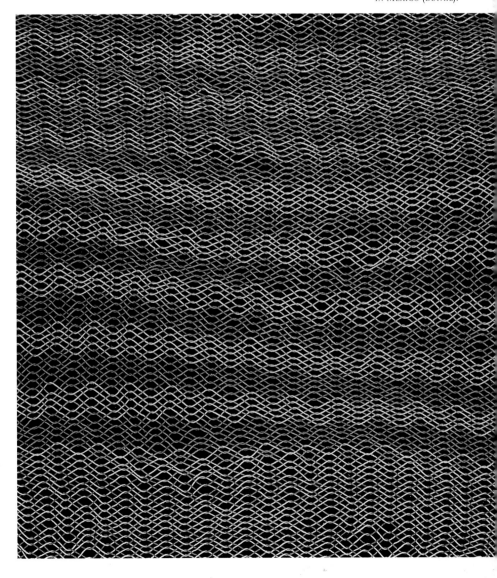

NON-LOOM TEXTILES

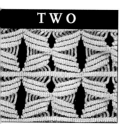

THE first textiles fabricated by mankind were made by manipulating fibres with the fingers. It has been suggested that the craft of basketry was invented by primitive man and that the techniques developed were then applied to constructing other fabrics. A number of techniques were developed that involved looping, knotting, interlacing or twining strands together. The major difference between early baskets and textiles was not so much in the techniques, but in the choice of materials. The more resilient and flexible a fibre used, the more supple the fabric constructed from it. Some of the methods that evolved are so effective that in parts of the world, such as central and eastern North America, the loom was never devised and even with the introduction of the true loom by colonists the techniques of working only with the fingers were not replaced.

PORTABILITY

WITH non-loom textiles the very fact that a bulky loom is not required and that equipment is minimal means that work in progress is often portable and easy to pick up at any convenient moment. This is, of course, of prime importance to those who do not have a sedentary lifestyle or who are unable to devote prolonged periods to a single task. The supreme example of a portable technique is knitting, a craft that is practised by men and women all over the world and is today one of the most common of all domestic textile crafts. On the Scottish islands of the Outer Hebrides there are still experts who are able to knit with one hand, while attending to their domestic

Above: *A young Breton knitter, from Finistère, France, wearing a lace cap.*

Above: *An English fisherman, from East Anglia, wearing a knitted pullover while mending his nets.*

Right: *Making bobbin lace in the streets of Burano near Venice in Italy.*

Right: *Amazonian Indians weaving baskets. Many techniques are common to both basketry and textile construction.*

Below: *French shepherd. Knitting can be carried out anywhere.*

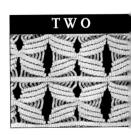

chores, nursing the baby or stirring the supper, with the other. In the days of whaling and global exploration, sailors, away from home for months or even years at a stretch, spent a considerable amount of time knitting themselves articles of clothing or knotting lengths of twine into useful articles.

FRAMES

To maintain their structure and regular shape many textiles, such as crochet, only need to be held firmly by the fingers, but others need to be attached to a fixed point or stretched on some form of frame, as is necessary in sprang. These simple devices are rudimentary relatives of the loom.

WARP AND WEFT

Most techniques that do not need a loom require only one set of elements – they are either weft-based like netting, knitting and crochet, or warp-based like sprang, macramé and braiding.

Right: *A Tongan woman making an apron from crocheted twine.*

Far right: *Ishwar Singh from Jaisalmer in Rajasthan, Western India – a great exponent of ply-split work – making a camel girth out of goat hair.*

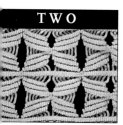

A NET is a structure built up horizontally by connecting each row of weft to the previous one. The connection may be linked, knotted or looped, but has the appearance of being structured on the diagonal. All textiles made like this have a fair degree of elasticity.

Technique

THE foundation of most netted fabrics is a horizontal thread or cord attached at either end to some sort of frame. A manageable length of yarn is then wound onto a shuttle or bobbin and loosely attached to the foundation cord in a series of loops. On reaching the edge, the yarn is worked back in the opposite direction, looping through the previous row and creating a new set of loops on to which the following row is attached. For a flexible structure the yarn is simply passed through the loops, but if a stronger fabric, such as that required for fishing, is being manufactured then the yarn may be attached to the previous row with a suitable knot like a sheet bend.

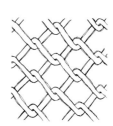

LINKED BAG FROM MEXICO.

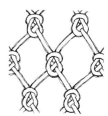

FISHING NET.

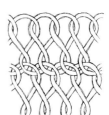

LOOPED BAG FROM ECUADOR.

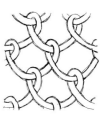

BILLUM FROM NEW GUINEA.

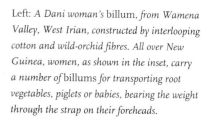

Left: *A Dani woman's* billum, *from Wamena Valley, West Irian, constructed by interlooping cotton and wild-orchid fibres. All over New Guinea, women, as shown in the inset, carry a number of* billums *for transporting root vegetables, piglets or babies, bearing the weight through the strap on their foreheads.*

There are many variations on this basic principle. The density and strength of a looped or netted structure may be greatly reinforced by linking several rows together at the same time, introducing extra horizontal elements, crossing the yarn in a figure of eight or simply pulling the work tighter.

Uses

The most obvious application of this technique is the manufacture of nets for fishing and storage or for use as hammocks. When the fibres or threads are worked tightly, strong, yet flexible, bags can be constructed. Such bags can be found all over the world, often incorporating fibres of several colours to build up decoration. Among the most interesting examples are the *billums* of New Guinea which are constructed in hourglass or figure-of-eight looping using a needle threaded with *Pandanus* fibre.

Above, left and centre: *Two bags, or* shigra, *from Ecuador, made by tightly looping yarn spun from fibres obtained from the cabuya plant.*

Above, right: *A general purpose bag, used by the Hani tribe of Yunnan in China, made from hemp fibres with a structure of interconnected looping.*

Right: *The embroidered border at the end of a Russian towel, embellished with a simple netted fringe and enhanced with beads threaded onto the yarn.*

Right: *Details of woollen socks, from North Afghanistan, with interlooped tops. They are intended to be worn inside riding boots at* bozkashi *contests, a form of free-for-all polo where a headless calf is used instead of a ball.*

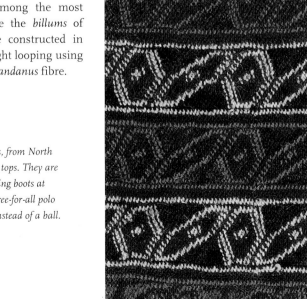

CROCHET

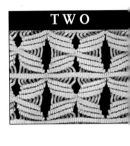

ᴄ ROCHET, which derives its name from the French for 'hook', is a doubly interlooped structure worked with a hook made of wood, metal, bone or plastic. As it is a simple technique requiring only a hook and yarn, crochet work can easily be carried around and worked on at any convenient moment.

Technique

ᴛʜᴇ foundation of every piece of crochet is a chain. First a slip loop is tied and then a loop is pulled through this with the hook. A succession of loops are then worked through each other, one at a time, until the chain has reached the required length. To build a crocheted fabric subsequent rows are added by working a new sequence of loops, each one of which is hooked through the previous loop and also through the previous row.

Variations on the basic stitch involve increasing the number of loops carried on the hook or linked together at the same time.

Uses

ᴄ ROCHET, usually worked in wool, cotton or silk, lends itself easily to the making of open work, and such is the variety of stitches and their possible applications that the number of different articles that can be crocheted is almost limitless. As crochet is such a simple, but versatile, technique and work in progress is so easily transported, it has been adopted by the inhabitants of many lands and adapted to local materials and requirements.

Below: *Tablecloths with crocheted borders made in England before the First World War.*

Opposite: *A selection of crocheted items, including a pair of socks, from Dubrovnik in the Former Yugoslavia; an English 'miser's purse' dating from the late 19th or early 20th century; and a pair of gloves from the Hunza Valley in Pakistan.*

Above: *A Spanish señorita wrapped in a crocheted woollen shawl.*

Below: *A tough bag with a narrow neck manufactured from crocheted cotton yarn in Kutch, North-West India.*

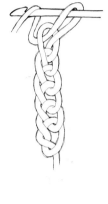

KNITTING

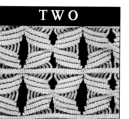

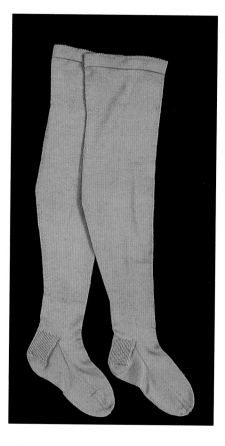

KNITTING is a technique where an interlooped textile is created by horizontally manipulating a weft yarn with two or more needles. Traditionally wool is used, although sometimes cotton. The Egyptian Copts, a Christian sect who became famous for their skill, are credited with inventing the first true knitting. As Christianity spread, knitting spread with it, travelling as far as Peru with the Conquistadores in the 16th century. Although it originated in a hot climate, knitting is now most often practised in temperate or cold countries and requires only an adequate supply of yarn. In Europe and Central Asia sheep or goat wool is used, but in the High Andes of Bolivia and Peru alpaca, llama or vicuña hair is more readily available and is knitted into beautifully soft garments. Plain, functional sweaters knitted with naturally oily wools are the choice of seafaring and fishing folk such as the inhabitants of Guernsey and the other Channel Islands.

Above: *A pair of woollen socks knitted in France. Seams can be avoided by circular knitting on three or four needles.*

Opposite: *A multi-coloured blanket knitted using recycled wool.*

Opposite, inset: *Scottish fisherman in a knitted hat.*

Above: *A knitted cotton altar cloth from Mexico.*

Technique

A FIRST row of stitches is cast on by looping the yarn onto one needle, pulling a second loop through the first with the other needle and picking the new loop up beside the first. A third loop is pulled through the second and so on until there are sufficient stitches for the required width. A second row is then knitted by pulling a new series of loops through the first, one stitch at a time. This is repeated until sufficient rows have been knitted to make one panel. When all the separate panels have been knitted they are stitched together to make the final garment. It is possible to knit tubular items like socks and hats in one go, without a seam, by using three or four needles.

The texture of the knit can be made more interesting by varying the stitch. For plain, or knit, stitch the loop of yarn is pulled through to the front, while for purl stitch it is pulled through to the back.

The most widely knitted fabric uses stocking stitch which makes a smooth fabric comprised of alternate rows of plain and purl. When it is reversed, with the purl side as the face, it is called reverse stocking stitch.

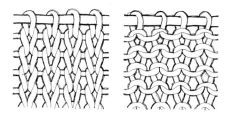

PLAIN OR KNIT STITCH.   PURL STITCH.

Popularity

THE fact that knitting is simple to learn, needs no special equipment, other than a pair of needles, and is portable has ensured the survival of knitting as a domestic, as well as a commercial, textile craft. In any moment of leisure or when the hands are not required for other work, whether while watching sheep or watching television, knitting can be done.

Far left: *Eastern European knitted and beaded hat.*

Near left: *English 19th-century knitted purse.*

TEXTURED KNITTING

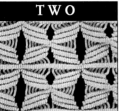

Tʜᴇ most famous textured knitting of all is Aran. Developed on the Irish Aran Islands to protect fishermen from the hostile elements, Aran sweaters are knitted in natural white wool which does not detract from the bold, raised patterns of cables and bobbles. It is possible to buy imitations as far away as Kathmandu in Nepal.

Technique

CABLES imitate plaited or twisted rope. To achieve this effect one set of elements is slipped onto an extra needle and pulled over or under another set of elements to change the order in which the stitches are knitted. To emphasize the texture, the cable is worked in stocking stitch on a background of reverse stocking stitch. Using a cable needle, a number of different patterns can be created. Although textured patterns can be built up without the use of cable needles, by comparison they are dull and two dimensional.

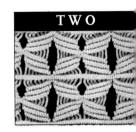

Uses

FISHERMEN all around the coasts of Britain have relied for generations on warm, weatherproof pullovers, knitted for them by their womenfolk. Navy blue is the most typical colour, but textured patterns on selected parts of the garment – neck, chest, sleeves or shoulders – were once a sure way of knowing whether a fisherman was from Whitby, Lowestoft or Guernsey. Sadly, these garments are now seldom made at home and plain, machine-knitted jumpers have become the usual mode of dress.

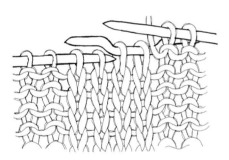

Opposite: *A child's woollen pullover from the Aran Islands off the Atlantic coast of Ireland. The panels are knitted in two-rib diamond cable. Warm woollens are considered indispensable for withstanding the harsh weather to which these islands are exposed.*

Opposite, inset above: *An English fisherman wearing a knitted pullover that identifies his home port as Lowestoft.*

Opposite, inset below: *An Aran Islander, from Inishmaan, wearing a textured pullover under his jacket.*

Above, right: *English knitted woollen socks, or stockings, with a ribbed texture. In some parts of England and Scotland women still make their families hand-knitted socks.*

Right: *A woollen pullover, from Kathmandu in Nepal, knitted in imitation of the Aran style. The central pattern is a horseshoe cable.*

MULTI-COLOURED KNITTING

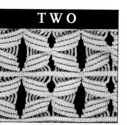

TWO

Just as the introduction of dyed yarn increased the range of effects that could be achieved in weaving, so did many cultures build up a treasury of motifs and patterns in knitting. To this day men in the Andes record their marital and social status in the hats and belts they knit and the repertoire of designs used in the Scottish Shetland Islands includes motifs (such as the Armada cross) supposedly derived from the wrecks of ships from the dispersed Spanish Armada of 1588.

In recent years knitting skills have been given a new lease of life amongst refugees, such as those from Afghanistan, who knit to their own designs using wool unravelled from garments given to them by aid organizations.

Above: *Guatemalan bag. By using different yarns and by varying the tension of the stitches, it is possible to produce delicate, gauzy fabrics or tough, hard-wearing objects like this bag knitted with a typically Guatemalan colour scheme.*

Technique

The process of knitting in colour is very much like weaving with a supplementary weft, in that an extra colour can float across the back of the knitting, surfacing when required to take over the pattern. It is possible to use several colours in a single row, but the more strands of yarn used, the harder they become to manipulate and the bulkier the fabric will be.

Because knitting is a horizontal process it is easiest to build up patterns in bands or rows of repeated motifs. This can be observed all over the world from Fair Isle in Scotland to Afghanistan and from Norway to Bolivia.

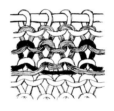

LEFT: MULTI-COLOURED KNITTING SEEN FROM THE BACK.

Opposite: *A knitted hat, or* chullo, *from Bolivia. Hats knitted from vicuña, alpaca or sheep's wool are worn by both sexes all over the Andes.*

Opposite, inset: *Villagers in Western Macedonia wearing hand-knitted socks.*

Above: *Bulgarian woollen socks. Patterned socks are knitted in many parts of the world, often by men while watching over their sheep. In Afghanistan, many socks are now knitted for export using recycled wool.*

Right: *Bag, puttees and socks knitted from woollen yarn by Sarakat nomads in Northern Greece.*

BRAIDS

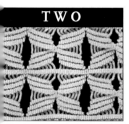

$\mathbf{A}$LTHOUGH the word braid is often used to describe any narrow textile, irrespective of the method of construction, technically, a braid is a band manufactured by interworking a group of warp strands together diagonally across the width of the fabric. When carried out with a large number of strands, the interlacing bears a strong resemblance to a woven textile using both warp and weft. A technically more precise term is oblique interlacing.

The three-strand plait has been universally used, particularly by women, for keeping hair tidy, sometimes in quite complex styles as can be observed in West Africa. One of the most elaborate plaited coiffures is that used by Khampa women in Tibet who braid their hair into 108 plaits, a religiously significant number for Buddhists.

RIGHT: SCOTTISH DIRK
WITH BRAIDED GRIP.

Opposite, above: *Khampa girl, from Eastern Tibet, with her hair plaited into 108 braids.*

Opposite, inset: *John Henry, the factor of the Hudson's Bay Company at Lower Fort Garry, Manitoba, Canada, wearing an Ojibway sash constructed by oblique interlacing.*

Below: *A Hazara woven storage bag, or* juval, *from central Afghanistan, embellished with tassels and a fringe of interlaced braids.*

Technique

A NUMBER of strands are suspended side by side from a foundation thread and each strand is interlaced diagonally to one edge, passing alternately over and under every other strand on the way. The strands originating on the left all travel to the right and all the strands on the right travel to the left. As each strand reaches the selvedge it changes direction and travels back across to the opposite side. In North America this is called double-band plaiting. In multiple-band plaiting a larger number of strands are used. These are divided into groups and from each group half the strands travel to the right and half to the left.

The introduction of coloured strands allows the creation of a variety of patterns which may be made more intricate by changing the direction in which selected strands are interlaced. Braids can be flat, tubular, solid and even three-dimensional.

ABOVE: MULTIPLE-BAND PLAITING.

Uses

As the technique of plaiting or braiding lends itself best to the manufacture of narrow fabrics a few inches wide, it is most often used for making straps, belts and bags. Quite often plaits may be used to make fringes to secure the ends of larger textiles. The finest examples of textiles made with this technique are the Assumption sashes made by the Native Americans of the Great Lakes area. These are made of finely spun worsted wool with colourful repeated zigzag patterns.

Above, left: *Wool sash, from Cherokee, North Carolina, North America, with linked elements to allow more complexity.*

Above, right: *A double-weave belt, or* chumpi, *from Bolivia, with a braided end.*

Below, left: *Tablet-woven band, from Turkey, finished with oblique interlacing and tassels.*

Below, centre: *Simple braided camel anklets acquired at Yalikavak market in Turkey.*

Below, right: *The braided end of a tablet-woven baggage strap, from Cappadocia in Turkey.*

55

SPRANG

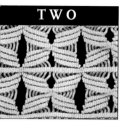

SPRANG is an ancient method of making a stretch fabric. Although similar in appearance to netting, it is constructed using only warp without any added weft elements. Much used before the invention of knitting, the earliest archaeological evidence of sprang is a hair-net made in around 1400 BC found in a Danish bog.

Opposite: *Three sprang pyjama cords from Sind in Pakistan. The fine band on the right is made with a circular warp and has a distinctive pattern of holes near each end.*

Technique

A SET of warp threads are always stretched between two beams or in a rectangular frame. A fabric can then be created by manipulating the warp threads, row by row, interlinking, interlacing or intertwining them. Small sticks may be set in to prevent the work in progress unravelling. Because the threads are fixed at top and bottom, any textile structure created at the top will also be created in mirror image at the bottom. If, after they have been worked, each row and the complementary row created at the bottom are beaten with a flat stick, forcing them to opposite ends of the warp, a compacted fabric will grow, one half growing from the top downwards, the other from the bottom upwards.

Eventually the two halves will grow until they almost meet in the middle. The unworked threads between them must be secured in place to prevent the whole structure unravelling. It is also possible to create two identical textiles by cutting the threads at this point.

Uses

ONCE used to make clothing, hats and gloves in many parts of the world, sprang is still in traditional use in Guatemala and Colombia for the making of bags and hammocks and in Pakistan for the construction of elaborately patterned silk draw-strings for trousers. Now almost universally superseded by knitting, it has experienced something of a vogue in the art-textile world as a medium for decorative hangings.

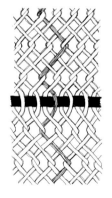

ABOVE: INTERLACED SPRANG WITH RETAINING BATTEN.

Right: *A small Colombian bag, a mechita, constructed from agave fibres in interlaced sprang. The warps are stretched on a portable frame with a central rod that is tucked under the left arm while work is in progress. Unravelling is prevented by inserting a roll of fibres into the final sheds and tucking it up inside the finished bag. The mechita is still manufactured and in everyday use, although examples constructed with synthetic materials are now appearing.*

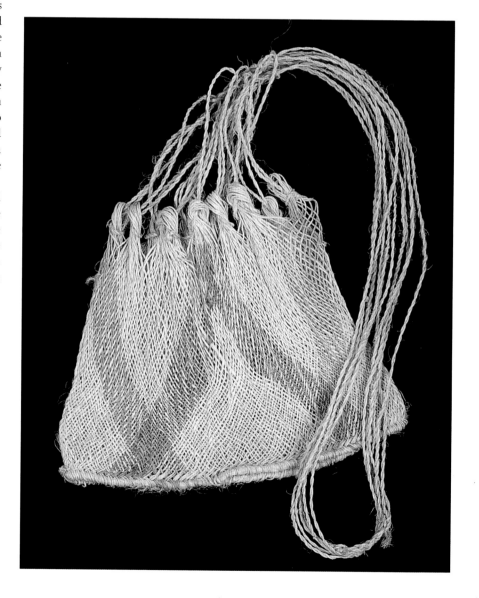

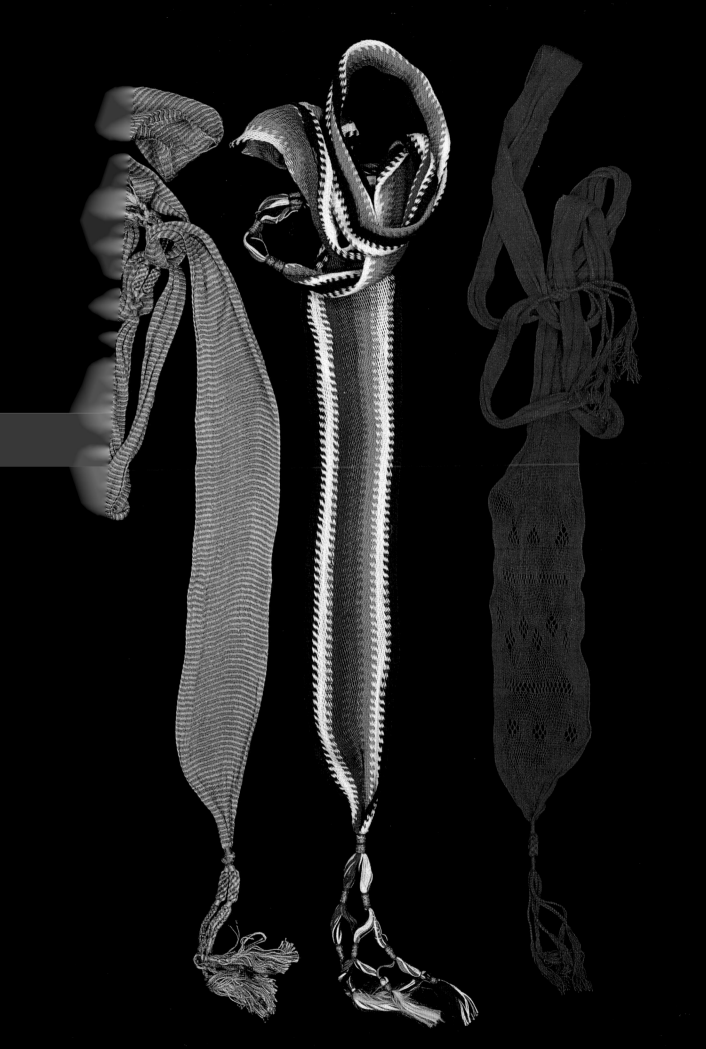
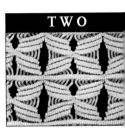

MACRAME

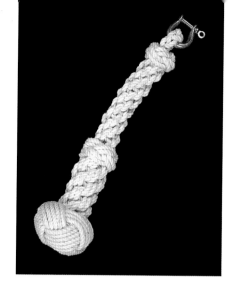

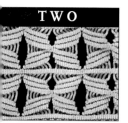

MACRAME is a knotting technique used to make fringes, decorative braids and other articles. It is of ancient Near Eastern origin and reached Spain through the Moorish invasions (8th century onwards) and Italy through the Crusades (11th to 13th centuries). From Europe it was disseminated to other parts of the world largely by sailors. It came into popular vogue in the 19th century and has been in and out of fashion ever since.

Above: *A ship's bell rope, acquired in Scotland, featuring three-dimensional knotting and Turk's heads.*

Below: *Cotton macramé fringes such as this were in widespread use in the 19th century as domestic decorations in Victorian England.*

Technique

MACRAME can be worked on a knotting board of cork or similar soft, but rigid, material on which the cords can be held in position. Every piece of macramé is started from a holding cord *(see diagram opposite)*. The working threads are doubled and attached to the cord using double half hitches, or larks heads, and packed closely together across its width. As a guide to planning the work, the doubled threads need to be four times

Left: *An embroidered apron, from Bulgaria, with a fringe dominated by rows of diagonal knotting.*

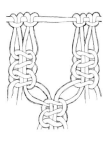

LEFT: INTERLOCKED
BRAIDS OF FLAT OR
SQUARE KNOT SINNIT.

as long as the finished work. However, some knots or sinnets (several knots worked in succession to form a bar) are likely to take up even more thread so allowance must be made for this. On the other hand, an open knotted pattern will take up less thread.

The work proceeds downwards, joining sets of cords at intervals using a few basic knots and many variations, the main ones being the square knot, half hitch, double half hitch and the Josephine knot. Common variants include the picot, square knot sinnet, corkscrew sinnet and alternating square knots.

To finish off, loose ends can be knotted into tassels or worked into horizontal cording.

Above: *A Victorian English mantlepiece fringe worked in unbleached cotton yarn, 19th century.*

Above, right: *Turkish blue glass 'eye' bead, or bonjuk, a good luck talisman, suspended from a macramé strap.*

Below: *Cotton macramé fringe from Spain.*

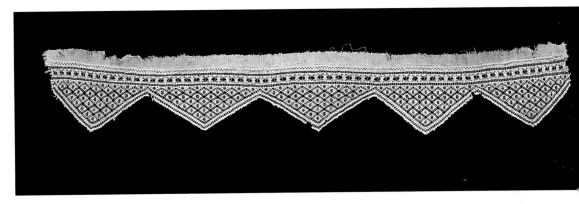

PLY-SPLITTING

PLY-SPLITTING work is one of the simplest forms of textile structure, a technique almost exclusively used in the manufacture of animal trappings. Cotton cord or sisal is sometimes employed, but the chosen material is most often goat hair.

Technique

IN Rajasthan in India a villager will spin out yarn from a bundle of either black or white goat hair. This yarn is doubled and then folded in four and twisted to make a four-ply cord. The looped ends of the four-ply cords are then slipped onto a wooden stick or spindle. An expert girth maker can use as many as sixty separate strands.

The basic structure of ply-splitting work is similar to plaiting in that the warp elements travel diagonally down the fabric from selvedge to selvedge. However, instead of passing over and under each other, one four-ply cord is untwisted sufficiently to allow another to be threaded through it. By varying the initial sequence in which the strands are attached and by choosing whether to thread one strand through another or have the other pass through it, it is possible to build up a range of patterns.

There are several basic pattern structures that can be formed using variations on this technique. The resulting girths can be monochrome (usually in black), have a black-and-white diagonally chequered pattern or alternately black-and-white horizontal waves. The most visually interesting structures, obtained with four-ply yarn that is half white, half black, are geometric or figurative with the pattern appearing in negative on the reverse.

Uses

THE villagers of Western Rajasthan in India are particularly adept at making camel girths using this technique. Ply-split darning is a similar technique in which one strand is used as a weft and threaded through a set of warp elements. Ply-split textiles can be found in Egypt, Turkey, Greece, Nepal, India and Japan.

Above, left: *A ply-split bottle bag from Rajasthan, North-West India. The intersections are concealed by mirrors.*

Above, right: *Two hollow, tubular straps, from Rajasthan, North-West India, constructed by ply-split darning with a needle.*

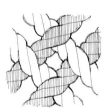

LEFT: INTERLACED DIAGONAL ELEMENTS.

Opposite: *Ply-split camel girths from Rajasthan in North-West India. Most camel girths are made using a combination of natural-coloured light and dark goat hair to create a two-colour pattern. The girth on the right has a polychrome pattern created by the diagonal interlacing of dyed cotton cords.*

Right: *Ply-split darning as used by the Sarakat nomads of Northern Greece for constructing borders for clothes.*

LACE

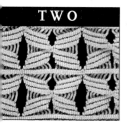

LACE is a European invention, made by the poorest of women to adorn the clothing of the rich. Probably the most recent traditional textile-making technique to come into existence, it seems to have originated in Italy or Dalmatia (the coastal region of the Former Yugoslavia) in the 15th century, but the technique and the fashion for its use spread rapidly to countries as far apart as England and Russia. It was later introduced to other parts of the world by Christian missionaries whose vestments were ornamented with lace cuffs and collars. Generally speaking, peasants are and were the lacemakers in Eastern Europe, but in Western Europe lacemaking was a profession. Hand-made lace was always expensive, and the death-knell of the lace-making industry in Western Europe was sounded in 1818 when the first bobbin net was machine-made in France. But in the conservative societies of Eastern Europe, peasant women continued to create bobbin lace to decorate their festival clothing. Tape lace was a speciality in Eastern Europe, especially in Russia.

Bobbin lace

Bobbin (or pillow) lace is worked over a firm pillow on to which a paper pattern has been fixed. Needles are inserted into the pattern to support the work and a number of threads, weighted by bobbins of wood or bone, are twisted and interlaced around them to create an open-work mesh. There are many regional styles, from that of the cottage industries of rural England to the sophistication of Brussels and the Mediterranean styles of the islands of Malta and Cyprus.

Needle lace

MORE time consuming than bobbin lace, needle (or needlepoint) lace has always been more expensive. Using a needle, long chains of buttonhole stitches are worked which are looped and linked up as the work progresses to form net-like patterns. Once known as the Queen of Lace, complicated figurative patterns can be created with as many as one hundred stitches to the inch.

Tatting

TATTING is a form of lace-making worked with a small shuttle. Knots and loops or picots are worked on a ground thread which is drawn into rings or semi-circles and built up into delicate patterns.

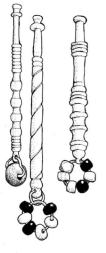

LACE BOBBINS.

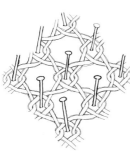

BOBBIN LACE.

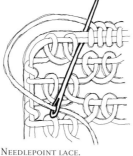

NEEDLEPOINT LACE.

TATTING SHUTTLE AND PICOTS.

Left, above: *Two Greek linen bobbin lace or copanelli valances in torchon technique. The top one is unbleached.*

Far left: *Branscombe tape lace from England.*

Near left: *A pair of Italian Reticella needle-lace collars.*

Opposite: *A tatted doily from Western Europe.*

Opposite, inset above: *Maltese girls learning the craft of lacemaking.*

Opposite, inset centre: *A 'bourgogne', a traditional lace headdress from Normandy, France.*

Opposite, inset bottom: *Russian peasants wearing tape-lace decorated skirts.*

TWINING AND WRAPPING

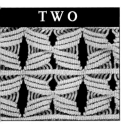
TWINING and wrapping need some sort of frame for their construction, use a warp and a weft and greatly resemble loom-woven textiles. The warps and wefts are, however, manipulated by hand and, therefore, need no system of heddles to open a shed. The similarities to basket-making methods suggest that these techniques may have been in use over a much larger area of the world before the invention of the true loom. In places, twining and wrapping techniques are used in combination with loom-weaving techniques.

Weft twining

FOR the manufacture of a weft-twined textile a set of warps are suspended from a fixed rod. To maintain tension, weights are often attached to the bottom. The weft strands are then worked in pairs. One strand passes over a warp, the other under. The strands are then twisted around each other so that the first strand will pass under the next warp and the other over it. In this way, the weft twists and twines across the fabric from one selvedge to the other. The most amazing textiles woven using this method are the Chilkat blankets made of cedar-bark fibre by the indigenous people of the North-West coast of Canada and Alaska, and the phormium fibre cloaks worn by the Maoris of New Zealand.

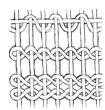

WEFT TWINING.

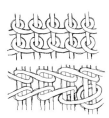

WEFT WRAPPING AND *SOUMAK*.

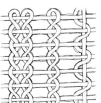

WARP TWINING.

Warp twining

MUCH as in weft twining, it is possible to bind in the weft by twisting and twining the warp. This is an ideal technique for the construction of long narrow bands. Warp-twined textiles can also be woven with tablets.

Weft wrapping

IN this technique the weft threads do not merely pass over and under the warps,

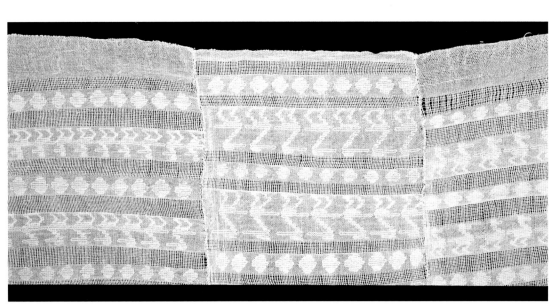

Left: *A loosely woven cotton textile from Mexico with raised patterns of supplementary wefts and openwork sections of gauze weave. The combination of different techniques has created interesting textures and patterns even though only one colour has been used.*

they are actually wrapped right around them. In the case of *soumak*, a technique popular in Balouchistan, Anatolia and the Caucasus, the weft wraps around several warps at a time. Fine, hard-wearing bags and rugs are woven in *soumak*, sometimes with the addition of a ground weft.

Gauze weaves

Gauze weaves, woven for centuries in China and South America, are very similar to warp-twined textiles except that the warps cross and are anchored by a pick of the weft and then uncross before the next pick. They do not twine around each other. Like *soumak*, gauze is often incorporated into a loom-woven ground weave.

Above: *A bag for transporting goods by camel, from Malatya in Eastern Turkey. The patterned areas are woven in soumak.*

Above, right, inset: *Pataragurai, a Maori chief, wearing a cloak of weft-twined phormium fibres.*

Right: *A narrow-necked bag, shaped like a tobacco pouch, made in Gujarat in North-West India from densely twined goat hair.*

Far right: *Ceremonial sling, or* honda, *made from wool and camelid hair by men in Bolivia. The cradle for the stone is wrapped and the cords are braided.*

THREE

LOOM-WOVEN TEXTILES

LOOM-WOVEN TEXTILES

WEAVING is quite simply the art of interlacing one element in and out of another. Interesting fabrics can be woven using the fingers alone, but the most complex and sophisticated results are achieved using a loom.

THE LOOM

THE most basic loom is a wooden frame which the warp threads are suspended from or stretched across. The weft threads are then woven in and out of the warp from side to side. To keep the warps tensioned evenly, thus ensuring a consistent piece of cloth, different solutions have been found. A suspension loom, as used by the Tlingit Indians of Alaska or the Lapps of Northern Scandinavia, is vertical with weights attached to the warp. The horizontal drag loom, used by the Yoruba of Nigeria, for instance, has the warps attached to a heavy weight on a sledge, while body-tensioned looms, such as those used in parts of Indonesia, rely on the weight of the weaver's body to keep the warp taut. Large cloth is usually woven on looms with the warp attached to a beam fixed to each end of the frame.

Above: *A Javanese woman weaving tabby-weave cloth on a semi-automized loom. A shed is open ready for the passage of the shuttle.*

Below: *An Ashanti weaver at Bonwire in Ghana using a double-heddle loom to weave narrow strips which are then sewn together to make* kente *cloth.*

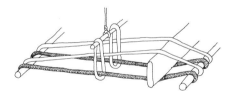

ABOVE: OPENING A SHED WITH A SHED STICK ON A SINGLE-HEDDLE LOOM.

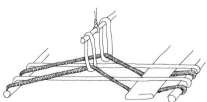

ABOVE: OPENING THE COUNTERSHED BY LIFTING THE HEDDLE ROD.

Right: *By an old Inca wall in Cusco, a Peruvian woman sits making double-weave belts, or* chumpi, *on a body-tensioned loom. She is using a heddle and three shed sticks.*

Left: *A Navaho woman, outside her hogan in Arizona, North America, making a tapestry-weave blanket on an upright loom. Although the Navaho use a very simple form of loom, they are famous for weaving blankets and rugs of great beauty and complexity.*

Above: *Weaving long narrow strips in Ghana on a drag loom. The warps are tensioned with a heavy stone on a sledge.*

Below: *An Ewe weaver at a double-heddle loom in Ghana. He uses his hands to manipulate the shuttle and his feet to operate the heddles for opening the sheds.*

OPENING THE SHED

To facilitate the interlacing of the weft, a shed stick is threaded over and under alternate warp threads to open a space, or shed, through which the weft can be passed more easily. A countershed then has to be opened and the sequence in which the weft passes over and under the warp altered. To do this, the threads pressed down by the shed stick are attached through loops or heddles to a rod that will pull them above the other threads when it is raised. This is called a heddle rod. By having two or more heddle rods, it is possible to raise a variety of combinations of warp threads and so weave increasingly complicated textiles.

BINDING SYSTEMS

THERE are three basic methods of interlacing the warp and weft together – tabby, twill and satin weave. They are called binding systems and differ in the number of warps the weft crosses before passing to the other face of the fabric.

TABBY WEAVE

Technique

Tabby or plain weave is the simplest form of woven cloth. Each pick, or passage of the weft from side to side, passes over one warp, under one, over one and so on. On its return passage the sequence is reversed. If the warp and weft are composed of yarn of equal weight they will be equally visible in the finished weave which will therefore have a balanced, criss-cross texture. By varying the colour of the warps, longitudinal stripes are produced and by varying the colour of the weft, horizontal stripes are produced. By varying the colours of both warp and weft a pattern of checks is achieved.

LEFT: WARP AND WEFT ARE BALANCED.

Uses

As tabby is the easiest cloth to weave it is also the most widespread and is universally employed for everyday wear and use. A balanced tabby weave provides an ideal surface for printing, painting or embroidery and is also easy to cut and sew.

Distribution

Tabby or plain-weave cloth is produced wherever people use a loom, but certain fabrics are produced with distinctive qualities. Examples of these are the light-weight, cotton muslin originally developed in Mosul in Iraq, tough calico from Calicut in India and heavy-duty canvas woven from hemp or flax and used for sails or as a base for fine embroidery.

Above: *English embroidery sampler, 1818. Balanced tabby weave is the ideal ground for counted-thread embroidery.*

Opposite: *A balanced tabby-weave silk shawl from Turkmenistan. The vertical stripes are created by the colours of the warp threads and the horizontal bands by the colours of the wefts. Where they cross, checks are formed.*

Opposite, inset left: *A Myanmarese (Burmese) youth wrapped in a comfortable, checked tabby-weave lungi.*

Opposite, inset right: *Tabby weave is cheap and easy to produce, but here it is worn by Foumba, a former king of the Kilema district of Uganda.*

Above: *A bandhani tie and dye shawl from Jamnagar in Gujarat, India. The material is a loosely woven, tabby-weave silk.*

Right: *Checked tabby-weave yardage, from Guatemala, with compound-ikat patterning created by resist-dyeing the yarn before weaving.*

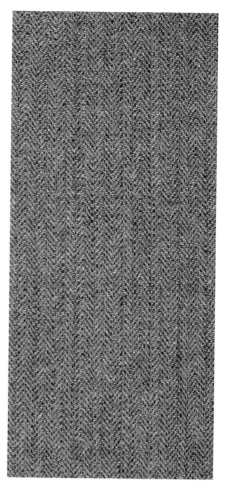

Left: *Twill-woven Scottish tartans, from left to right, Royal Stewart, Dress Gordon and Lindsay. The colours normally used for tartans are sombre and harmonious because they were originally based on the available natural dyes.*

Top: *Tweed cloth woven in a herringbone pattern on the Isle of Harris in the Outer Hebrides.*

Above: *Woollen cloth, from Gilgit in Northern Pakistan, woven in herringbone twill.*

TWILL

Technique

IN twill each passage of the weft through the warps goes over two, under one, over two, under one. In the next passage the same sequence is repeated, but staggered, to produce a textured effect with raised diagonals. The degree of staggering will affect the angle of the diagonal. A number of variations are possible and by careful sequencing different patterns such as chevrons, lozenges and herringbone can be made.

LEFT: TWILL WEAVE.

Above: *Tapestry-weave cloth with a twill binding system from Kirman in Iran. A similar technique is often used in the manufacture of Kashmir shawls.*

Below, left: *A Scottish piper in full costume.*

Uses

TWILL weaving produces a thick, firm fabric ideal for outdoor and working clothes such as the tough, woollen Harris tweed made on Harris Island in the Outer Hebrides, the tartan plaid used by Scottish highlanders for kilts, shawls and blankets or cotton denim first used to make overalls in the California gold rush of 1849.

Tartan

THE simple technique of weaving checked woollen cloth allows for an enormous number of combinations with the limited range of colours available from natural dyes. During the 17th century distinctive arrangements began to be associated with specific families, and districts in Scotland. By the 18th century wearing tartan had become a sign of clan allegiance and national identity to such an extent that after the defeat of Bonnie Prince Charlie at Culloden in 1746 an Act of Parliament was passed banning the wearing of Highland dress.

Today, the sale of tartan cloth to tourists ensures the survival of this textile. Although not often worn as daily attire anymore, many Scotsmen still choose to wear a kilt on special occasions.

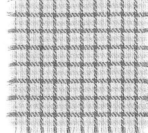

Above: *Four samples of tweed cloth, from the Isle of Mull, Scotland, showing some of the patterns that can be created with a twill binding system.*

SATIN WEAVE

Technique

SATIN has a much more loosely bound weave than tabby or twill. The weft thread passes over one warp thread, under four or more, over one and so on. This produces a weave in which the face shows virtually only the warp and the reverse is nearly all weft, so the texture is particularly smooth, especially if the warps are silk or viscose. The weft threads are often of cotton, both for strength and economy.

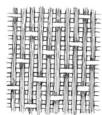

ABOVE: WARPS LIE
OVER SEVERAL WEFTS.

Uses

SATIN textiles are widely used in Europe and Asia for blouses, skirts and pyjamas because of their glossy sheen and texture. *Mashru* fabric woven in Turkey, Syria and India is a luxury fabric with a silken warp and a cotton weft. The literal meaning of *mashru* is permitted. According to Islamic custom, silk should not be worn against the skin; with the satin

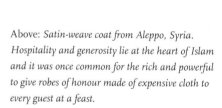

Above: *Satin-weave coat from Aleppo, Syria. Hospitality and generosity lie at the heart of Islam and it was once common for the rich and powerful to give robes of honour made of expensive cloth to every guest at a feast.*

Left: *Indian* mashru *was once exported to the Middle East in large quantities. This contemporary example, from Aleppo, shows a style with plain and patterned bands popular in the 19th century. The fuzzy effect is created by dyeing the warps with the ikat-resist technique, so that they vary in colour along their length.*

Left, inset: *Armenian teachers and pupils in the 1920s. Until the early 20th century,* mashru *was the everyday costume worn by many inhabitants of Asia Minor, whether scholar, chief or Kurdish mountaineer.*

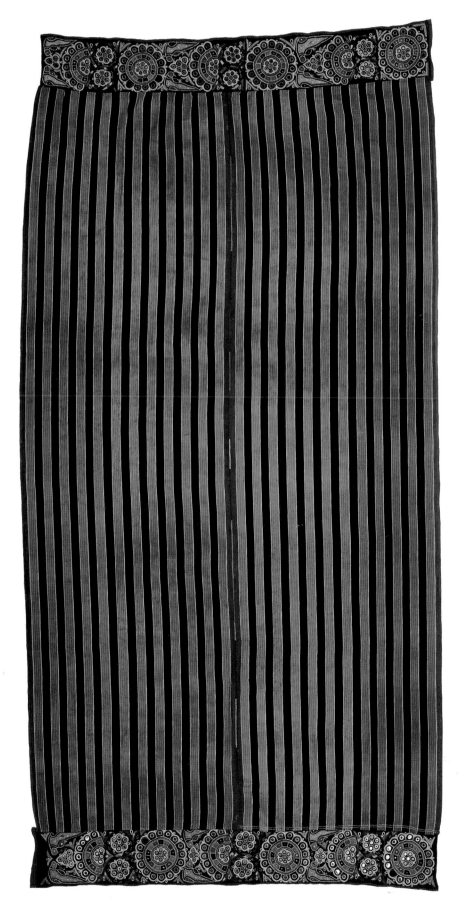

weave of *mashru*, silk is only shown on the face of the fabric and it is cotton that brushes against the skin. In this way the proprieties of custom are preserved.

In Central Asia, as well as in the Middle East, *abr* (satin-weave ikat-dyed) robes of honour are traditionally given at feasts or worn by the wealthy. The Tajik and Uzbek women of Central Asia still wear *abr* trousers and tunics on a daily basis.

Left: *A festive* mashru *shawl, or* odhni, *from Kutch in North-West India. The margins are decorated with sparkling mirrorwork and embroidered with patterns of flowers and parrots.*

Below: *Silk coat from Damascus in Syria. The leaves of two mulberry trees are required to feed enough silk worms to spin sufficient silk to make one coat. Several coats may be worn when the weather is cold.*

TAPESTRY WEAVE

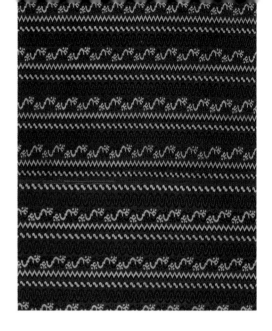

Above: *A silk sarong, from Amarapura, Myanmar (Burma), woven in a variation of tapestry weave known as* Lun taya *or thousand bobbin.*

Above: *A subtly coloured, tapestry-woven cotton kerchief, or* pis, *from the Sulu Islands in the Philippines.*

Below: *A brightly coloured, tapestry-woven woollen* serape, *or shawl, from Mexico.*

Technique

WHEN weaving a weft-faced textile it is not necessary for a weft thread to pass all the way from one edge to the other (selvedge to selvedge). At any chosen point a new weft thread of a different colour may be substituted and woven in. In this way, any number of colours may be introduced and blocks of pattern built up. This technique may also be described as using a discontinuous weft.

Uses

BECAUSE this technique has so few practical restrictions it has been used to create decorative and pictorial clothing, carpets, rugs and tapestries, often on a large scale. The word tapestry, now used to mean a woven wall hanging, actually comes from the French *tapis* meaning a carpet. When speaking of carpets, the term *kilim* is often used to denote a rug executed in tapestry weave.

Distribution

TAPESTRY weave is practised in many parts of the world. Some of the oldest and most beautiful decorative textiles were woven in Ptolemaic Egypt using the tapestry method. Many examples survive from the early Christian era and are popularly known as Coptic weavings. This tradition is kept alive in contemporary Egypt with the fine tapestries woven in the

workshops of Wissa Wassef at Harrania near the pyramids at Giza. Also of surpassing beauty were the famous twill-tapestry shawls of Kashmir, Northern India. Of very complex design, in the 19th century work on a single shawl was split between two or more looms. These shawls, known as *jamawars*, are still woven at Basohli near the North-West Indian town of Jammu. Particularly fine prestige textiles are woven in tapestry in Iran, South-East Asia and South America.

LEFT: TAPESTRY WEAVE.

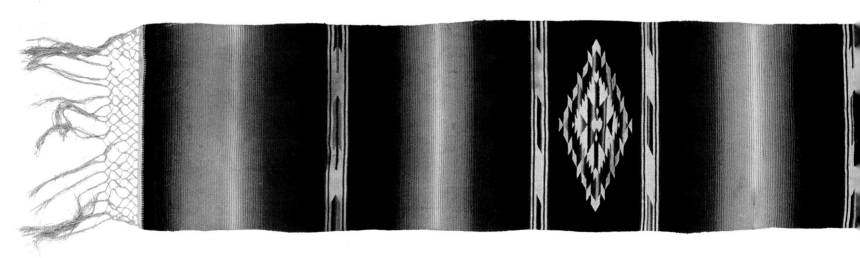

Above: *Chinese 19th-century insignia.*

Below: *Early 19th century Kashmiri* jamawar.

Bottom: *Woollen shawl with tapestry-woven borders from Kulu in India's Himalayan foothills.*

THREE

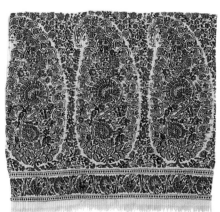

Above: *A modern Egyptian tapestry-weave panel from the workshop founded by Dr Ramses Wissa Wassef at Harrania.*

Right: *A fragment of tapestry-woven cloth made by Christian Copts in 6th-century Egypt.*

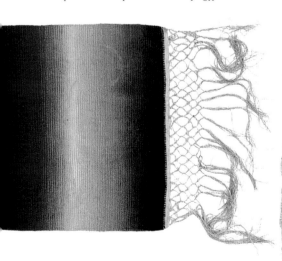

WARP-FACED WEAVE

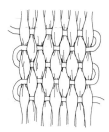

A WARP-FACED weave is one in which the weft has been obscured by the warp threads and any pattern, most commonly longitudinal stripes, is therefore carried by the warp.

Technique

THE pattern of a warp-faced fabric is laid down in the initial setting up of the warps – the colour of the yarn is changed at intervals to ordain the width and frequency of the stripes. To ensure its dominance, the warp must be more densely packed than the weft or made of a thicker yarn. More complicated patterns can be woven if selected warp strands are periodically made to float across the weft or behind it, as in satin weave.

LEFT: WARPS OBSCURE WEFTS.

Complementary warps

IF more than one set of warps is used, floating short distances on opposite faces of the fabric, these can be made to change places periodically to create a pattern, one face the reverse of the other.

Below: *Yoruba indigo-dyed, warp-striped cloth from Nigeria.*

Distribution

WARP-FACED, longitudinally striped textiles are found in all parts of the world where any kind of loom exists. The popularity of striped textiles is ensured not only by the ease of their construction, but also by their dynamic effect. Serviceable, hard-wearing items such as blankets and cloaks intended for day-to-day use are frequently decorated with warp-faced stripes. In both rich and poor countries, the variations possible in the colour and width of stripes has often been used as a means of differentiating affiliation, whether tribal or collegiate.

Belts, bands and sashes for securing loads or fastening clothes are frequently woven with warp-faced patterns and often elaborated with floats and complementary warps.

Above: *Bolivian coca bag with complementary warp patterns.*

Below: *An Uzbek* ghudjeri, *from Afghanistan, made from narrow woven strips sewn selvedge to selvedge.*

Opposite: *Warp-striped cotton blanket from Guatemala.*

Opposite, inset: *A Mende chief, from Sierra Leone, wearing warp-striped cloth.*

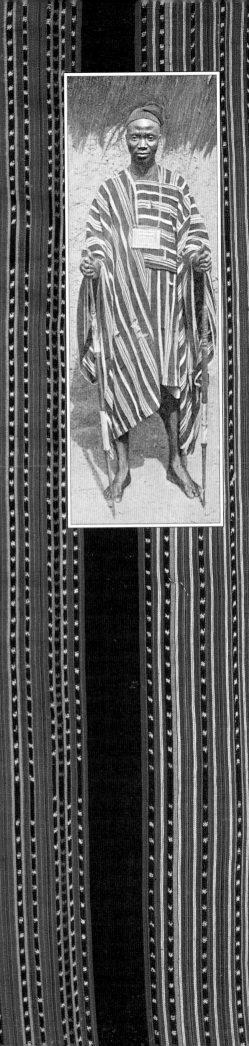

WEFT-FACED WEAVE

A WEFT-FACED weave is the reverse of a warp-faced weave. The wefts are more densely packed than the warp or are of heavier weight and so the warp threads are obscured and dominated by the wefts, which therefore carry the pattern. A weft-faced pattern will run across a textile in horizontal bands.

Technique

FOR a textile to be weft-faced, the weft threads must be appreciably thicker than the warps or more densely packed. A common example of the former is the combination of a woollen weft and a cotton warp. To achieve the latter, although warps and wefts may be of equal thickness, the wefts are beaten down hard with a comb or beater, so that in any given surface area they predominate.

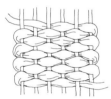

LEFT: WEFTS OBSCURE WARPS.

Complementary wefts

JUST as a pattern can be created with complementary warps, if more than one set of wefts is used, floating short distances on opposite faces of the fabric, these too can be made to change places periodically to create a pattern, one face the reverse of the other.

Opposite, left: *A woman's shawl, from North-East Thailand, woven in two pieces. The pattern of horizontal bands is enhanced with supplementary weft details.*

Opposite, right: *A Mexican blanket woven in two pieces. The weft-faced pattern has been emphasized with weft ikat that shows as white dashes.*

Right: *A Kano luru stripweave from Nigeria. The textile is made up of strips that run vertically, but the weft-faced pattern appears to run horizontally.*

Uses

SHAWLS and ponchos are most commonly woven in weft-faced weaves. Weft-faced weaves keep their shape better than warp-faced ones and are most often used for complex patterning.

Above, right: *Aprons with weft-faced stripes can be found all over the world, from Wales to Tibet. These two matrons are from Hardanger in Norway.*

Right: *A Tibetan woman's weft-striped woollen apron sewn together from three pieces. The stripes are seldom perfectly aligned.*

Below, right: *A Kano luru stripweave cotton cloth from Nigeria. The details are worked in supplementary weft.*

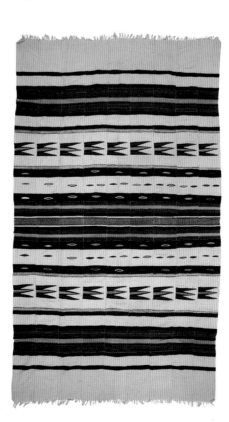

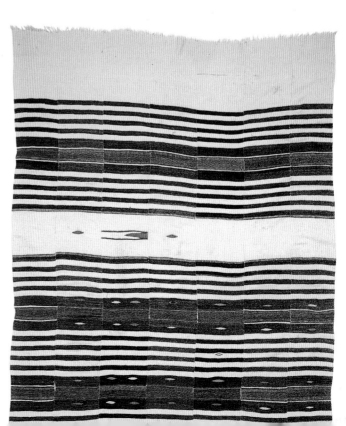

DAMASK

THE Chinese had been weaving figured silk fabrics for hundreds of years before they were introduced to Europe via the Middle East. They became known as 'damask' after the Syrian city of Damascus, which may have been where these textiles were first encountered by the Crusaders.

The play of light

DAMASKS are self-patterned textiles woven, most often, in silk or linen in one colour. The pattern motifs are thrown into relief by the way light falls on the fabric and is reflected differently by the lustrous fibres of areas of pattern and ground. The effect is subtle, shimmering and glamorous.

ABOVE: THE DOMINANCE OF EITHER THE WARP OR WEFT CHANGES TO CREATE THE PATTERN.

Left: *Korean damask pojagi used to wrap gifts given to a bride by the groom's parents.*

Above: *A silk damask duffle bag, from Korea, used for carrying a bottle of spirits. In Korea, special cloths are used to carry or protect many things. They may be made of silk, cotton or ramie and are decorated according to the means of the owner.*

Technique

DAMASKS are essentially satin-weave textiles, although on occasion a twill binding system may be employed. While the pattern motifs are being woven, the silky warps float over a number of wefts before being bound in. When an area of background is reached the warps are made to float across the wefts on the reverse face. This results in the motifs being shown in warps (which lie vertically) and the background being shown in wefts (which lie horizontally). Light falling on vertical and horizontal threads is reflected differently and so as the fabric moves and light strikes it at different angles it seems to shimmer.

The Chinese pioneered the use of a drawloom equipped with a large number of heddles. This enabled the weaver to lift warps individually, with the help of several assistants, and so weave very complicated patterns. At the beginning of the 19th century Joseph Marie Jacquard of Lyons in France invented an automated apparatus 'programmed' with a system of punched cards that selected and lifted the warps in a desired sequence. The process of weaving damask and other fancy weaves subsequently became quicker, easier and cheaper.

Uses

WOVEN in silk, damask makes a glamorous dress fabric. In Europe linen damask continues to be the classic choice for tablecloths and napkins. Damask woven with warp and weft composed of different fibres has often been used for curtains and upholstery.

Above: Silk damask dress fabric woven in Europe in about 1800. European damasks have often featured bold patterns of flowers and birds.

Above, right: A Chinese woman wearing a wide-sleeved damask jacket decorated with auspicious symbols.

Right: English tablecloth from the 1920s with damask-figuring thrown into relief, in places, by contrasting colours in the warp and weft.

Below: A detail of a Chinese robe made of silk brocade fabric. Motifs of flowers and auspicious symbols are common features of Chinese brocades.

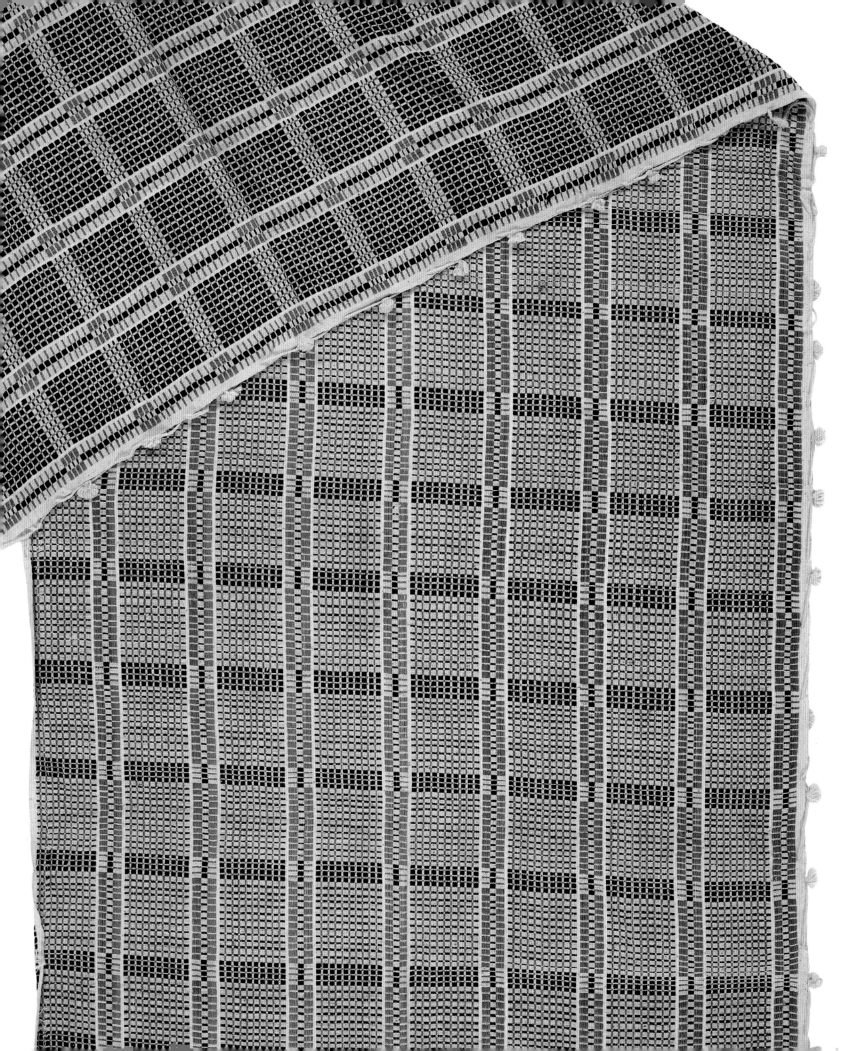

SUPPLEMENTARY WARP

DECORATION can be incorporated into a ground weave with the use of extra, or supplementary, warps which play no part in the basic structure.

Technique

IN Indonesia the ground warp threads are laid out on a two-heddle, continuously warped body-tension loom and the supplementary warp threads which are thicker and lighter in colour are laid over them. The weaver then places a bamboo stick between the ground and extra-warps, near the warp beam, to ensure that the two sets of warp do not get entangled. A small model of the pattern made of string and sticks is used as a guide to setting out the extra-warp pattern. Many small wooden splints are then set into place, picking up the appropriate supplementary warp threads to form a pattern as the weft is introduced. As weaving progresses, the splints are lifted in sequence to form a supplementary pattern in twill weave. Where the splints are lifted, the extra-warp threads will appear on the surface to form the pattern, otherwise they appear on the underside as a continuous float. Weaving with extra warps causes problems with tensioning, so constant adjustments have to be made with both the ground and supplementary warps.

Distribution

SUPPLEMENTARY-warp textiles are woven in very few parts of the world – they are most prevalent in Eastern Indonesia, particularly on the islands of Bali, Timor and the Moluccas, and most notably in Sumba. In East Sumba, noblewomen weave a sarong known as *Lau pahudu*. Its lower border has mythological motifs worked in a supplementary warp of heavy, light-coloured yarn against a dark background weave. Long sashes are also woven in the same technique. The tourist demand for these pieces is now so high that, breaking with tradition, young men as well as young women weave them on back-strap looms with very long warps.

Above: *The border of a woman's* tapis, *from Sumba, decorated with men at prayer worked in supplementary warps.*

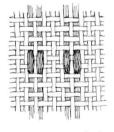

LEFT: THE PATTERN HERE IS CREATED BY SUPPLEMENTARY WARPS FLOATING ABOVE THE WEFTS.

Opposite: *Syrian bath towel. The supplementary warp pattern appears in negative on the reverse.*

Right: *Antoni weaving, from Timor, an Indonesian island, with the borders and lizards created by supplementary-warp floats.*

Far right: *Supplementary-warp* selendangs *from Sumba, an eastern Indonesian island. Human figures appear on many Sumban weavings.*

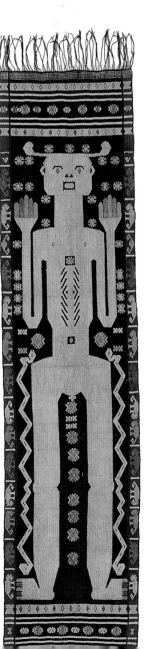

Extra or supplementary wefts can be introduced into a weave to add decoration to an otherwise plain cloth. As with supplementary warps, these are decorative and are not an essential part of the structure. The supplementary weft is usually of a different colour and thicker than the yarn used for the ground weft. A continuous supplementary weft is one that passes right across the weave from selvedge to selvedge.

THREE

Technique

To build up a pattern an extra-weft thread must be made to appear or disappear by floating it across several warp strands at strategic points. This type of weave is called a weft float. The supplementary weft, when it does not appear on the face of the cloth, floats on the reverse and is periodically bound in to the ground weave to maintain the integrity of the structure.

With elaborate continuous supplementary weft designs the decorative motifs characteristically appear as a dark pattern against a lighter ground, whereas on the reverse the design will appear in negative, a light pattern against a dark background. A supplementary weft may be woven in with the ground weft or by the opening of a separate shed.

WEFT INLAY.   WEFT FLOATS.

Distribution

Elaborate and beautiful continuous supplementary weft cloths are woven in many parts of the world. Weavers in Europe, Asia, North Africa and Latin America are the producers of almost all of these fabrics. Probably the most beautiful are those woven in the remote hills of Sam Neua in Northern Laos for use as sashes, stoles and curtains.

Far left: *A cotton belt, from Timor, with decorative elements worked in silk supplementary wefts.*

Above: *Moi tribesman from Annam, Vietnam. The man's shirt is decorated with supplementary wefts.*

Right: *Laotian silk and cotton shawl, from Sam Neua, with continuous and discontinuous supplementary weft patterns.*

Opposite, above, left: *Detail of a Mexican shawl with bird pattern.*

Opposite, above, right: *An Itneg mantle from Luzon in the Philippines.*

Opposite, below, left: *Cotton curtain, from central Laos, decorated with supplementary weft threads.*

Opposite, below, right: *A woven cotton square, from Lombok, Indonesia, with a simple pattern of supplementary wefts.*

JUST like a continuous supplementary weft thread, a discontinuous weft thread is decorative and not an essential part of the textile's structure, but is woven into selected places only, as in tapestry weave, and not into the full width of the cloth from selvedge to selvedge.

Technique

THE most effective way of employing discontinuous supplementary wefts is with the use of floats, introducing them either into the same shed as the ground weft or into one of their own. They are not entered at the selvedge, but at the point at which the pattern is to be begun, unlike continuous supplementary wefts which must traverse the full width of the fabric.

For a different effect a weft inlay may be employed. This consists of a supplementary weft that is laid in with the ground weave. As it does not float the effect is more subtle, although stronger as it is less likely to snag.

DISCONTINUOUS WEFT INLAY.

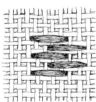

DISCONTINUOUS WEFT FLOATS.

Distribution

TEXTILES with a pattern woven with a discontinuous supplementary weft are found all over the world, often in combination with continuous supplementary wefts. Weft inlay is used with particular vigour for working the motifs of animals and domestic objects in the stripweaves of the Ashanti and Ewe peoples of Ghana.

Opposite: *Bhutanese textiles. Discontinuous supplementary weft patterns frequently appear as isolated motifs rather than in bands as is typical of continuous supplementary weft weavings. The sash on the left has been woven using both techniques.*

Opposite, inset: *A girl, from Mixan, in the 1920s. Her cotton blouse, with discontinuous supplementary weft patterns, is of a type that can still be seen in Guatemala today.*

Right: *A Kach'in woman's apron, from Myanmar (Burma), worn with the wefts, and therefore the bands of patterns, running vertically.*

Left: *Coverlet, from Laos, in which the use of discontinuous supplementary wefts has created an effect resembling tapestry weaving.*

Above: *Discontinuous supplementary weft weaving from Laos.*

Above, right: *A Guatemalan head wrapping made by surface weft packing, a cross between tapestry and supplementary weft weaving.*

89

BROCADE

BROCADES are finely woven luxury fabrics worn in many parts of the world on ceremonial occasions or as an indication of status. Although the term 'brocade' refers to a textile woven with a supplementary weft of a material different to that of the ground weft, it is generally used to signify a silk textile with rich figuring worked with gold or silver supplementary weft threads.

Metal thread

IT is possible to draw gold and silver out into very fine wire. This wire is wound tightly around a silk or cotton core to produce a thread sufficiently flexible and durable for weaving or embroidery. When metal threads are utilized as supplementary weft threads they catch the light with a subtle shimmer suffused with mystery and enchantment.

Above: *Silk* songket *brocade from Singaraja, Bali. Balinese* songket *is most often woven in gold and mulberry.*

Left: *Minangkabau* songket *brocade, from Sumatra, woven in typical gold and red.*

Distribution

FINE brocades are woven in Europe, all over the Muslim world, and in India and South-East Asia. The vast majority of these are worked with metal thread. China and parts of South-East Asia have a tradition of silk brocades. The opulent and beautiful *kinkhab* of Benares, India, and the *songket* of the Indonesian islands of Sumatra and Bali are so complex that a specialist is employed to set up the intricate system of heddles required.

Opposite: *The sumptuous silk brocade pallav of a Baluchar sari woven at Murshidabad in Bengal, Eastern India. It features a pair of* butti *cones and a border of galloping horsemen.*

Opposite, inset: *A Palestinian elder wearing a brocade turban.*

Left: *Supplementary-weft Bulgarian apron woven on a narrow loom in two strips. To qualify as brocade the supplementary wefts must be of a different material from the ground weft.*

Right: *A 19th-century Chinese sleeveless coat made from floral silk brocade with auspicious calligraphy on the shoulders.*

STRIPWEAVE

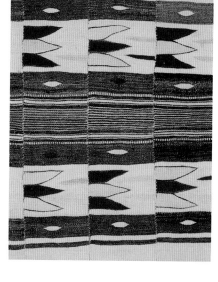

IT is a widespread practice to sew two separately woven pieces together to make one textile which is too large to be woven in one piece on any available loom. This is the method of construction, for example, of rugs made by the Balouch in Afghanistan or of *hinggi* mantles woven on Sumba in Indonesia. In a very few places textiles are made by sewing together a large number of very narrow strips. Apart from the *ghudjeris*, or horse blankets, of Uzbekistan virtually all stripweaves are to be found in West Africa. The best known is the *kente* cloth of Ghana.

Above: Detail of a Kano luru stripweave, from Nigeria, with both continuous and discontinuous supplementary-weft patterning.

Opposite, above: Arkilla jengo wool and cotton cover woven by the Fulani for the Tuareg Mali.

Opposite, below, left: An Ashanti woman's rayon kente cloth woven in Bonwire village, Ghana.

Opposite, below, right: An Ashanti kente cloth.

Opposite, inset: Prempeh, last of the Ashanti kings, wearing a cotton stripweave.

Technique

CLOTH is woven on double-heddle looms in extremely long strips from 4–10 inches (10.2 x 25.4 cm) wide which are cut into shorter strips and sewn together, selvedge to selvedge. Woollen blankets are woven in Mali, but usually cotton, silk or rayon is used to weave a voluminous toga-like garment for men and a smaller cloth for women.

The stripweave *kente* cloths woven in Ghana by the Ashanti and Ewe tribes have a distinctive checkered appearance. This is achieved by alternately weaving a section warp-faced, and therefore showing the longitudinal stripes of the variously coloured warp threads, and then a section weft-faced, which shows as a horizontal band. An extra pair of heddles is used with the warp threads grouped in sixes so different sheds can be opened for weaving the weft-faced sections. Supplementary weft floats are used to introduce motifs depicting animals, drums, combs, hands and so on into the warp-faced sections.

ABOVE: ALTERNATING WARP-FACED AND WEFT-FACED WEAVES.

Left: *Ewe stripweave cloth from Ghana. Ewe weaving can be identified by its restrained use of subtle colours. A wide variety of motifs, representing objects such as chickens, drums and combs, are woven with supplementary-weft inlay.*

Right: *A Fulani sheep's wool khasa, or blanket, from Mali, constructed from strips about 20 cm (7⅞ in) wide. Second-hand Fulani blankets are traded all over West Africa.*

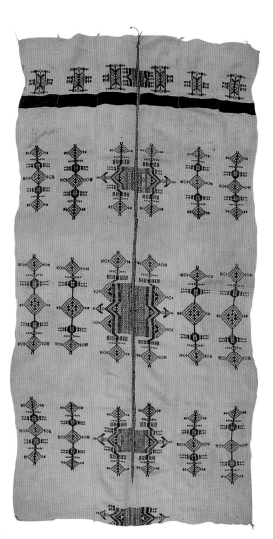

93

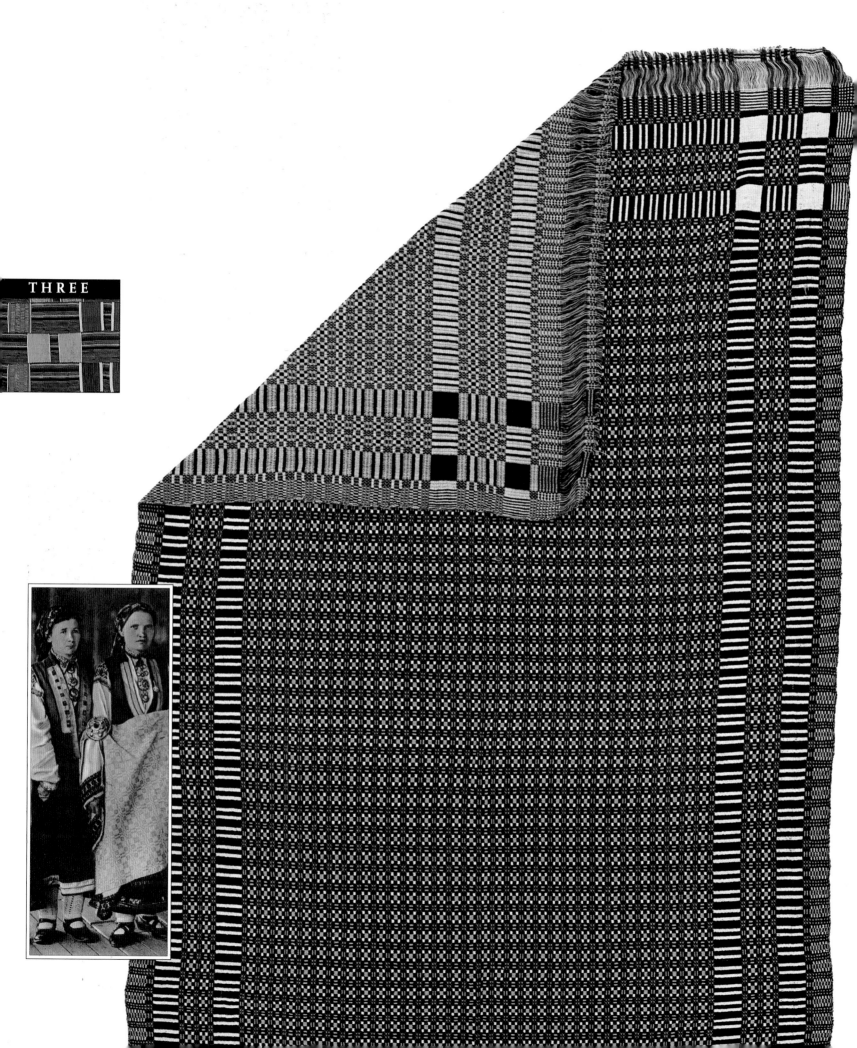

THREE

DOUBLE WEAVE

MANY textiles are woven in such a way that the front and back are quite different in appearance. Double weave or double cloth, however, is an unusual technique in which the 'front' and 'back' are actually woven as independent layers, one above the other, occasionally swapping places to interlink and create a pattern.

Technique

TWO sets of warps are set up one above the other and either separate wefts are woven in or one weft is used for both layers which links them at one selvedge (double-width weave) or at both (tubular weave). With the aid of four or more heddles, the warps are periodically lifted from one level to the other, causing the two layers to change place. As the two layers are composed of different colours or materials, a pattern is created with one face of the fabric the negative of the other.

LEFT: A PATTERN IS CREATED WHERE THE LAYERS INTERSECT.

Uses

TEXTILES woven in double weave, particularly when made of wool, are thick and warm. They have, therefore, been widely used in cooler climates for shawls, blankets and coverlets.

Distribution

DOUBLE weave is a technique in widespread use in Europe and examples can be found from Scotland, Spain, Germany, Poland and Italy. The

manufacture of traditional blankets continues to be a thriving industry in central Wales.

Emigrants took the knowledge of how to make double-weave cloth to the New World where it continued to be manufactured by colonists, such as those in Virginia in the USA and Ontario in Canada.

Archaeological excavations in central Peru have shown that double weaves were produced by the Chancay people who thrived between AD 1000 and 1476. The Quecha and Aymara of Ecuador, Bolivia and Peru continue to produce intricately woven double-weave belts and hat-bands to this day.

In the Punjab and the Pakistan province of Sind, cotton double-weave textiles, known as *khes*, are woven in sections and sewn together and used as bedding.

Above: *A double-weave throw, from the Blue Ridge Mountains in North America, incorporating wool dyed in the distinctive Williamsburg blue. The technique was probably introduced to the region by settlers from the British Isles.*

Below: *Double-weave woollen belts, or* chumpi, *from La Paz in Bolivia. Andean textiles include motifs derived from indigenous wildlife and fabulous creatures taken from myth and heraldry.*

BELOW: HOWLING SPIRITS FROM A PERUVIAN DOUBLE-WEAVE FRAGMENT WOVEN SOME TIME BEFORE AD 1450.

Opposite: *A simple, but boldly patterned, double-weave blanket, or* khes, *from Panipat in India. The pattern can be seen in negative on the reverse.*

Opposite, inset: *Latvian women, one with a double-weave blanket. Double-weave cloth is most often woven in symmetrical, geometric patterns.*

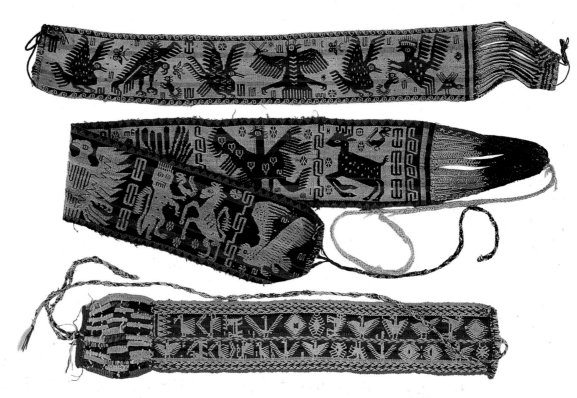

VELVET

VELVET is a luxury fabric with a short, densely piled surface traditionally woven from silk. The pile may uniformly cover the face of a textile (solid velvet) or it may produce a pattern by only appearing in selected places (voided velvet). The pile can be very long (plush) or of two or more lengths (pile on pile). Velvet textiles are often of several colours, may have a pattern stamped onto them and may even be printed.

Technique

THE distinctive pile of velvet is produced by means of supplementary warps which are raised over grooved metal rods inserted into an open shed just like the weft. When weaving has proceeded far enough for the raised warps to be secure they are cut along the groove in the rod with a sharp knife to form dense tufts and the rods are then removed. Sometimes the loops are left uncut for a coarser effect or patterns may be made up from a combination of cut and uncut areas ('cisele' velvet).

Right: *English machine-made upholstery velvet of about 1880, printed with a pattern in the Jacobean style.*

Other piled textiles

FABRICS similar to velvet can be woven with a supplementary weft – for instance, velveteen, which has a solid pile, and corduroy, which has a ribbed pile. Particularly interesting pile cloths are the embroidered raphia textiles made by the

LEFT: PILE OF CUT AND UNCUT LOOPS.

Above: *English Jaspé velvet made in 1640. The patterns are created by areas of cut and uncut pile and void ground.*

Right: *Spanish table carpet, from Alpujarra, woven in about 1750 with wool pile and linen ground weave.*

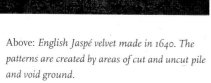

Above: *Russian roller-printed velvet. Mass-produced fabric, like this, was printed with contemporary versions of traditional motifs, such as the medallion, or gul, to be sold to the Central Asian market.*

Above: *Kasai velvet, Kuba cut-pile raphia cloth from the Congo (formerly Zaire).*

Kuba of the Congo (formerly Zaire), sometimes referred to as Kasai velvet. The pile is created by sewing a fine raphia strand under the warp thread of a ready-woven base cloth, so that both ends are above the surface, and then they are cut off short with a knife.

The pile of many fine rugs and carpets is created by knotting or wrapping yarn around the warps of a ground weave. The denser the knots, the higher the quality of the carpet.

Left: *A skilfully woven child's hat, from Uzbekistan, with an ikat pattern with a velvet pile.*

Above: *Opulent Hazara velvet gown, from central Afghanistan, embellished with gold-thread embroidery.*

Right: *A Moroccan woman in a velvet gown with a luxurious texture reminiscent of fur.*

TABLET WEAVING

TABLET weaving is an ingenious method of making narrow bands, belts and straps. The earliest known textiles that were irrefutably woven with tablets were found in a grave at El Cigarellejo in Spain and have been dated to around 375 BC. Although requiring only a small work station, weaving in progress is not readily transportable as it is essential that tension is maintained to prevent twisting. The most sophisticated exponents of this technique are therefore sedentary rather than nomadic.

Turkish tablet woven bands, from top to bottom: Goat hair animal strap from Western Turkey.

Camel bag tie, from Cappadocia, Turkey, with a wavy pattern produced by turning all the tablets in the same direction.

A long, finely woven band from Eastern Turkey.

THREE

Technique

WARPS are stretched on a long narrow loom or between the weaver and a fixed point and not threaded through a system of heddles, but through the corners of tablets made of card, wood or bone, which lie flat against each other like a pack of cards. The tablets are most often square, although many shapes including triangles, hexagons and octagons have been used. According to the intricacy of the pattern anything between seven and three hundred may be used to weave a single band. Each tablet separates the warps threaded through it, lifting some and forcing others down, thus effectively opening a shed through which to pass the weft. By twisting the tablets, individually or in groups, different warps are raised and lowered and different sheds can be opened.

Each time a tablet is rotated, the warp threads twist around each other and so most tablet weaving can be identified by this distinctive warp-twined appearance.

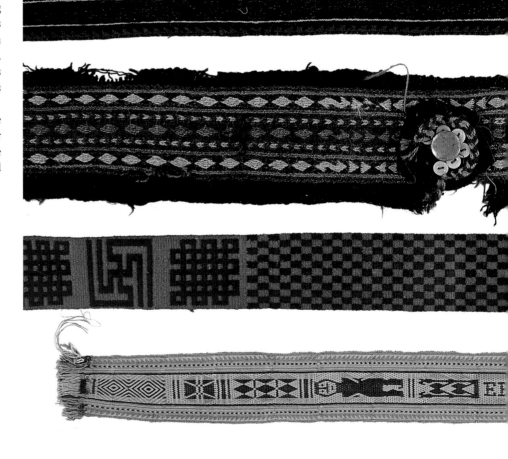

LEFT:
THREADED
TABLET.

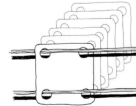

ABOVE: TWINING
WARPS.

Camel bag tie, from Sivas in East Turkey, mounted on a plain wool band for reinforcement.

Double-faced cotton belt from Bhutan.

Double-faced Greek cotton band depicting two of the Evangelists.

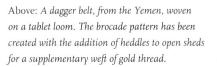

Above: *A dagger belt, from the Yemen, woven on a tablet loom. The brocade pattern has been created with the addition of heddles to open sheds for a supplementary weft of gold thread.*

Uses and distribution

THE high ratio of tablets to warp threads (far higher than is practicable with heddles on a loom) means that a diverse range of complex and intricate warp-faced patterns can be woven, such as the magical cotton belts of Sulawesi in Indonesia worked with Arabic lettering. It is even possible to open two sheds at the same time and produce double weave.

Tablet weaving is employed all over the world from Norway to Morocco and from China to Spain for the construction of narrow bands to be used as belts, sashes, straps and animal trappings.

99

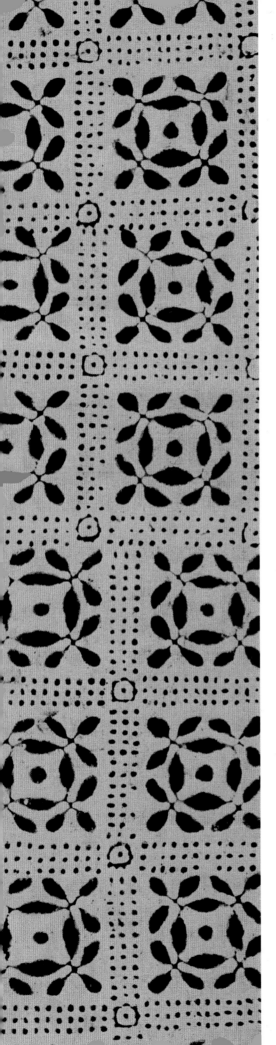

FOUR

PAINTED AND PRINTED TEXTILES

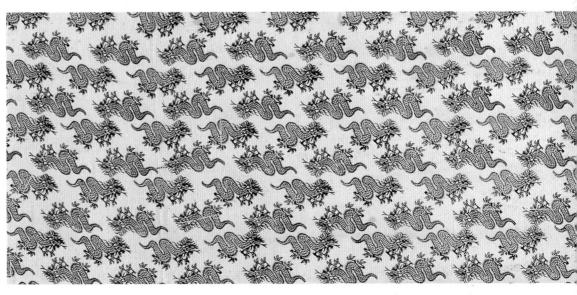

PAINTED AND PRINTED TEXTILES

P AINTINGS from prehistoric times survive on the walls of caves in many parts of the world. A large number of the images depicted served a magical purpose, attracting good luck through the medium of sympathetic magic, the process whereby imitating an action can cause it to happen in reality.

Left: *Tonga islanders playing spillikins in a hut decorated with a large bark cloth painted with geometric patterns with the sap of local trees.*

Above: *Until the disruption of their lifestyle by white colonists, the indigenous inhabitants of Australia disdained the use of clothing. On ritual occasions they decorated their bodies with paint and flowers.*

The first personal decoration was the painting of the body with earth pigments to provide magical protection, denote status or to enhance personal beauty. Tattooing is an extension of this process. Similar designs could be applied to hide or cloth with fingers, sticks or knives. To this day, textiles that serve a particularly esoteric purpose, like the hunting cloths of Herat in Afghanistan or the ceremonial initiation shirts of the Poro men's society of the Côte d'Ivoire, are painted by hand by choice because the high concentration required focuses the life force or thaumaturgic energy and endows the textile with a power of its own.

Left: *Using a* kalam *to draw the ink outlines on a* kalamkari *cloth in Kalahasti, Andhra Pradesh, India.*

Right: *Bakoumba Coulibaly, a Bambara artist, painting the patterns on a bogolanfini mud cloth at Fanimbongou in Mali.*

Left: *An Indian textile artist, outside the G.P.O. in Ahmedabad, Gujarat, India, drawing the outlines of a* mata-ni-pachedi *using lampblack. A finished example of his work hangs on the wall behind him.*

EARTH PIGMENTS

THE colouring agent most readily available to primitive peoples was mud. By selecting mud from different sources and mixing it with a variety of substances, a subtle range of shades of black, red, yellow, brown and white could be made. One of the strongest earth pigments is ochre, prized to this day by the Masai of Kenya for the rich red it yields which they use to colour their garments, hair and bodies. Earth pigments, such as umber, sienna and ochre, are also still used in the manufacture of paint for artists and decorators.

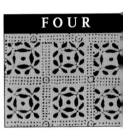

TECHNIQUE

THE first application of pigment to cloth was most probably by hand, and then in progressive order with a stick, a chewed stick and animal hairs attached to a stick to form a brush. All these implements could be used to create a flowing linear pattern. Alternatively, a design could be created by printing onto the cloth with an object such as a shell, stick or hand dipped into pigment. From these primitive origins it did not take man long to make a stamp from clay, wood or metal, shaped to any particular design that took his fancy.

Above: *A Ghanaian craftsman carving stamps from calabash, a large gourd, for printing* adinkra *motifs onto cloth. Every stamp has a symbolic meaning.*

Right: *Printing metallic patterns onto cloth at Indore, Madhya Pradesh, India. Brightly coloured cloth like this is used for shawls and saris by Indian women from all walks of life.*

Far right: *A Muslim woman, from Jodhpur, in the Indian state of Rajasthan, printing patterns on cotton cloth with a wooden block.*

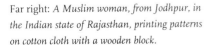

DAUBED TEXTILES

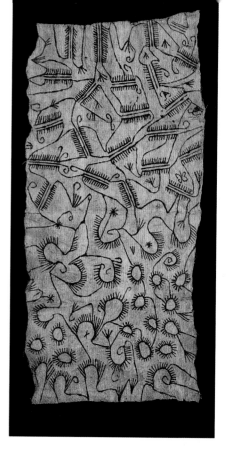

Just as prehistoric peoples painted their magical images on the rock walls and caves of every continent, they painted the skins and hides that they wore.

Native American hide paintings

On the prairies of North America, until late in the 19th century, the Plains Indians continued to record and commemorate the great events and adventures of their lives, as well as their magical visions, on the buffalo-hide robes they wore and on the covers of the tipis in which they lived. The humble medium they used was pigment derived mainly from earth and rocks applied with a stylus of bone or wood. The final painting was often protected with size made from boiled horn, hide scrapings or cactus juice.

Painted magic

Although the Native Americans of the Plains were adept at decorating clothing and equipment with beads or quillwork, like the artists of many other cultures, when decoration took on a magical significance they preferred to

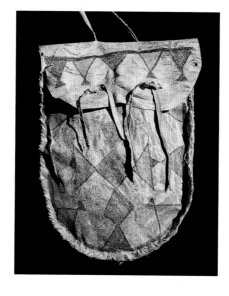

Above: A painted rawhide pouch acquired at the Sioux reservation at Pine Ridge in South Dakota, North America.

paint the motifs directly by hand. The Ghost Dance shirts worn in the 1880s and 1890s, hand painted with motifs of birds, animals and stars, were believed to render the wearer bulletproof.

Bogolanfini mud cloths

One of the most striking of all daubed textiles are the bogolanfini 'mud cloths' of Mali. These are decorated with geometric patterns in white on a black background – the result of painting previously dyed cloth with river mud, applied with a bamboo splint or metal spatula, and bleaching colour from the exposed, unpainted areas with a solution of caustic soda, peanuts and millet. 'Mud cloth' is traditionally worn as ceremonial costume at rites of passage.

Top: Loincloth of bark cloth made by a pygmy tribe in the Congo (formerly Zaire). The mysterious, flowing, linear pattern appears to have been applied with a stick.

Left: A tapa bark cloth from Tonga. A brush, made by sharpening the dried key of a pandanus fruit, is sometimes used to paint patterns with pigment made from the bark of the koka tree, Bischovia javanica.

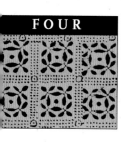

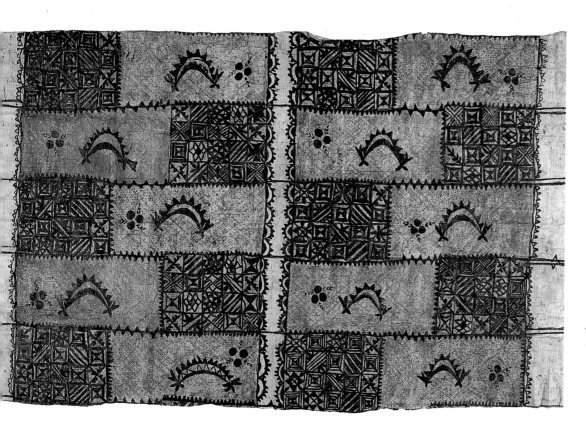

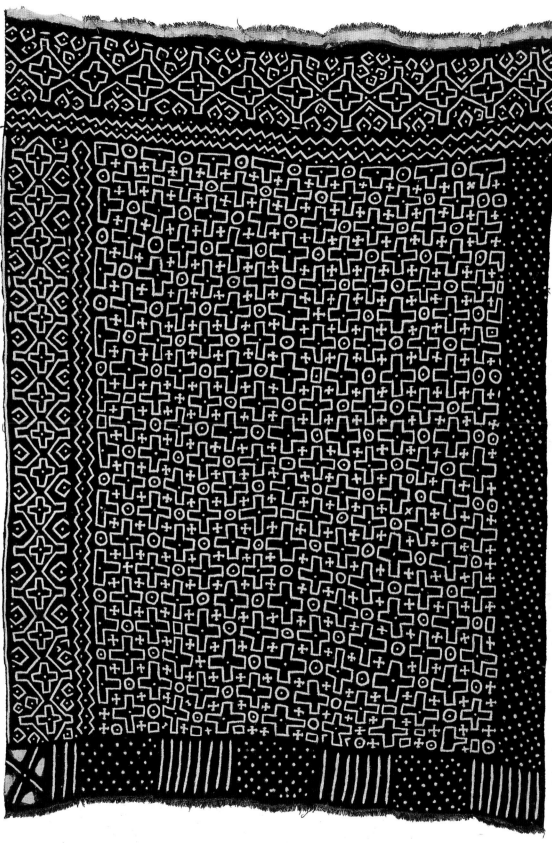

Above and below: *Bogolanfini mud cloths made by the Bamana of Mali. The ground is made by sewing together narrow strips of cotton cloth.*

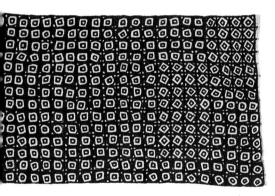

Other daubed textiles

MEMBERS of the Senufo's Poro men's society of the Côte d'Ivoire wear daubed cloths for ceremonial dress which are decorated with crocodiles, turtles, snakes and masked figures. The designs are drawn out with a green paint made from leaves and with mud applied with the edge of a knife. Some of the bark *tapa* cloths of Tonga are also decorated by daubing on the patterns freehand.

Above: *The dense application of mud on this Bamana mud cloth from Mali results in an intricate negative pattern of exposed, bleached areas.*

PAINTED TEXTILES

The introduction of a brush or absorbent applicator that will hold a reserve of pigment and can be manipulated with fluidity allows a much greater degree of sophistication than a finger, knife or stick.

Paints

Pigments are the raw materials of colour. They may be derived from earth, minerals, animals, insects or plants, but all need to be mixed with other substances, usually oils or fats, to achieve a sufficiently fluid consistency for controlled painting. Gum arabic, exuded by certain acacia trees, is a particularly good medium.

Technique

Textile painting for religious and educational purposes is frequently carried out according to very strict rules about composition and colour. The sequence of painting is also often scrupulously adhered to – so that the colours will not run, the cloth is first coated with starch or size, a sort of glue. Outlines are drawn in and then painting proceeds, one colour at a time over the whole fabric, beginning with the lightest colour and ending with the darkest. The outlines are then repainted over in black. Finally, the eyes of the focal figure are painted and the picture brought to life.

Uses

Paints remain on the surface of fabrics and are therefore vulnerable to wear and tear. For this reason painted textiles are seldom used for clothing – more often being employed for religious, educational or decorative purposes. In many places large, painted cloths are used as illustrations and backdrops by professional storytellers for the recitation of epic tales such as that of the Pabuji in Rajasthan, India, or of the Paladins in Sicily. Great care is also taken over the painting of spiritual works such as the thankas of Tibetan Buddhism.

Roghan

Roghan work was once practised in many places in the Indian subcontinent, but is now restricted to the village of Nirona in Kutch. Roghan is a thick, bright paste which is used to decorate inexpensive textiles with geometric patterns. Safflower, castor or linseed oil is boiled up until it forms a thick residue which is then mixed with chalk and coloured pigment. This is applied to the cloth with a stick or metal rod. It may also be printed on with a metal block.

Above: *A section of a painted* par, *from Bhilwara in Rajasthan, India, used in the telling of the story of the folk hero Pabuji, who appears in the centre.*

FOUR

Below: *A mata-ni-pachedi* shrine cloth, from *Ahmedabad in Gujarat, India, depicting the mother goddess in her fearsome form of Durga. These painted cloths are used to decorate shrines visited by low-caste Hindus to ask for help from the goddess during times of misfortune. On this cloth she is shown armed with the weapons of the other gods to fight the buffalo demon, Mahisha. The outlines and details may be printed or drawn on, while the large areas are painted in with a brush made from a chewed stick.*

Opposite, above, left: *Painted bark cloth from Colombia.*

Opposite, far left: *Delicately patterned cotton textile made by the Shipibo-Conibo in northern Peru.*

Opposite, right: *Roghan work* odhni, *or shawl, made in Kutch, North-West India, to be sold in Sind, Pakistan.*

PEN WORK

FOUR

Kalamkari

THE Persian word 'kalamkari' can be literally translated as 'pen work'. The use of a Persian name for these Indian fabrics proves their popular demand as trade items. They have been exported from the south-east coast of India since the 16th century to Persia, South-East Asia and Europe.

Technique

COTTON cloth that has been specially prepared is spread out on the ground or on a low bench and outlines are sketched out freehand with charcoal. The lines are then carefully drawn over with a *kalam*. The *kalam* is a sharpened length of bamboo with a felt or wool pad tied to the point. The flow of ink is controlled by finger-tip pressure on the ink-soaked pad. Larger areas are then filled in with another *kalam* with a flattened and softened tip. The colours are achieved partly with paint and partly with the application of dyestuffs and mordants.

Uses

LIKE all painted cloths, *kalamkaris* are vulnerable to wear and so they are primarily reserved for use as religious hangings. They are often decorated with scenes from the Hindu epics, the *Mahabharata* and the *Ramayana*. The craftsmen of Masulipatnam in Andhra Pradesh in India, however, concentrated on the production of floral and geometric patterns demanded by Muslim customers and later by Europeans. These fabrics, that we think of as chintzes (from the Hindi word for 'painted'), were often glazed to make them more durable.

A large Persian kalamkari, *from Isfahan, used by storytellers to illustrate the adventures of the kings and heroes of the great Persian epic, the* Shahnama.

Three kalamkari *paintings from Kalahasti in the eastern Indian state of Andhra Pradesh.*

Above: *In an episode from the Ramayana, Ravana, the demon king, creates a magical deer to lure Rama and his brother, Lakshman, into the forest, leaving Sita, Rama's wife, unguarded.*

Right: *Before the battle of Kurukshetra, Krishna recites the* Bhagavad Gita *to teach his hesitant cousin, Arjuna, his duty.*

Below: *The avatars, or incarnations, of Vishnu, top row, from left to right, Matsya, Kurma, Varaha, Narasimha and Vamana; bottom row, Parashurama, Rama, Balarama, Krishna and Kalki, who is yet to come.*

WOODBLOCK PRINTING

THE idea of using an object or utensil to impress repeated and identical designs into pottery can be traced to prehistoric times. The Chinese developed the use of wooden blocks for letterpress printing about two thousand years ago and soon after cloth was being printed in both China and India. Today, printed fabrics are produced all over the world.

Woodblocks

To ensure crisp carving and sharp detail, woodblocks are made by cutting into the end grain of densely grained hardwoods such as ash, box, sycamore or pearwood. To avoid excessive weight, the pattern may be divided up and different sections of it carved on different blocks.

Technique

First a sheet of cloth, most often cotton, is laid out on a level surface. Then, a tub or bowl is filled with pigment and a cloth pad placed over the surface to soak it up. The printing block is pressed on this pad with sufficient pressure to pick up just the right amount of colour. The block is then placed carefully on the cloth to be printed and struck with the heel of the hand or with a mallet. This process is repeated, carefully aligning the block each time, until the entire cloth has been patterned.

Uses

Because block-printing can be employed to produce patterned cloth so quickly and efficiently, it is both cheap and popular. As the colours can be created through the application of resilient inks and dyes, hard-wearing textiles can be made suitable for everyday use as clothing, bedspreads or decoration.

Adinkra

The Ashanti of Ghana use stamps cut from calabash gourds to print *adinkra* cloth. There are many different motifs, each having magical or allegorical meaning, and these are printed in groups on a large cloth that has been marked out in squares. The ink, derived from bark and iron slag, is always black or dark brown and the background is usually either white or bark dyed blue-black. *Adinkra* cloths are not used on a daily basis, but on ritual and special occasions such as funerals.

Above: *A Shiah Muslim shrine cloth with medallions of Arabic calligraphy printed in Ahmedabad, Gujarat, India.*

Below: *Detail of Indian block-printed yardage from Madhya Pradesh.*

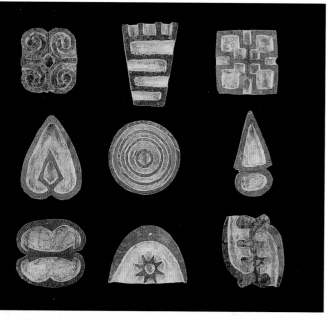

Far left: *Stamps carved from calabash shells for printing* adinkra *cloth.*

Left: *Block-printed prayer flags, from Bhutan, featuring* lung ta *wind horses.*

Opposite: Adinkra *cloth from Ghana. The cloth has been divided into squares, each of which has been filled with prints of one allegorical motif.*

Opposite, inset: *A Ghanaian schoolmaster. The double ram's horn motif means, 'It is the heart and not the horns that leads the ram to bully.'*

By using a number of printing blocks, each cut to print a different part of the pattern, it is possible to produce sophisticated, multi-coloured designs. It is not uncommon for nine or ten colours to be used on a single textile. Of course, the more colours used, the greater the time and labour required for cutting the blocks and printing and, therefore, the more expensive the product.

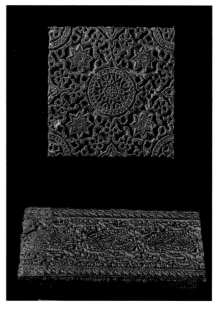

Above: *Wooden printing blocks from Gujarat, India. The Gujaratis are expert carvers and crisp, floral carvings can be found ornamenting the façades of the family palaces of merchants and princes.*

Technique

THE process for printing with several blocks is the same as for printing with one. One colour is applied at a time using the appropriate block or blocks. To ensure that each subsequent colour registers properly whole blocks are often cut to shape or have registration notches cut in their sides. The most efficient method is to set brass pitch pins into the corners for accurate alignment.

Mass production

THE invention of multiple block-printing opened the doors for manual mass production. The economy of India

Left: *Printed cotton, Masulipatnam, Andhra Pradesh, India. Patterns like this may use ten or more differently carved blocks.*

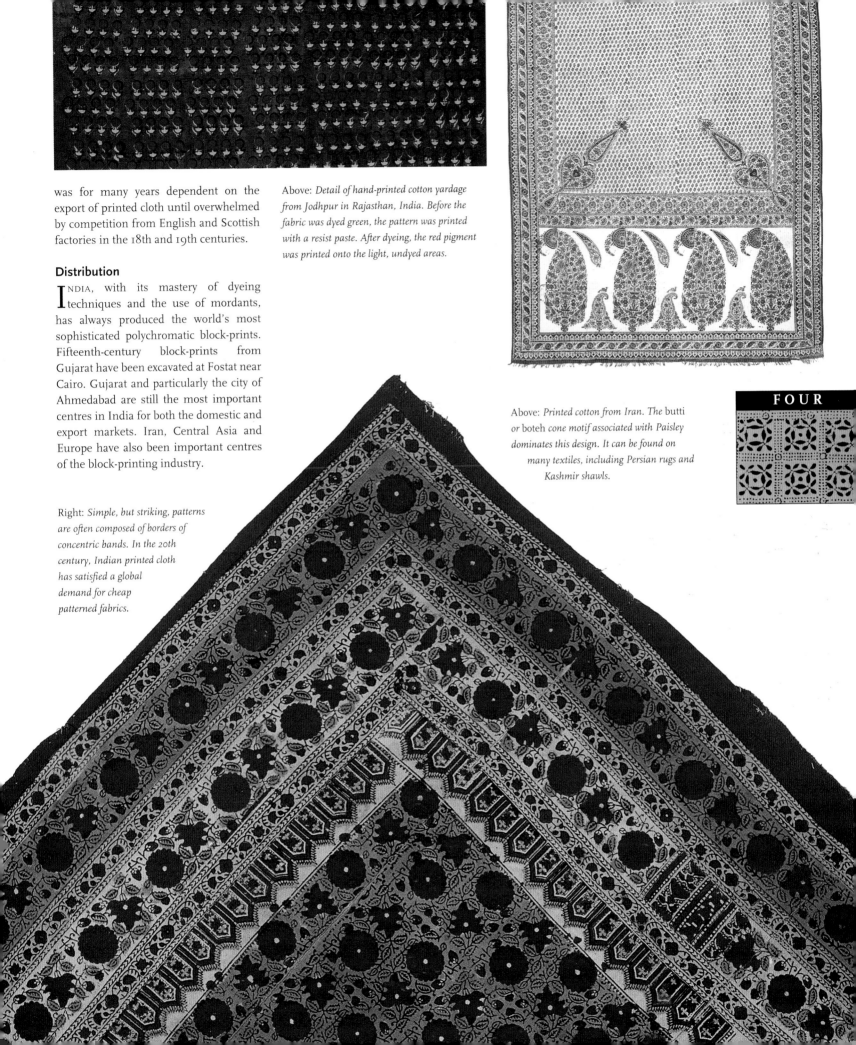

was for many years dependent on the export of printed cloth until overwhelmed by competition from English and Scottish factories in the 18th and 19th centuries.

Distribution

INDIA, with its mastery of dyeing techniques and the use of mordants, has always produced the world's most sophisticated polychromatic block-prints. Fifteenth-century block-prints from Gujarat have been excavated at Fostat near Cairo. Gujarat and particularly the city of Ahmedabad are still the most important centres in India for both the domestic and export markets. Iran, Central Asia and Europe have also been important centres of the block-printing industry.

Above: Detail of hand-printed cotton yardage from Jodhpur in Rajasthan, India. Before the fabric was dyed green, the pattern was printed with a resist paste. After dyeing, the red pigment was printed onto the light, undyed areas.

Above: Printed cotton from Iran. The butti *or* boteh *cone motif associated with Paisley dominates this design. It can be found on many textiles, including Persian rugs and Kashmir shawls.*

FOUR

Right: *Simple, but striking, patterns are often composed of borders of concentric bands. In the 20th century, Indian printed cloth has satisfied a global demand for cheap patterned fabrics.*

STENCILLING

S TENCILLING is a widespread technique used either to implant a design directly, or to apply starch in the dye-resist process. The stencil is in essence a mask with a carefully cut hole in it so that pigment can be applied to selected areas only. This mask might be made of metal, oiled paper or even banana leaves. The most sophisticated stencils of all are made in Japan.

Technique

T HE Japanese learned how to use stencils in the 8th century. The weakness of stencils was the ties that had to be left once the pattern had been cut out. These were fragile and broke easily, so stencils were previously bold and clumsy. The Japanese came up with an ingenious solution that transformed stencilling into the art form now known as *katazome*. Sets of identical stencils are cut with a long, thin knife from sheets of paper made from waterproofed mulberry fibre. One sheet is brushed with adhesive and silk threads or strands of hair are glued on in several directions like a net. A second sheet is then glued on top. The hairs reinforce the stencil and make it possible to cut very intricate shapes that will not fall apart. Ink (or starch when resist dyeing) is then pounced through the stencil with a soft brush. Great subtlety can be achieved by varying the amount of colour on the brush or the pressure applied.

LEFT: INUIT STENCIL FROM BAFFINLAND, 1961. 'TWO MEN DISCUSSING THE HUNT.'

Above: *A 19th-century Japanese stencilled kimono. More frequently, the Japanese stencil on a resist paste and then dye the cloth. This would have produced a light pattern on a dark background.*

Below: *Nineteenth-century tent decoration from Rajasthan, India. The details and outlines are printed and the large red areas filled in with a stencil.*

Opposite: *Detail of bark cloth from Fiji. Pigment is rubbed through a banana-leaf stencil with a wad of* tapa.

Screen printing

S CREEN printing is a development of the Japanese stencil. Silk or organdie is stretched across a wooden frame and parts of it are masked off with paper or acetate which subsequently sticks to the silk because of the printing ink. Ink is then poured into the frame and forced through the silk with a rubber squeegee onto a sheet of fabric. Where the silk has been masked, the ink is unable to penetrate and cannot reach the fabric beneath. The wooden frame, or screen, is then lifted clear and the design can be repeated on a further section of cloth. Several screens may be used to build up as many colours as are required.

Left: *A painted 'hunting cloth', from Herat, Afghanistan, intended to appease the spirits of hunted animals. The flowers and details of the pattern have been applied with a stencil.*

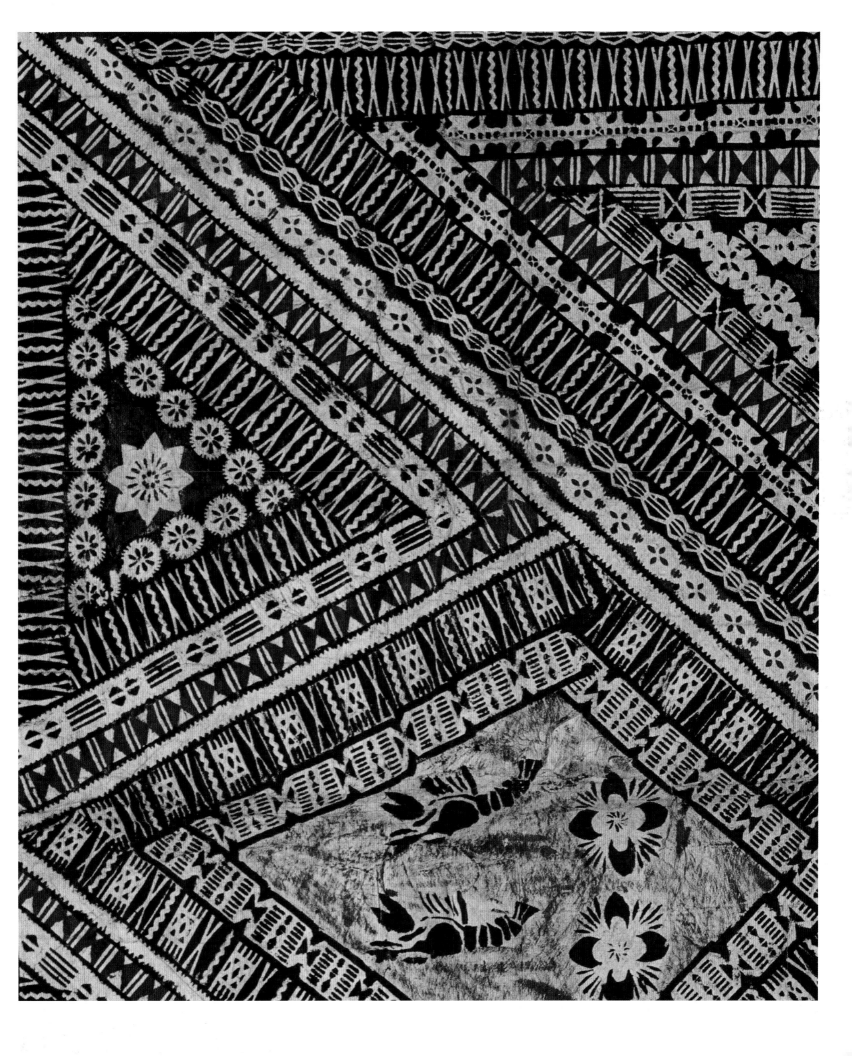

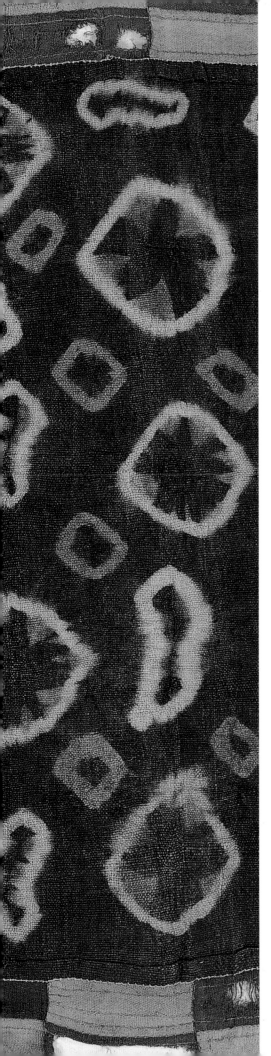

LEFT: KUBA RAPHIA
SKIRT WITH STITCHED-
RESIST DECORATION,
THE CONGO
(FORMERLY ZAIRE).

BELOW: BAGOBO
MAN'S TIE AND
DYE KERCHIEF
FROM MINDANAO,
PHILIPPINES.

BOTTOM: ERSARI
JALLAR DYED
WITH MADDER
AND COCHINEAL,
TURKMENISTAN.

RIGHT: DYED TURBAN
LENGTHS, RAJASTHAN,
INDIA.

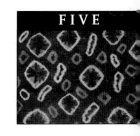

FIVE

DYES

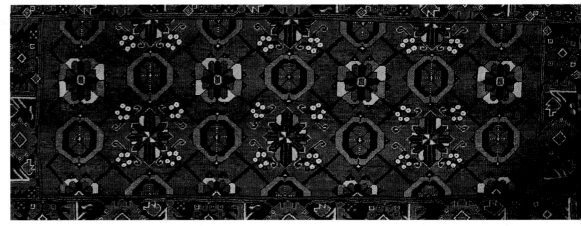

DYES

YES are absorbed into the very fibres of textiles, ensuring a much longer lifetime than paints and pigments which are applied to the surface of a textile and are therefore vulnerable to wear and tear. At its most basic, dyeing is a process in which yarn or fabric is immersed in a solution produced by boiling up selected raw materials or dyestuffs. In origin these may be animal (*murex* shell for purple), vegetable (onion skins for yellow) or mineral (iron oxide for red).

Above: *A dyer at Barmer in Rajasthan, India, mixing together the ingredients for a yellow dye. He is in the process of adding myrobalan flowers to the mix. Many dye recipes are closely guarded secrets.*

FIVE

Above, right: *Black walnut, a source of black and brown dye.*

Right: *Dyed woollen yarn for sale at the Kashgar yarn market in Xinjiang, China.*

Below: *A woman, from the village of Biashia, Guizhou, China, drawing out wax-resist patterns on cotton cloth with a Chinese knife.*

SUBSTANTIVE DYES

ANY substances are capable of yielding colours or stains, but few are resilient enough to withstand repeated washing or exposure to sunlight. Those dyes that give a fast, lasting colour without the need for extra chemical processes are known as substantive dyes. Amongst these highly prized dyestuffs are walnut (for black), orchil lichens (for mauves), and, the king of dyes, indigo.

ADJECTIVE DYES

OST natural dyes such as cochineal or madder are not fast unless the yarn or fabric to be dyed is first treated with a mordant which makes it more absorbent and helps the dye to bite. Different dyes require different mordants, but most mordants used today are of mineral origin such as alum, tin, chrome or iron, although the oldest and most widespread is urine.

ANILINE DYES

I N the 1850s, as the result of a search for a use for coal tar (the waste product of coal gas) and analysis of the chemical structure of indigo, the first reliable alternative to natural dyes was developed in Britain. These aniline dyes (from *anil*, the Arabic word for indigo) became available in an astounding range of colours which, combined with their fastness, consistency and ease of use, made them so popular worldwide that in many places the craft of dyeing with natural dyes was virtually forgotten.

Above: *Woman drawing batik with a canting, Java.*

Above: *Man printing batik patterns with a cap in Jogjakarta, Java. The pattern is known as* parang *and was once reserved for use only by members of the court.*

Above, right: *Using a wooden block to print the red onto* ajrakh *cloth at Dhamadhka, Kutch, North-West India.*

THE SURVIVAL OF NATURAL DYES

A LTHOUGH the use of aniline or chemical dyes is now the norm, in a number of places, such as the Highlands and Islands of Scotland, the subtlety of natural dyes is still appreciated and there has been a resurgence in their use. In other places where particular dyes are used for reasons of beauty, prestige, custom and symbolism their use has never been threatened.

Left: *Untying wefts for weft-ikat cloth at Sukarara, Lombok, Indonesia. The pattern was resist dyed into the wefts before they were woven. This may involve tying, untying and retying the yarn several times to dye different parts of the pattern in different colours.*

Right: *Weaving double ikat, where both the weft and warp have been resist dyed, Tenganan, Bali.*

INDIGO

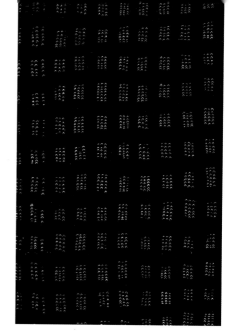

Indigo is the oldest dyestuff known to man, having been in use since 2500 BC, if not before, during the Old Kingdom of Ancient Egypt. Requiring expertise and patience to produce, indigo-dyed textiles have been valued the world over for their fast, deep blue colour and until the advent of aniline dyes indigo was the most widely used dye of all. Various plants growing in tropical regions are used to make indigo, including members of the genus *Indigofera* in India, China, the Americas and the East Indies, *Baptisia tinctoria* also in the East Indies, *Lonchocarpus cyanescens* in West Africa and *Polygonum tinctoria* in Japan. Woad, *Isatis tinctoria*, with which Ancient Britons so famously painted themselves, is a form of indigo.

Technique

The preparation of indigo for dyeing is an arcane and complicated process. The indigo dyestuff is almost always extracted from plants by boiling, but in West Africa the leaves are sometimes simply rolled into a ball and dried. Although indigo is a substantive dye and needs no mordant, it must be fermented and deoxidized in an alkaline solution to make it soluble so that it can be absorbed into the fibres to be dyed. This is carried out in deep vats, which are often buried in the ground. Cloth or yarn may be repeatedly dipped in the vats or soaked for as long as six days depending on the intensity of colour required. On removal from the vats, the dyed fibres initially appear pale yellow, but as the indigo once more becomes oxidized as it is exposed to the air it turns blue and becomes insoluble again which renders it fast against washing. To add sheen, dyed cloth may be beaten with a wooden mallet or polished with shells.

FIVE

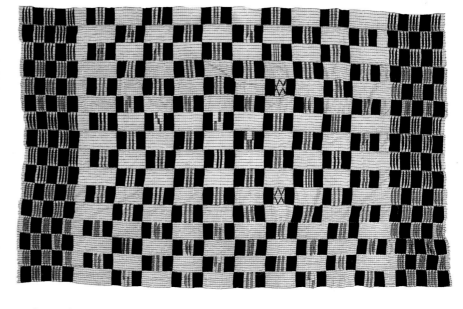

Indigo today

Indigo dyeing remains a living art to this day, notably in West Africa and South-East Asia where indigo cloth is used for ritual purposes, to express tribal identity and to show status. Ironically, synthetic indigo is used to dye denim jeans, the common man's modern working attire.

Above: *An Ewe woman's cotton stripweave mourning cloth woven from undyed and indigo-dyed yarn, Ghana.*

Left: *Girls of the Blue H'mong tribe wearing their distinctive indigo-dyed costumes at Sapa weekly market in Vietnam. The sheen on their skirts is achieved by beating indigo-dyed cloth with a mallet.*

Top: *A woman's loincloth from Burkina Faso. The pattern was created by resisting the indigo dye with stitching.*

Opposite, above, left: *Woman's tapis with a warp-ikat pattern of horses, worn by the Ngada people, Flores, Indonesia.*

Opposite, below, left: *Yoruba hand-drawn adire cloth from Nigeria. The pattern is created by resisting the indigo with starch paste.*

Opposite, right: *A woman's stitched-resist loincloth from Burkina Faso. Strong blues are built up by repeated dippings in the indigo vat.*

Opposite, inset: *Tuaregs, the Blue Men of the Sahara, wearing the indigo-dyed veils that stain their skin blue.*

TIE AND DYE

Dye resist

DYEING only selected parts of a piece of cloth is a tricky process as dye's natural tendency is to run along the fibres of a piece of cloth. It is easier to prepare the cloth before dyeing in such a way that in certain areas the absorption of the dye is resisted. Tie and dye is one of the simplest dye-resist techniques.

Technique

IF twine is bound tightly around a bunch of fabric before it is dyed the twine will resist the penetration of the dye and upon unbinding an undyed circle will be revealed. Binding the bunch at intervals will produce concentric circles, while tying a series of independent bunches (see diagrams on right) will create a pattern of small rings. In India and Indonesia the cloth is poked up with the fingertip and tied. In West Africa the cloth is sometimes tied around a stone or stick to control the shape of the resist area, whereas in Japan very delicate patterns can be produced by tying tiny bunches with a grain of rice inside to hold the twine in place.

If the cloth is folded or pleated and then tied before dyeing, as is often done by the Yoruba of Nigeria, the result is a zigzag or criss-cross pattern.

FIVE

Above, left: *Japanese* shibori *silk scarf. A border has been made at each end by tying a series of closely placed knots in a cloud pattern.*

Above: *A Japanese short-sleeved, silk* shibori *jacket, with a simple pattern of tiny diagonal rings.*

LEFT: TYING KNOTS FOR SEPARATE RINGS.

LEFT: TYING KNOTS FOR CONCENTRIC RINGS.

In Senegal and the Gambia a marbled effect is created by bunching up the whole cloth before binding it ready for dyeing.

By repeating the tie and dye process a number of times, using a different dye each time, a multi-coloured effect is achieved. In Indonesia this is known as *plangi* which means rainbow.

Left: *Dyed cotton dress, from Hama in Syria, decorated with a simple, but striking, geometric pattern of small tie and dye rings.*

Right: *A Sindhi woman's shawl from Khipro Sangar in Pakistan. In the Indian subcontinent tie and dye is known as* bandhani, *from the Hindustani word meaning 'to tie'. The demand for 'bandannas' has been so great that dyed or printed imitations are today produced as far afield as North America and Java.*

Above: *Rabari girls, from Kutch, North-West India, one is wearing a tie and dye shawl.*

Distribution

Traditional tie and dye textiles are found in Latin America, the Middle East, the Caucasus, Africa and all over Asia. It is known as *plangi* in Indonesia, *shibori* in Japan and *bandhani* in India and Pakistan.

In the 18th century Indian *bandhani* was in such demand that 'bandanna' entered the English language as the word for a spotted kerchief. In the 1960s the technique spread to the Western world and tie and dye garments became a popular mode of dress worn by the hippies of San Francisco in North America.

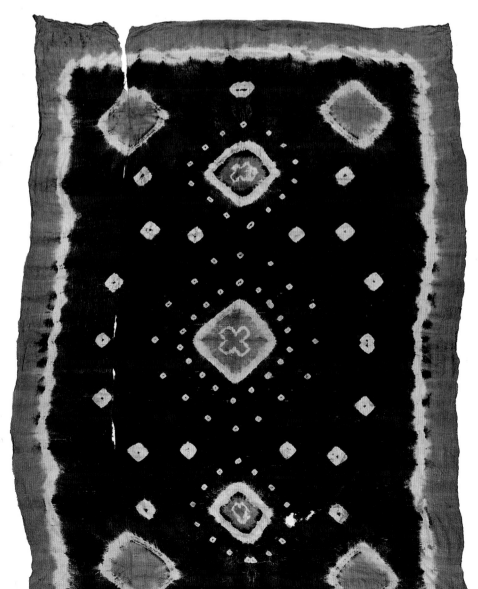

Left: *A woman's silk shawl from Tajikistan. To tie the resist bindings to produce squares, the sections of fabric must be pinched up and then carefully folded or pleated before tying.*

Above: *A tie-dyed yashmak of loosely woven woollen cloth, worn to hide their faces by women from San'a, the capital of Yemen. Here, the cloth has been folded, pinched up and then tied in concentric circles before dyeing.*

123

STITCHED RESIST

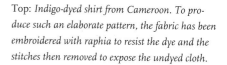

STITCHED resist, like tie and dye, prevents dye reaching parts of the cloth. In Indonesia this technique is known as *tritik* and in Nigeria as *adire alabere*. It is a commonly used technique in Japan, Indonesia and the West African countries of Senegal, Mali, the Gambia, Sierra Leone, Burkina Faso, Nigeria and Cameroon.

Technique

To create a symmetrical pattern, and incidentally reduce the amount of work involved, the cloth to be dyed is normally first doubled up or pleated. Strong thread or raphia is sewn in and out of the fabric and then pulled very tight, causing the cloth to compress and resist the dye. The pattern is revealed in negative when the stitches are removed and the cloth opened out.

Distribution

In Sumatra and Java *tritik* is generally linear, but in West Africa a wide variety of bold patterns are produced with different arrangements of stitching. Indigo-dyed *adire alabere* textiles are produced in Nigeria, Gambia and other parts of West Africa by machine-sewing, as well as by hand.

West African stitched resist is almost always either blue or brown. Kola nut can be used for brown and the blue is obtained from either natural or synthetic indigo.

STITCHING FOLDED CLOTH.

PULLING STITCHES TIGHT.

The import of fine European mill cloth and smooth sewing threads has also meant that finer work can now be done.

In Java, Japan and Cambodia *tritik* is often combined with other methods of resist dyeing. One method is to stitch the outlines of a resist pattern, draw the threads tight, and then cover the portion of fabric within with vegetal matter, plastic or paper, which is then tacked into place. The most notable examples of this are the beautiful *selendangs* of Palembang in Sumatra which are worked on Shantung silk. As this silk is loosely woven, to save time on an arduous task, the *tritik* workers can tie them three layers at a time.

Top: *Indigo-dyed shirt from Cameroon. To produce such an elaborate pattern, the fabric has been embroidered with raphia to resist the dye and the stitches then removed to expose the undyed cloth.*

Above: *Cotton cloth, from the Gambia, stitched resist dyed in indigo. The cloth has been folded three times before stitching to ensure symmetry.*

Far left: Tritik *shawl from Palembang, Sumatra. To resist the dye, the dot patterns have been tied, but the egg shapes and linear motifs stitched.*

Left: *Indigo-dyed cloth made by the Dogon people of Mali with a pattern created by the stitched-resist technique.*

Opposite: *Dance skirt, worn by a member of the Dida tribe of the Côte d'Ivoire, made of silky raphia cloth with stitched-resist patterns.*

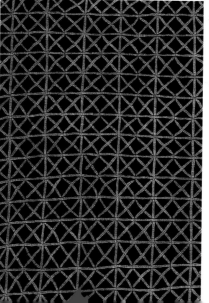

LEHERIA AND MOTHARA

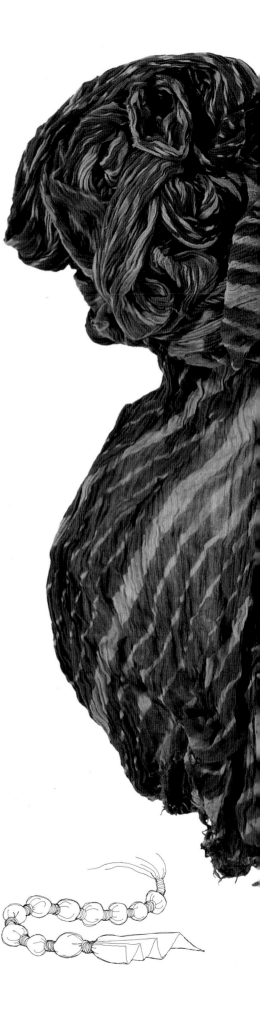

IN the 19th and early 20th centuries, the Marwaris, merchants of Rajasthan and the dominant business community of India, wore elaborately tied, brightly coloured turbans as their distinguishing mark. These turbans were made by the leheria technique ('leheria' in Hindi literally means 'waves') and this process continues to be practised in the dyeing quarters of the Rajasthani towns of Jodphur, Jaipur, Udaipur and Nathdwara.

Technique

LEHERIA is a method of tie and dye. Fabrics, generally turbans or sari lengths, are rolled diagonally from one corner to the opposite selvedge, and then tied at the required intervals and dyed. The result is a pattern of diagonal stripes. To produce a zigzag wave pattern the fabric is folded like a fan across its width before tying.

After dyeing, the fabric may be untied, refolded or rolled, this time on the other diagonal, and retied. Fabric prepared in this way reveals a pattern of checks called mothara, named after the spaces left which are the size of a lentil ('moth' in Hindi). Further colours may be introduced with a succession of tying, dyeing in different dye baths and by bleaching back.

Colour must penetrate right through the tightly rolled cloth, so this technique can only be applied to highly permeable, thin, loose cottons or silks.

Leheria is sold with its ties still in place to show that it is the genuine article. A small end portion is unravelled to display the pattern to potential buyers.

LEFT: MAHARAJA GAJ SINGH OF JODHPUR (REIGNED 1620–38) WEARING A LEHERIA TURBAN.

Below: *A turban length, from Jaipur, Rajasthan, India, with the end untied to reveal a pattern of diagonal stripes and dots. Leheria and mothara turbans are sold with the ties still in place.*

Right, from left to right: *Three leheria turban lengths from Jaipur, India. The cheap turban on the left is made of coarse, loosely woven muslin that has been stretched on one diagonal, rolled up and then tied with resists to create a pattern of simple diagonal stripes. The second is of much finer quality and has been carefully pleated before the resists have been tied in order to produce the distinctive* leheria *'wave' pattern. The third turban has been dyed like the first, the resists have been removed, and then the cloth has been stretched and rolled on the other diagonal before a new set of resists has been tied. This results in a pattern of* mothara *dots.*

Opposite, right: *Two cotton turban lengths, from Jodhpur, India, showing the result of repeated tying and dyeing in different colours.*

STARCH-RESIST BY HAND

I N Nigeria and Japan starch is used as a resist medium for designs on cloth to be dyed with indigo. In both countries it can be applied either by hand or through a stencil. In Nigeria, starch-resist is the speciality of the Yoruba people and is known as *adire eleko*.

Above: *A Toraja banner, from the Indonesian island of Sulawesi, with panels decorated with rice-paste resist patterns.*

Below: *A sake seller's* happi *from Honshu, the largest island of Japan. In the past, indigo-dyed jackets were worn by workmen of many professions with the insignia of their employer emblazoned on the back by means of a rice starch-resist.*

Technique in Nigeria

I BADAN is the main Nigerian centre for hand-drawn adire cloth. The cloth to be dyed is always divided into squares and the designs drawn within each square. The starch used is known as *lafun* or *eko* and is made from either cassava or cornflower. It is boiled with alum and then applied to the cloth by women using a palm-leaf rib or a feather. After the starch dries, the cloth is dyed in indigo. It must be handled very carefully during the dyeing process so the starch is not rubbed off.

The cloth is dried and the starch is scraped or flaked off, leaving a pattern in negative in the same manner as Javanese batik. Because the starch does not completely resist the dye, indigo-dyed adire cloth has a pattern in light blue on a dark blue background.

Adire eleko is decorated with stylized motifs based on birds and everyday objects.

Technique in Japan

I N Japan a sheet of cotton is stretched out on a bamboo frame and a pattern is drawn on both sides using a resist paste made from rice starch. The process is

Above: *The crane and the tortoise are both symbols of longevity and appear on many Japanese textiles. Here, the patterns have been created by resisting the dye with rice starch applied with a* tsutsu.

Opposite: Adire eleko, *from Nigeria, with a pattern created by applying a resist-paste of cassava flour by hand. This pattern, made up of two particular motifs, conveys the messages, 'I'm getting my head together'.*

Opposite, inset: *Japanese workmen wearing traditional indigo-dyed* happi *with starch-resist insignia, while making barrels.*

known as *tsutsugaki* after the tube (*tsutsu*) with which the paste is applied. This is made from a length of bamboo with a metal tip at one end and a paper cone at the other. The cone is gently squeezed so that the starch with which it has been filled will flow out of the metal tip in a controlled line.

Indigo-dyed *tsutsugaki* cloth traditionally features designs of auspicious symbols, and figurative patterns.

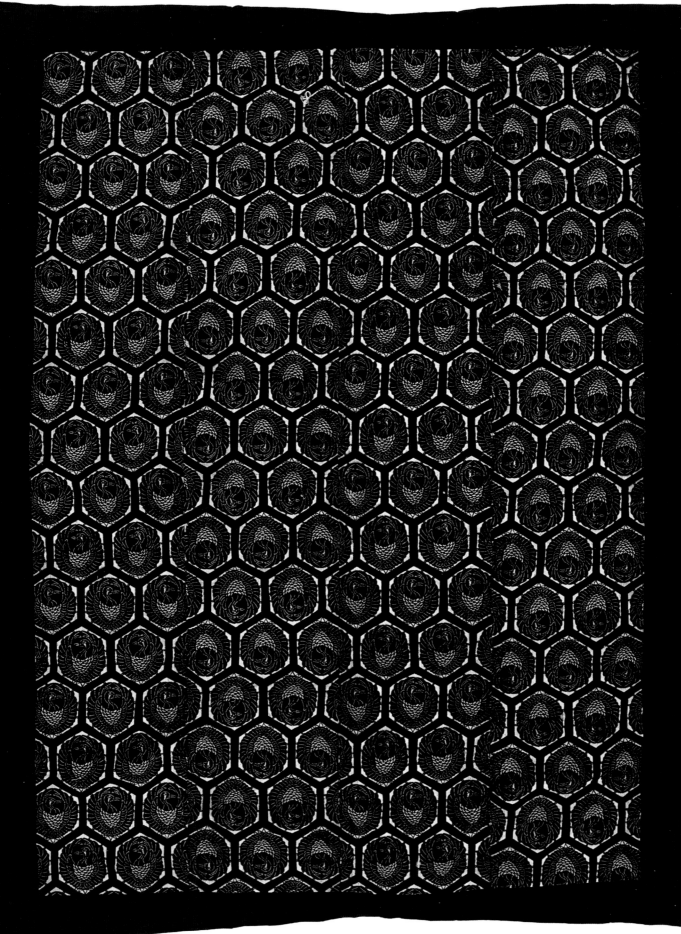

STENCILLED STARCH-RESIST

In both Nigeria and Japan starch can be applied for resist dyeing either freehand or through a stencil. The use of stencils facilitates the precise repetition of motifs as well as making the process much quicker. In Japan several sheets of paper, made from the inner bark of the paper mulberry tree, are stuck together with well-aged persimmon juice. Patterns are then cut out accurately to ensure that the repeat design matches perfectly. Stencils with large sections of paper cut out are reinforced by sandwiching a mesh of silk threads between the layers of paper. To apply the resist, the fabric is laid out on long boards and rice starch or bean paste is spread through the stencil with a wooden spatula. After the resist paste has been dried, the fabric is dyed and the dyes are set by steaming. Finally, the rice paste is washed away.

LEFT: A KIMONO WITH STENCILLED STARCH-RESIST MOTIFS, FROM A PRINT BY KUNISADA, 1851.

RIGHT: STENCILLED JAPANESE FAMILY CRESTS OR MON.

Technique in Nigeria

FIRSTLY, a piece of metal is cut into a rectangle, commonly 12" x 8" (30.5 x 20.3 cm), and the required motif is cut or punched into it. The first stencils, dating back to the late 19th century, were cut out of the lead linings of tea chests and other containers.

The cloth to be stencilled is nailed flat to a table. The stencil is placed firmly on top of the cloth and cassava starch is applied and pressed into the cloth using a metal spatula. Any surplus is scraped back into a bowl. Both the stencilling and the cutting of stencils is the work of men. Abeokuta is the main centre for stencilled adire cloth.

Technique in Japan

THE centre of the Japanese craft of stencilled resist dyeing, or *katazome*, has always been the small towns of Shiroko and Jike in Mie prefecture. It is thought to have evolved from the stencilling of armour and leather in Japan's medieval period, but is now widely used for the decoration of clothes and domestic textiles.

FIVE

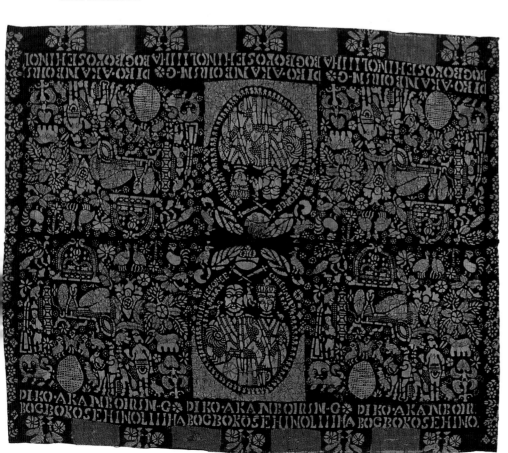

Top: *An indigo-dyed textile, from Japan, with a pattern of mythical beasts created with a stencilled starch-resist that imitates sashiko stitching.*

Left: *Stencilled* adire eleko, *from Nigeria, showing King George V and Queen Mary in 1935 when Silver Jubilee celebrations took place all over the British Empire.*

Right: *A Japanese trapping, tied around a horse's belly, decorated with both freehand and stencilled starch-resist patterns.*

Opposite: *A Japanese indigo-dyed futon cover with a stencilled resist pattern of cranes, a symbol of long life.*

WAX-RESIST: CHINESE KNIFE

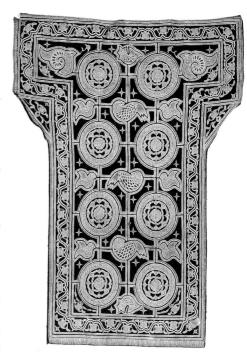

THE oldest known example of wax-resist dates from 10th-century China. The tradition of hand-drawn wax-resist still flourishes amongst the hill tribes of South-West China. It is known as the *ladao* or wax-knife technique. The *ladao* knife consists of a bamboo handle to which two or more small triangular layers of copper are attached with enough space in between them to trap a small amount of molten wax.

Technique

NEW beeswax is mixed with wax recovered from a previous dyeing. The latter retains some blue from the indigo and makes the drawn patterns more visible. After being dipped in molten wax, the knife is held at an oblique angle to a piece of smooth cotton or hemp cloth pinned to a board. Wax is dripped from the bottom edge of the knife onto the cloth, blocking out geometric or figurative patterns. The waxed cloth is then dyed in a cold vat of indigo to prevent the wax from melting. After dyeing, the wax is removed by boiling, resulting in a pattern of white motifs against a blue ground.

The number of copper leaves on the knife determines the amount of wax that can be held; the more leaves, the larger the reserve of wax held and the thicker the line drawn. A practitioner will have a whole

Left: *Tie for a baby carrier, from Guizhou, China, with a pattern of stylized birds executed with a Chinese knife.*

Above, right: *Indigo-dyed baby carrier, from Guizhou, China, with wax-resist patterns.*

Below: *Jacket from Pojao, Guizhou, China. The pattern around the neck and arms has been executed with a Chinese knife on fine cloth which is then sewn onto a coarser ground of glazed indigo.*

Below, left: *A design, known as 'grouped snails', popular amongst the Blue H'mong of Laos.*

Left: *A baby carrier, from Laos, reinforced with coarse cotton cloth. Arranged on it are a selection of* ladao, *Chinese knives of copper and bamboo, used to draw out wax-resist patterns. Different* ladao *may be used on one textile to draw fine, broad or even multiple lines.*

Above: *A baby carrier of the type used around Sapa in Vietnam, decorated with geometric patterns drawn with a Chinese knife. Baby carriers are one of the most elaborately decorated types of textile found in Indo-China.*

Below: *A Zhao woman's skirt, from Vietnam, dyed in indigo with a striking wax-resist zigzag pattern.*

FIVE

collection of *ladao* knives – ones with more leaves for drawing lines of different thicknesses and special ones for the border, dots and cross-hatching.

Distribution

THE same method of batik is practised amongst the hill tribes of Indo-China and Thailand. As in China, the women mainly work on hemp or now often on cotton cloth. The main item produced is the prized many pleated skirt.

Opposite, below, right: *Intricately patterned apron panel with wax-resists applied with a Chinese knife from Guizhou, China. Wax-resists frequently appear on the aprons, sleeves and baby carriers of women from this region.*

WAX-RESIST: CANTING

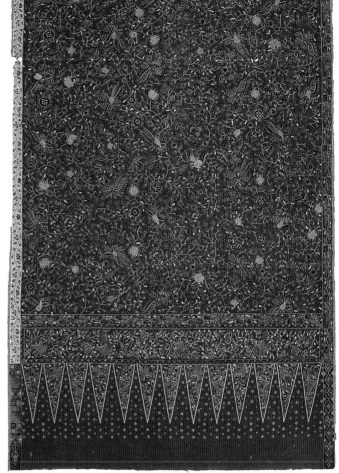

Above: *A batik* kain *from north Java. The art of hand drawing wax-resist patterns with a* canting *is known as* tulis.

THE application of a wax-resist before dyeing to form a pattern in negative is most often referred to by the Javanese word batik. Batik is practised in India, Sri Lanka, China, South-East Asia, Turkestan and West Africa, but in Indonesia, on the island of Java, the craft has been brought to an acme of refinement. Nowhere else has wax-resist cloth been so finely detailed.

The origins of batik are obscure, but what is certain is that the Javanese invention of the *canting* waxing instrument enabled the finest hand-drawn batik to be produced.

Technique

HAND-DRAWN batik is known by the Javanese word *tulis* which means writing. The *canting* consists of a wooden handle inset into a small copper reservoir with single or sometimes multiple spouts. This is dipped into a bowl containing molten wax, which is kept at a constant temperature. The female batiker dips her *canting* into the bowl of wax and glides it over the surface of a piece of fine cotton cloth, dripping wax in a smooth continuous flow as she goes. For quality batik, the resist is always applied first to one side and then to the other. The completion of a piece of batik involves a series of stages of waxing, then dyeing, waxing fresh areas of the cloth, taking off some portions of the first waxing and then dyeing in another colour. The more complex the desired colour scheme, the more stages there are. Finally, all the wax is boiled out.

Opposite: *A dua negri* batik sarong *from Java. Dua negri (meaning two country) indicates that different parts of the process were carried out in two places, in this case Lasem and Pekalongan.*

Opposite, inset: *A Malay woman, from Singapore, wearing a batik sarong.*

Left: Kalligrafi *batik, based on Koranic verses, made in Cirebon, Java, to be sold in Sumatra.*

Right: *A silk sarong made in Juana, Java, intended for festive use in Bali.*

Uses

PRODUCING high-quality, hand-drawn batik is a time-consuming, and therefore expensive, process. Some particularly fine pieces may take as long as a year to wax and dye and are therefore only worn by the wealthy. In Java, batik is traditionally worked on rectangular pieces of cotton which are not tailored, but worn by both women and men wrapped around the body as a *kain panjang*.

WAX-RESIST: PRINTED

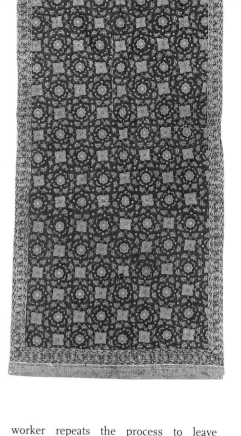

I N Java in the middle of the 19th century the technique of wax-resist batik using a copper block or *cap* was developed because the supplies of European machine-printed imitation batik had been interrupted due to the economic disruption caused by the American Civil War. The structure of the *caps* was inspired by European block-printing stamps, but they were constructed according to local Chinese jewelry-making techniques.

This was truly a revolution in the making of batik. Previously a woman using a *canting* could take months to wax and dye a batik cloth, but workshops were then set up and men hired to undertake the arduous and unhealthy work. Each worker could produce up to eight batik cloths a day.

Technique

C AP printers stand at a tightly padded-out rectangular table. Beside them on a small stove sits a circular flat-bottomed pan containing the wax. A filter made of a percolated copper plate and a fibrous mat is set in the molten wax and covered with an absorbent cloth. Any impurities in the wax are strained out by the filter. The *cap* is pressed onto the filter pad to load it with wax and then stamped onto the cloth. The

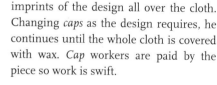

Above, right: *A cap-printed* selendang, *from Jambi, Sumatra, with a pattern that imitates textiles from the Coromandel coast of India. These batiks were often printed with wooden blocks.*

Below: *A cap-printed* kain, *from central Java, boldly patterned with storks.*

Below, right: *A large silk shawl from Central Asia. The* boteh *motifs, familiar to Europeans through Paisley shawls, are the result of crudely printing a wax-resist with a wooden block.*

worker repeats the process to leave imprints of the design all over the cloth. Changing *caps* as the design requires, he continues until the whole cloth is covered with wax. *Cap* workers are paid by the piece so work is swift.

Uses

T HE production of patterned cloth employing *cap*-printing is both quicker and cheaper than with a *canting*, so it has become possible for members of all strata of Indonesian society to afford batik textiles. In modern times European factories have begun mass-producing cheap imitation batik cloth to cash in on the demand. These days most 'batik' cloth worn in West Africa is actually machine-printed in Holland.

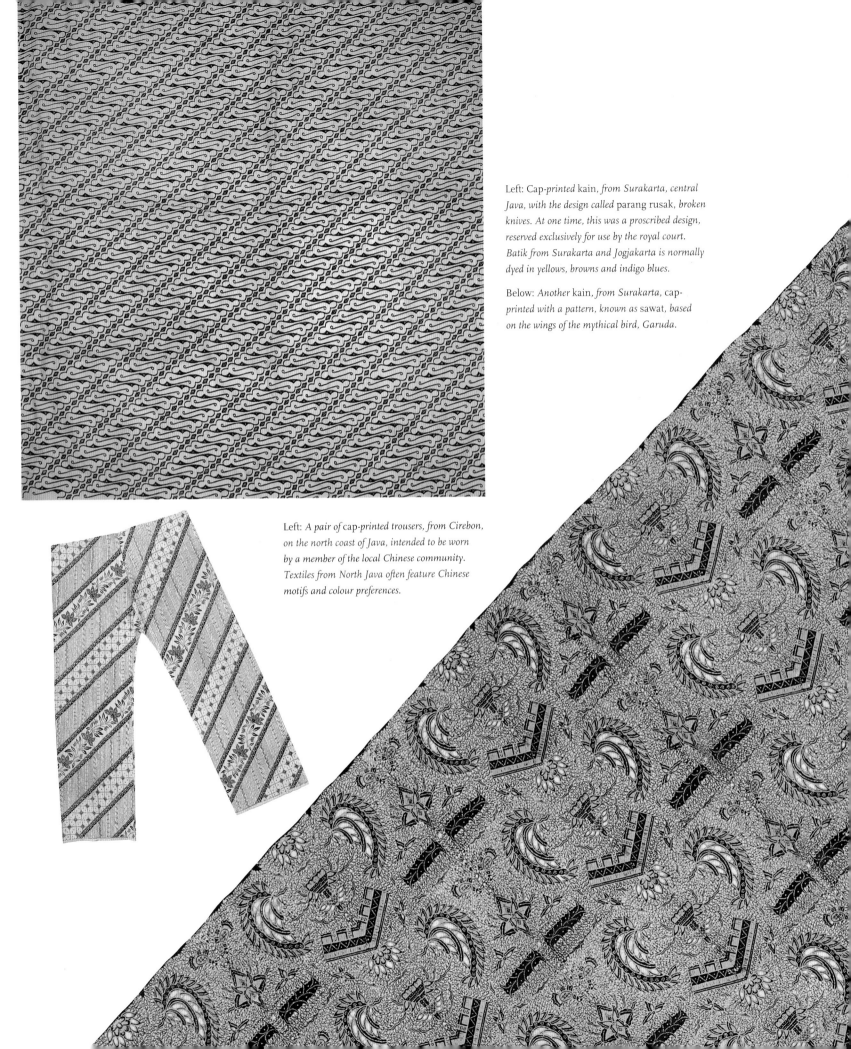

Left: Cap-*printed kain, from Surakarta, central Java, with the design called* parang rusak, *broken knives. At one time, this was a proscribed design, reserved exclusively for use by the royal court. Batik from Surakarta and Jogjakarta is normally dyed in yellows, browns and indigo blues.*

Below: *Another kain, from Surakarta, cap-printed with a pattern, known as* sawat, *based on the wings of the mythical bird, Garuda.*

Left: *A pair of* cap-*printed trousers, from Cirebon, on the north coast of Java, intended to be worn by a member of the local Chinese community. Textiles from North Java often feature Chinese motifs and colour preferences.*

138

MORDANT TECHNIQUES

A MORDANT is an agent, such as alum or urine, which is used to make an, otherwise fugitive, adjective dye permanent. Various techniques that exploit this principle have been developed for the decoration of cloth. The most basic method of all is to soak cloth in a mixture of dye and mordant or to soak it first in mordant and then in dye. This will produce an evenly distributed colour.

Central Asian woodblock printing

IN Central Asia black dye made from an iron solution stiffened with flour or vegetable gum is printed with wood blocks onto cotton cloth that has been soaked in a mordant made from pistachio galls. An alum mordant is then printed onto the cloth which is immersed in a red-madder dye bath. The cloth is rinsed out to wash the excess dye from the unmordanted areas. The result is a pattern in black and red on a light background.

Kalamkari

IN the Indian state of Andhra Pradesh the makers of *kalamkari* cloths use a similar method. At Masulipatnam cloth which has first been bleached in a solution of dung is soaked in a mordant of myrobalan. Designs of birds and animals are then drawn or printed with mineral dyes mixed with gum which, on contact with the mordant, turn black or red. Further dyes are then painted on before being fixed by immersion in an alum solution. In the temple town of Kalahasti,

craftsmen paint religious images entirely by hand using a bamboo pen, or *kalam*, with an absorbent pad bound to the tip. The final background colours are applied by painting on a mordant solution and then immersing in dye, the reverse of the method used in Masulipatnam.

Ajrakh

A JRAKH cloth is produced by Muslim communities in the Indian regions of Kutch and Rajasthan and in the adjoining Pakistani province of Sind. The name comes from the Arabic word *azrak*, meaning blue, and refers to the dominant colour. Wooden blocks are used to print the mordant and a resist paste onto cotton. The cloth is then immersed in a red alizarin dye bath and a blue indigo vat. The mordanted areas take the red dye, the areas printed with resist remain white and the rest of the fabric is coloured by the indigo which is a substantive dye and needs no mordant. A similar, predominately red cloth called *malir* is made for Hindus in the same region.

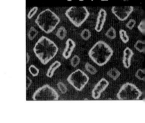

FIVE

Above: *A detail of the lining of a Turkoman woman's* chyrpy *coat. The pattern is the result of printing a resist paste of flour or mud onto cloth that has previously been soaked in mordant. On dyeing the cloth, dye is only absorbed by the unresisted areas.*

Below: *A woman's cotton shawl, from Syria, with a pattern of resists on mordanted cloth. Aniline dyes have done away with the need for mordants and in modern Syria patterns are usually printed directly in coloured dye or in negative using a resist paste made from slaked lime mixed with starch.*

Opposite, left: *Woman's cotton shawl, from Deesa, Gujarat, India, enhanced with embroidery. The light-coloured patterns are formed where a resist paste has been applied to stop dye being absorbed.*

Opposite, above, right: *Block-printed* malir *cloth, from Barmer, Rajasthan, India, made for Hindus using the* ajrakh *technique.*

Opposite, below, right: *Two* ajrakh *cloths, the one underneath is from Barmer and the other one is from Tando Mohammed Khan, Sind, Pakistan. A resist has been printed to create the white areas, then mordant has been printed on to take the red dye and the indigo blue has been absorbed by the remaining fabric.*

WARP IKAT

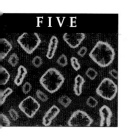

UNTIED YARN.

FIVE

WARP ikat is reputed to be one of the most ancient of the resist-dyeing techniques. It is practised on the threads of cloth before it is woven, in much the same way as woven cloth can be resist dyed using the tie and dye method.

Technique

THE word ikat is derived from the Malay word *mengikat* (to tie or to bind) and is a method whereby the patterning of a textile is obtained by tying fibre resists tightly around the warp threads that have been stretched out on a frame and then immersing the tied hanks in a dye bath. If, for example, the original thread is white and the dye bath blue, the tied portions form a white pattern against a blue background. By tying up further sections of the warp threads, untying certain sections of the original tied resists, and then immersing the tied hanks in a dye bath of a different colour, a pattern emerges that is of four colours, the first of which is the original undyed colour of the warps, the second and third the colours of the successive dye baths and the final colour the hue produced by the combination of the two dyes. When the dyeing process is completed the yarn is woven up to produce a warp-faced, patterned cloth. During the 19th century Japanese craftsmen applied the *itajime* technique to yarn, a method previously employed for resist dyeing whole sheets of cloth. This involves clamping the unwoven warps between boards to resist the dye. By carving patterns into the blocks, as in block-printing, it is possible to create repeated patterns much more quickly and easily than by resist tying.

Materials

FOR climatic reasons warp ikat is usually woven on cotton, rarely on bast, although some interesting ikat textiles are woven in the Philippines from abaca fibre.

In modern times synthetic twine has been adopted for resist tying because of its excellent water-resistant properties.

Distribution

WARP-ikat textiles are produced in South and South-East Asia, Central Asia, the Near East, West Africa and Central and South America.

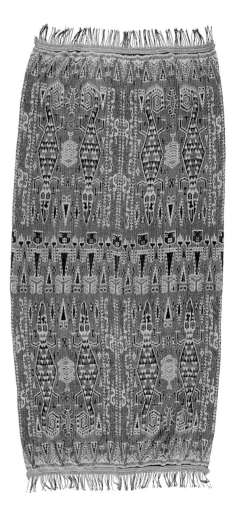

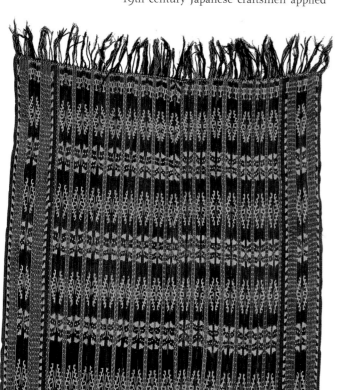

Left: *A cotton* selendang *made by the Lesser Blossom clan from the small Indonesian island of Savu. On Savu, warp-ikat textiles are made in various sizes and shapes, but normally using the same subtle colour scheme and patterns laid out in grids or rows. Geometric forms are most common, but some patterns show the influence of Dutch colonists in the use of floral and figurative motifs.*

Top right: *A warp-ikat* hinggi, *from east Sumba, Indonesia, worn by men around the waist or shoulders. Each* hinggi *is made in two halves, which are woven separately, and then sewn together along the length, selvedge to selvedge. Most often dyed in browns, reds and ochres, they feature images of monitor lizards, skeletons, chickens and sea creatures.*

Above: *An Iban woman's warp-ikat* bidang *skirt, from Sarawak, Malaysia, with lizard motifs. Iban textiles are decorated with abstract interlocking patterns inspired by local flowers and wildlife or human figures.*

Opposite: *A cotton mantle made by a group of Toraja women in Sulawesi, Indonesia.*
Inset above: *Iban woman in a* bidang *skirt.*
Inset below: *Women, from Uzbekistan, wearing ikat fabric known as* abr *or 'cloud' cloth.*

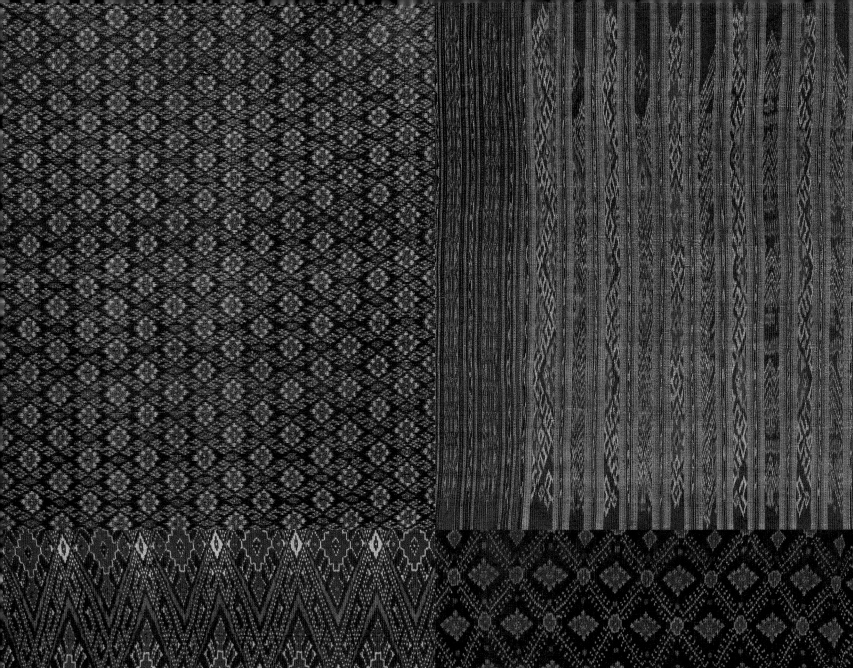

WEFT IKAT

WEFT ikat is a sophisticated process requiring more paraphernalia than warp ikat. Its origins most probably lie in the Arab world – particularly the Yemen, from whence it travelled to India and South-East Asia where the majority of its practitioners are still Muslims. Knowledge of the technique may have evolved independently in widespread locations, but it reached as far west as Majorca where a fabric called Roba de llengues, or cloth of tongues, is woven. The preferred medium is silk, but the technique can just as readily be practised on cotton or rayon. In most parts of the world weft-ikat weaving is organized on a commercial workshop or factory basis.

Technique

THE weft threads must be wound on to a simple rectangular frame that is approximately the same width as the finished cloth. This can be done by hand, but is now most usually achieved by drawing off threads from a rack containing twenty to thirty bobbins and wrapping them around a revolving frame. Threads that are to be given identical motifs are bunched together on the tying frame, and the resist patterns are then tied in using fibre or plastic thread. The tied yarn is dyed and as with warp ikat certain sections may be untied, fresh sections may be tied and further immersions in different-coloured dye baths may be carried out to produce multi-coloured yarn.

This yarn is then woven in as the weft on a plain warp using a semi-mechanized loom. Care must always be taken that each succeeding pick of the weft is correctly aligned with the preceding one.

Above: *Weft-ikat cotton sari length, from Orissa, India.*

A quicker method of producing multi-coloured weft-ikat cloth is now much practised in India and South-East Asia – different-coloured chemical dyes are daubed on sections of the yarn which are then tied over. This means the yarn only needs immersion in one dye bath. In Indonesia this is known as the *cetak* process.

FIVE

Opposite: *The top right-hand textile is a vertically striped weft-ikat sarong from North-East Thailand. The other three textiles are exquisite examples of Cambodian silk weft ikat. The geometric diagonal trellis layout* *of the pattern is reminiscent of the fabled double-ikat weaves of Gujarat, India, which were traded widely in South-East Asia and subsequently imitated in Laos, Cambodia and parts of Indonesia.*

Above: *A Thai silk textile, dyed and woven with great skill into a pattern generated by small swastikas, a Buddhist good luck symbol.*

Left: *Pidan,* a long figurative weaving in distinctly Cambodian style, featuring temples, dancers and elephants. This fabric is viewed on its side, with the weft running from top to bottom.

143

COMPOUND AND DOUBLE IKAT

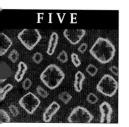

prestigious of all is *patola* – the vividly coloured and patterned, silk double ikat is now only woven by two families in Patan in Gujarat, although it was once woven in many parts of Western India and widely traded, particularly to South-East Asia where it became a symbol of royalty and was much imitated.

LEFT: DETAIL OF A JAPANESE PRINT BY UTAMARO SHOWING A WOMAN, DRESSED IN A DOUBLE-IKAT KIMONO, FOLDING TIE AND DYE CLOTH.

Technique

DOUBLE ikats are always woven on very simple looms in plain-balanced weave. *Patola*, for instance, is woven on a single-heddle, frameless loom set at an angle to catch the light. The time-consuming part of the weaving is the adjustment of each pick of the weft, so that the pattern dyed into the weft matches exactly with the pattern dyed into the warp.

FIVE

Compound ikat

WHEN both warp and weft threads are tie and dyed and then woven in plain-balanced weave the resulting fabric is known as compound ikat. Usually the warp and weft sections of patterning are in distinct areas of the textile, although sometimes they overlap to form random motifs.

Double ikat

WHEN warp and weft patterning are designed in such a way that they can be combined to form integrated motifs, the resulting textile is known as double ikat. This is without doubt the most complex and most time-consuming of all the resist-dyeing arts. Craftsmen can spend months tie and dyeing a pattern into both warp and weft threads and then painstakingly weaving the double-ikat cloth so that the pattern fits together without looking disjointed.

Double ikat is only woven in India where it is known as *patola*, on the island of Bali, in Indonesia, where it is known as *geringsing*, and in Japan where it is known as *kasuri*. In all these countries double ikat is a prestigious and expensive textile. Most

Above, left: *A cotton sari, from Orissa, India, with a warp-ikat border and panels of double ikat.*

Above, right: *A Japanese man's indigo-dyed cotton sleeveless jacket with patterns created by the* kasuri, *double-ikat, method.*

Below, left: *A double-ikat head cloth or telia* rumal, *from Chirala, Andhra Pradesh, India.*

Right: *An indigo-dyed cotton textile from Japan. The auspicious cranes are the result of weft-ikat resists (yokogasuri or e-gasuri) and the geometric motif is the result of double-ikat resists (kasuri).*

Opposite, above, left: *A compound-ikat textile from Guatemala. Both the warps and wefts have been resist dyed, but as the two patterns created do not interlock they create a disjointed, blurred effect.*

Opposite, below, left: *A textile from Andhra Pradesh, India. Here, it is easy to see the sections of compound-ikat pattern that have been created by weft ikat or warp ikat worked independently and the sections where the two intersect and register to create double ikat.*

Opposite, right: *Double-ikat* patola *cloth, from Patan, Gujarat, India, one of the world's most widely admired and copied textiles.*

Opposite, far right: Geringsing *from Tenganan, Bali.*

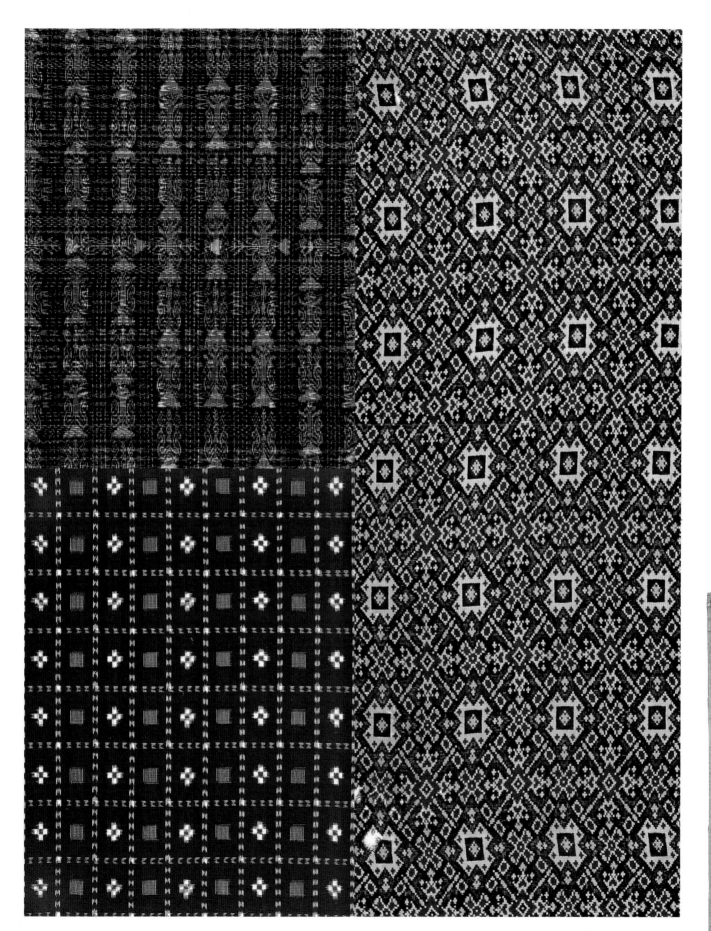

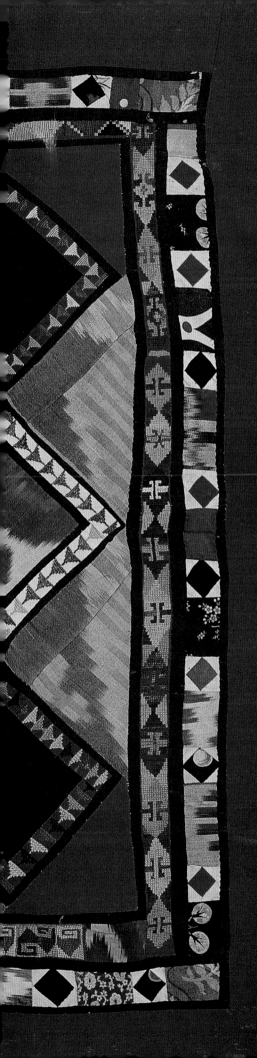

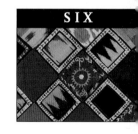

SIX

SEWING

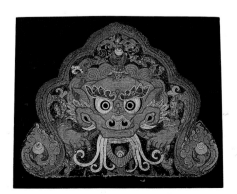

SEWING

Above: *Tailors outside a shop in the backstreets of Cairo, Egypt. Scenes like this can still be observed in many parts of the world, although the sewing machine has largely supplanted the needle.*

ALL loom-woven textiles are rectangular. This shape is exploited to the full and draped, gathered or tied in an enormous variety of ways for clothing and other uses. Prime examples of this are the Indian sari and the Javanese sarong. However, by cutting cloth into sections and sewing them together the range of possibilities, particularly for clothing, is greatly extended. The by-products of this tailoring are scraps and offcuts too valuable to waste.

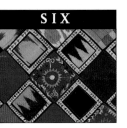

Above: *A cemetery on the South Sea island of Tonga where many of the graves have been decorated with lovingly sewn patchwork quilts – it was not only Christianity that missionaries introduced to the South Seas.*

Left: *A Sami mother and child from the north of Norway in 1932. These nomadic reindeer herders still decorate their colourful costume with bands of appliquéd braid.*

Right: *A Kuna Indian woman from Aligandi in the San Blas Islands off the coast of Panama. She is wearing a blouse with a mola-work panel and on her lap is a mola panel that she has just begun.*

Above: *The fascination with Ancient Egypt aroused by the discovery of the tomb of Tutankhamun in 1922 provided the tent and awning makers of Cairo and Luxor with a boost to their income with demand for appliqué versions of tomb paintings.*

SCRAPS AND PATCHES

THE addition of a patch is the strongest way to mend or reinforce holes and vulnerable areas in textiles and garments. The decorative possibilities offered by adding patches of different colours quickly become obvious and over the centuries a repertoire of inventive techniques exploiting these possibilities has been built up. Textiles constructed from layers of cloth, felt or leather found in tombs at Pazyryk in the High Altai of Siberia provide evidence that sewing techniques such as appliqué were in use as long ago as the 4th century BC, if not before.

THRIFT AND POVERTY

POVERTY has lead to the recycling of old textiles and the exploitation of left-overs. From these humble origins sophisticated techniques have developed. Amongst these are *kantha* work from Bangladesh, the patchwork quilts of colonists in North America and the *molas* sewn by the Kuna Indians of Panama. In contrast, the dervishes of the Sudan, followers of the Mahdi in the 19th century, wore patchwork garments specifically to show their rejection of the material world.

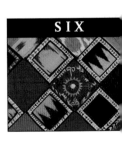

Left: *Before the First World War, an English housewife sits sewing outside her cottage in Shropshire.*

LEFT: A MEDIAEVAL EUROPEAN TAILOR MEASURING A CUSTOMER FOR A DRESS.

APPLIQUE

APPLIQUE, a technique in which pieces of material are sewn onto a ground fabric for decorative purposes, was developed out of the possibilities presented by sewing patches onto damaged cloth.

Technique

HEMMED appliqué is the simplest form of appliqué. Motifs are simply cut out of fabric and tacked onto the ground. Edges are then turned in and hemmed or slip stitched, leaving the ground fabric visible between the applied pieces.

More complicated techniques include reverse appliqué and *mola* work. The range of materials that can be employed in appliqué is considerable – including most notably cloth, felt and leather.

Uses

THE bold and dramatic effects that can be achieved using appliqué have led to the adoption of the technique by martial organizations in the manufacture of uniforms and banners. The dervish army of the Mahdi in 19th-century Sudan dressed in distinctive patched robes which varied according to rank and status, while to this day the Asafo men's societies of Ghana parade spectacular flags bearing allegorical messages.

Patched cloth has also been used by many religious and mystical groups as a symbol of poverty and material renunciation. Amongst these were the Sufis who inspired the Mahdi and his dervishes.

ABOVE: SAWTOOTH EDGING IS A COMMON APPLIQUÉ DEVICE WIDELY USED FOR BORDER PATTERNS. CUTS ARE MADE AT EVENLY SPACED INTERVALS IN A STRIP OF FABRIC WHICH IS TUCKED UNDER TO LEAVE A ROW OF TRIANGULAR POINTS. THE STRIP IS THEN NEATLY SEWN ONTO THE BACKING.

SIX

Top right: *Appliquéd* dharaniyo *used to cover a pile of quilts when they are not in use, from Saurasthra, North-West India. Depicted in appliqué on this cloth are a Tree of Life and elephants, lucky because of their association with the god Ganesh. Repetitive parts of the pattern are created by folding the fabric before cutting out the shapes.*

Middle right: Chakla, *or square hanging, with dense appliqué, mirrorwork and embroidery, made by Rabari shepherds in Saurasthra, North-West India. Between the ubiquitous elephants are stylized peacocks.*

Left: *A member of the Guild of the Young Folks of the Pear Garden. A Chinese male actor, playing a leading lady, dressed in a costume of boldly appliquéd cloth.*

Right: *Appliqué picture of peasants labouring in the fields in Colombia. The peasant lifestyle, however arduous for those living it, has an enduring appeal to tourists.*

Above: *Ox-cart tent. In Rajasthan and Gujarat in Western India brides are traditionally taken to their new husband's village in a cart pulled by oxen covered with boldly appliquéd textiles. On the cart itself is a cube-shaped appliqué tent to hide the bride from prying eyes.*

Left: *Tent hanging, Cairo. Ceramic tile patterns and appliquéd cloths are both built up from small segments and it is possible to produce similar designs in either technique. As tile work is more expensive, it is common for appliquéd tent hangings to imitate them in style and colour with arabesques and Arabic calligraphy.*

Above: *Kanduri cloth, Bahraich, Uttar Pradesh, India. The tomb of Salar Masud, a Muslim prince who died on Krishna's birthday, is a place of reverence for both Hindu and Muslim pilgrims. They buy appliquéd cloths, decorated with scenes from Indian mythology, to leave as offerings at the shrine depicted at the bottom of the cloth.*

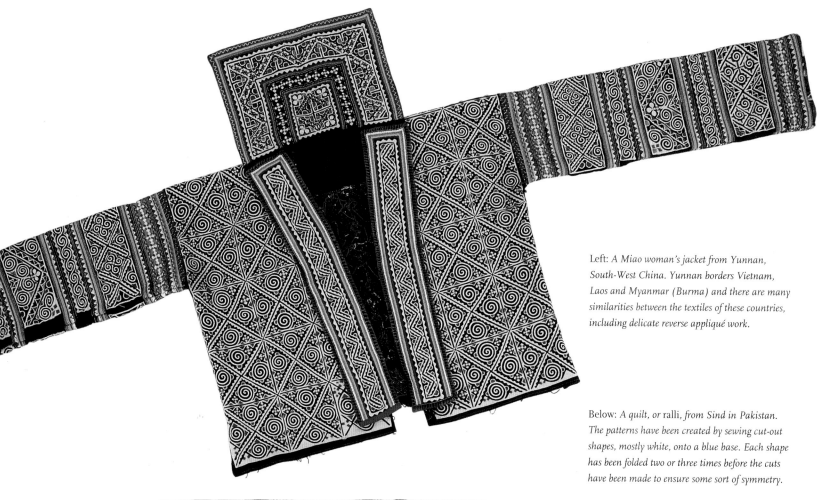

Left: *A Miao woman's jacket from Yunnan, South-West China. Yunnan borders Vietnam, Laos and Myanmar (Burma) and there are many similarities between the textiles of these countries, including delicate reverse appliqué work.*

Below: *A quilt, or ralli, from Sind in Pakistan. The patterns have been created by sewing cut-out shapes, mostly white, onto a blue base. Each shape has been folded two or three times before the cuts have been made to ensure some sort of symmetry.*

REVERSE APPLIQUE

Whenever one shape is superimposed on another, as is the case in appliqué, a negative shape is also created by the background. This effect can be reversed if the top – superimposed – layer of fabric is regarded as the background and shapes are cut out of it to reveal the layer below. This is known as reverse appliqué or cutwork appliqué.

Technique

A LAYER of fabric is tacked onto a base layer of a contrasting colour. Cuts are made in the top layer and the edges are turned back under and sewn down with small stitches. Thread that matches the colour of the top layer is used so that the stitches will be invisible. The main pattern is thus created by exposing the bottom layer.

Distribution

QUILTS from Sind and Rajasthan in the Indian subcontinent are often worked with bold floral and abstract patterns in a combination of appliqué and reverse appliqué. Sections of the top layer are folded and cut before sewing down to create a repetitive or symmetrical design.

Women of the hill tribes of China, Thailand and Indo-China decorate their costume and baby carriers with panels worked in reverse appliqué. These are often sewn so finely that it is almost possible to mistake them for embroidery.

Above: *A Vanya* chakla, *from Gujarat, India, with sawtooth edging and coloured appliqué and reverse appliqué on a white ground. The stylized motifs include birds, plants, elephants and horses.*

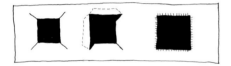

ABOVE: CUT EDGES ARE FOLDED UNDER AND SEWN DOWN.

Near right: *An appliqué and reverse appliqué cushion cover in the rusts and blues preferred by the Banjara of South India.*

Far right: *A woman's apron, from Yunnan, South-West China, with reverse appliqué motifs. The white fabric has been tucked under to reveal the dark spiral patterns.*

Below: *A woman's apron, from Yunnan, South-West China, with long ties. Sections of aprons or jackets are worked independently before the garment is assembled.*

SIX

MOLAS

ABOVE: A *MOLA* PANEL DEPICTING A KUNA MOTHER SEWING A *MOLA*.

Off the Caribbean coast of Panama lie the beautiful San Blas islands. Here the Kuna Indian women wear blouses known as *molas* which are decorated, front and back, with appliqué designs made by a unique and very sophisticated technique. The finest *molas* are sewn for their own use, but many women now considerably supplement their incomes by selling *molas* to tourists. Kuna Indian *molas* are unique, although work that resembles them is produced by the White H'mong of Laos.

Technique

Mola work is essentially reverse appliqué, but it can be worked with three or more layers of different-coloured cloth, portions of the lower layers of cloth showing through to the surface to form a multi-coloured pattern. Work begins by applying the central part of the final shape to a base and then superimposing and cutting away further layers until the final shape is revealed.

The effect can be elaborated upon by making up one layer of many colour patches which are exposed by cutting back to them on the next layer.

Cut-out cloth from the front of the *mola* is often counterchanged with cloth from the back. This results in the back and front having similar designs, although with a different colour sequence. Traditional *molas* are most often a deep red on a black base with brightly coloured layers between them.

Motifs

All *molas* are decorated with designs that are to some extent abstracted and stylized. Many of the most popular figurative motifs are of natural objects, flowers, birds and lizards. Some *molas* are illustrated with scenes from the everyday life of the Kuna people such as initiation, marriage and death, while others show episodes from their myths and legends. One story tells of the albino Moon Child who, during an eclipse, saves the moon when it is supposedly being devoured by the dragon-monster.

Opposite: *Detail of a mola, in three layers, depicting three stylized lizards.*

Opposite, inset: *A Kuna woman wearing a blouse with* mola *panels on the front and back.*

SIX

Right: *Four* mola *panels. Traditional Kuna designs depict aspects of their daily lives, such as wildlife, ceremonies and mythology. The puppy in a basket (above, right) shows the influence of the outside world.*

LEATHER AND FELT APPLIQUE

THE excavation of tombs at Pazyryk in Siberia and at Noin Ula in Mongolia has shown that both leather and felt were in use in the 4th century BC for the manufacture of everyday items such as carpets and saddle covers, as well as magnificent hangings commissioned by the élite.

Leather appliqué

LEATHER has a naturally integrated structure so it can be cut without fear of fraying. This makes it ideal for use in appliqué and especially for the making of hard-wearing clothes and covers. Long, decorative, appliqué jackets and waist-coats are favoured by peasants in Eastern Europe, while animal and baggage covers in the same technique are widely used in Northern India and Pakistan.

Below: *A pair of* babouches, *the traditional Moroccan leather slippers, decorated with embroidery and leather appliqué.*

Above, right: *The status of this Hungu official, from Manchuria, China, is emphasized by the appliqué decoration on his coat. Similar designs were discovered in the frozen tombs of Pazyryk and Noin Ula.*

Right: *Detail of a Hungarian sheepskin coat decorated with tassels, braid, pom-poms, floral embroidery and leather appliqué.*

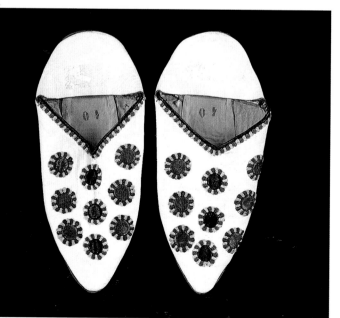

Felt appliqué

Felt is also a very suitable material for appliqué as the edges of any cut-out motif will not fray, and thus the motifs can be applied to a ground without the necessity of turning under any edges. Felt also lends itself to the art of counterchange appliqué where two different-coloured sheets of felt are laid one on top of the other to be cut. Identical motifs are cut out of both by simply cutting through both layers at once. The motifs from one felt are sewn into the voids in the other felt and vice versa. This process results in two appliquéd felt pieces of exactly similar designs, but the mirror image of each other in terms of colour.

Felt appliqué has traditionally been used by the nomadic tribes of Central Asia, such as the Turkmen and the Uzbek, in the manufacture of bags for the struts of their yurts (or tents), camel trappings and most notably for their counterchange floor coverings.

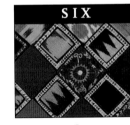

Above: *Three-coloured felt appliqué mat from Hungary. The crisp shapes have been cut out with a punch and then stitched together with a sewing machine.*

Left: *A Hungarian apron with a border of appliquéd felt strips. Women's aprons are frequently given special attention as they are thought to provide magical, as well as physical, protection.*

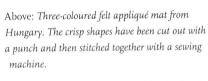

RIGHT: A
FELT APPLIQUÉ MOTIF
FROM PAZYRYK.

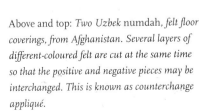

Above and top: *Two Uzbek* numdah, *felt floor coverings, from Afghanistan. Several layers of different-coloured felt are cut at the same time so that the positive and negative pieces may be interchanged. This is known as counterchange appliqué.*

157

BRAID AND RIBBON WORK

BRAIDS and ribbons are used in many parts of the world to add decorative details. The most complex and sophisticated technique is employed in China by the Miao.

Chinese braid embroidery

IN the remote mountains of Guizhou in South-West China the women of the Miao hill tribe create a unique style of embroidery, using silk braids of one or two colours couched down on rectangles of cloth. These panels are used to decorate the collar, cuffs, shoulders and lapels of the festive courting jackets that the Miao women so lovingly craft for their daughters. Folded and pleated ribbons are also employed to create dynamic designs composed of rows of triangles.

Technique

THE braids are made on a curved-top stand using weighted bobbins with eight threads of two-ply silk. The structure of the braid allows it to be manipulated into tight curves which gives it a textural appearance. The braids can either be laid flat or pleated to make a raised surface and are always stitched down with the same face of the braid showing. They may be used as either a single line, a double line or as an outline to be filled with flat or pleated braids. Two-colour braids with colour maintained as a single band on each side are not used for pleating, but solely as outlines or for zigzag filling.

Flat braids are couched down with zigzag oversewing, while pleated braids are held in place with a single stitch across the braid for each pleat. The sewing thread used is the same two-ply silk that is used to make the braids.

Opposite: Sleeve panel, from Guizhou, China, with pleated braids and a folded-ribbon border.

Opposite, inset left: Miao girl in festive costume, Guizhou, China.

Opposite, inset right: A Croatian couple with rickrack aprons.

Native American ribbon appliqué

AFTER the introduction of commercially produced silk and satin ribbon by traders in the 1780s many tribes quickly incorporated them into their decorative repertoire. While the Apache sewed ribbons and rickrack braid directly onto their shirts and skirts, Indians of the Plains, Plateau and Woodlands developed a more elaborate style with complicated counterchange patterns built up in strips which were used to decorate women's robes and skirts. The Seminole Indians of Florida began, in the 19th century, to employ imported cotton ribbon to make patchwork borders for their clothing.

Right: A Dong man's jacket, from Guizhou, China, decorated with overlapping strips of cloth pleated into triangles. Folding and layering is also used to work intricate silk panels for Miao costumes.

Below: Banjara skirt from South India. Skirts have been decorated with ribbon and braid by women from far-flung places, for instance, the Banjara of India, the Lapps of Finland and the Apache of South-West America.

Right: A glittering nuptial shawl, from Hyderabad, India, made of tinsel and metallic ribbon pleated and sewn onto a loose net base.

159

PATCHWORK

PATCHWORK is a method of constructing a textile by sewing together small pieces of fabric into a geometric design. The patches are most often of identical shapes such as squares, rectangles or hexagons. Although it is most commonly used to produce the decorative top-sides of quilts, patchwork is often also used in the making of clothes, banners and other articles.

Technique

TWO methods have evolved – one once widespread in Britain, the other popular in North America. With the former, now known as 'English piecing', pieces of stiff paper are cut as templates and the chosen fabric (a little larger than the template) is tacked over the paper. The separate pieces are then joined together by oversewing. Once all the pieces have been joined together the paper templates are removed.

As with the British method, the stitching of American patchwork is a relatively simple affair, the main difference being that a template is used to mark the fabric for cutting, but is not sewn onto it. The patches are joined along a plain seam using very small running stitches.

For ease of handling, patchwork is usually worked in sections, sewing together a number of patches into a block. In general, when a block is made the design is worked from the centre outwards.

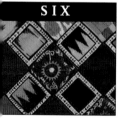

SIX

Left: Rumal, *from Sind, Pakistan, sewn together from strips of cloth edged with sawtooth appliqué.*

Below, left: *English Victorian 'crazy patchwork' made from left-over scraps of material, 19th century.*

Right: *Kuba patchwork, raphia dance skirt decorated with embroidery from the Democratic Republic of Congo. The rectangular patches are made of alternately dyed and undyed raphia.*

Opposite: *A Meghwal* ralli *from Rajasthan, India. The use of geometrically shaped patches, for ease of construction, puts restrictions on the design that often lead to the creation of bold, colourful patterns.*

Opposite, inset left: *A pair of girls from Georgia doing their laundry. They are dressed in patchwork outfits made from brightly coloured Manchester cotton.*

Opposite, inset right: *A mendicant mystic, from Bokhara, Uzbekistan, in the patchwork costume of a dervish, a statement of holy poverty.*

Crazy patchwork is a method in which irregularly shaped pieces are sewn together to create a random, but hopefully attractive, effect.

Distribution

As patchwork is an ideal way to use up scraps of cloth left over from other projects it is a very economic and popular technique. Particularly in North America and Western Europe patchworking and quilting are very popular forms of needlework. As the American patchwork method lends itself to machine stitching, machine-sewn patchwork is now very common in many other parts of the world.

QUILTING

QUILTING is the process of stitching layers of cloth together to form a cover of some kind. In colder climates they may be padded or stuffed with cotton waste, wool, feathers or even horse hair. In warmer climes they are often merely made up of layers of material between the surfaces. Quilts have from time immemorial been repositories for old, nearly worn-out cloth that has become surplus to requirements and quilting is often combined with patchwork and even appliqué.

Technique

THE technique of quilting is basically very simple. Layers of cloth are laid on top of each other and tacked together, often incorporating padding or stuffing. Using running stitch or back stitch they are then sewn together securely around the edges and at intervals across the central area which holds the filling layers in place and gives a padded effect.

Uses

QUILTING is most often used for protection from the elements – as warm bedding and clothes. However, padded and quilted garments have also frequently been worn under armour or on their own as protection against weapons. In sub-Saharan Africa both men and horses wore quilted armour.

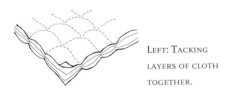

LEFT: TACKING LAYERS OF CLOTH TOGETHER.

The decorative possibilities

THE rows of stitching suggest their own decorative possibilities. The stitching can be sewn in patterns to give a subtle background pattern (as in the Durham quilts of North-East England) or the colour of the threads can be varied (as in the quilts of the Sindi Sami caste in east Pakistan on the border with India). Quilting has been brought to the acme of refinement in the highly figurative *kanthas* of East Bengal (now Bangladesh).

Kanthas

KANTHAS are made up of layers of discarded white dhotis or saris sewn together with predominantly white thread. Where areas of pattern are required, they are outlined (usually in black chain stitch) and then filled in with running stitch in a different colour. Motifs are of animals, flowers, circus figures, scenes from rural life and even historical figures such as William Shakespeare, Queen Victoria and Lenin.

Opposite: A distinctive ralli *with rows of concentric stitching made by the Sami caste from Sind, Pakistan. Sami quilts are normally worked on a base of one or two strong colours and rely on the contrasting stitching to provide interest.*

Opposite, inset: A cheerful Chinese man protected from the cold by a padded and quilted jacket of a type that has been used in the colder parts of Asia for thousands of years.

Below: A Banjara rumal, *from Madhya Pradesh, India, embellished with cowrie shells. The dense quilting stitches give the cloth great strength.*

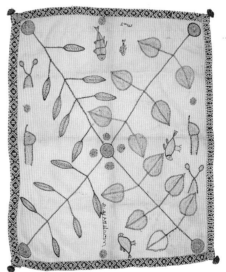

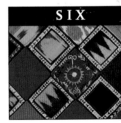

SIX

Top: *A fine* kantha *from Bangladesh. The patterns are picked out with coloured stitching.*

Above: *A* kantha *from West Bengal, India. Although this* kantha *appears quite plain, the background is worked intensively with white-on-white stitches.*

PATCHWORK QUILTS

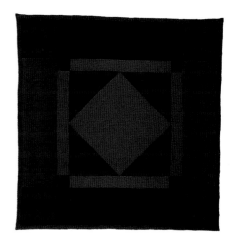

A PATCHWORK quilt is a combination of patchwork, quilting and sometimes appliqué. Warm, functional and attractive, these textiles, traditionally sewn **painstakingly from recycled materials, show the triumph of invention over poverty.**

Technique

PATCHWORK quilts are normally built up from repeated design elements which are made from individual patches, so blocks of these are sewn up separately and stored until all of them are ready. They are then sewn up into the overall pattern and the whole fabric is attached to the filling and backing layers for quilting.

American patchwork quilts

THE patchwork quilt has a special place in the heart of Americans. Introduced by colonists from the British Isles who made a virtue out of necessity, quilts kept the early settlers warm in their log cabins, packed and cushioned the valuables of pioneers travelling west in wagon trains and acted as shrouds for the lonely graves of those who did not survive the trip.

Making up a quilt became a social event, an opportunity to catch up on news, eat, sing and even dance. Women would bring along blocks they had already made and would then collectively join them together and sew the quilting stitches. The motivation for making a quilt was sometimes charitable, but most often marked a coming of age, a wedding or the departure of a friend.

SIX

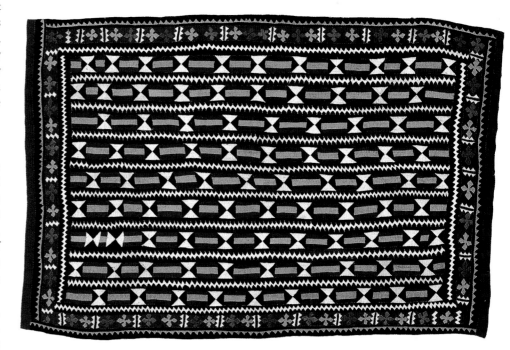

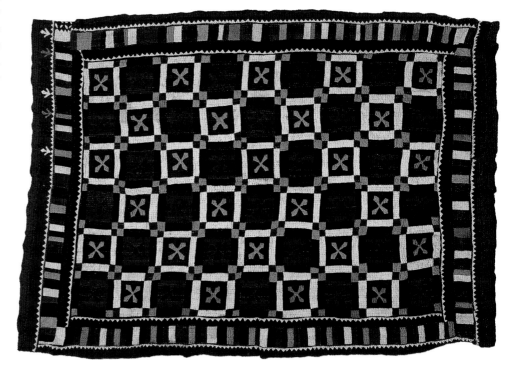

Top right: *An Amish 'diamond in a square' quilt made in Pennsylvania, North America, in 1880. The design is simple and powerful, but the feather-wreath quilting stitches are tiny and intricate.*

Above, centre and right: *Two quilts, from Sind, Pakistan, made by members of the Chauhan caste. The Chauhan use a limited colour range to create patterns with considerable visual impact.*

Above: *A tufted quilt made from patchwork squares by volunteers in Canada for the Canadian Red Cross and intended for use in English hospitals during the First World War. In North America quilting 'bees' have often provided quilts during emergencies.*

Right: *A 'log cabin' quilt made in England in 1890. The 'logs' are narrow rectangles of fabric sewn together into squares. In North America many patterns have developed based on this format. Frequently the square is divided into light and dark sections which, when separate squares are joined, form bold patterns of diamonds, zigzags and squares.*

Designs

OVER the last hundred and fifty years quilters have built up a large repertoire of patterns based on the repetition of certain motifs constructed from geometric shapes. These provide a basic design structure within which the seamstress can improvise. Popular patterns have evocative names like Log cabin, Star of Bethlehem, Tree of Life and Whig's defeat.

Distribution

STRIKING patchwork quilts are made in North-West India and Pakistan using triangles, squares and rectangles of three or four colours sewn in abstract patterns, but the most famous are those created in North America.

Stump work

STUMP work is a form of appliqué in which the applied pieces of cloth are padded out with materials such as horse hair or cotton waste to form designs in high relief. The three-dimensional effect can be enhanced with textural embroidery stitches and couching. The heyday of stump work was in England during Elizabethan times in the second half of the 16th century when stump-work boxes and other trinkets were extremely fashionable.

Above: *Two* kalagas, *from Myanmar (Burma), worked on a central field of black velvet edged with cloth saved from the discarded robes of Buddhist monks. The images of people or animals are padded and embellished with couched cords, glass studs, sequins and metal thread.*

Left: Nariyal, *a part of the wedding paraphernalia in Gujarat, India. It is made from a coconut wrapped in a bead net decorated with good luck symbols such as the swastika.*

Above, right: *Inca stuffed doll wrapped in double-weave cloth.*

Opposite, below: *A 'whimsy' made by Native Americans from the Tuscarora reservation in New York State, North America, in 1890.*

Above: A padded Ottoman horse trapping embellished with gold thread, made in 1897 for Lord Curzon's visit to Oman.

Whimsies

DURING the late 19th and early 20th centuries Native Americans in the Niagara Falls region considerably boosted their incomes by manufacturing 'whimsies'. These were stuffed and padded objects shaped like hearts or high-heeled boots and embellished with crystal glass beads. Their only purpose was decorative and they greatly appealed to *fin de siècle* taste.

Kalagas

IN recent times the most popular form of stump work has been the Myanmarese (Burmese) *kalaga*. Readily available to a wide tourist market in Thailand, they are smuggled across the long-porous Thai–Myanmarese (Burmese) frontier. Revived in the 1970s by aid groups, the centre of the craft is in workshops in Mandalay and Amarapura. *Kalagas* were made originally in Myanmar (Burma) from 1830 until approximately 1880, particularly during the reign of King Mindon at Mandalay, but even then they were partially an export item, though they never really caught on in 19th-century Europe. Myanmar (Burma) is a devout Theravada Buddhist land and *kalagas* are used as temple decorations. They often depict the story of the Buddha's life or feature the protective *nat* spirits or the ubiquitous Myanmarese (Burmese) elephant. *Kalagas* are padded with layers of cotton waste and the designs are picked out in lines of couched cords. Further embellishment is added with sequins and studs of glass.

LEFT: HAUSA
EMBROIDERY ON A
'TWO KNIVES' SHIRT
FROM NIGERIA.

ABOVE: BLUE
H'MONG
EMBROIDERED
APPLIQUÉ COLLAR
FROM SAPA,
VIETNAM.

RIGHT: SATIN-STITCH
SKIRT BORDER FROM
ATTICA, GREECE.

BELOW: GATHERED
SMOCKING ON A
DRESS FROM MEXICO.

EMBROIDERY

EMBROIDERY

EMBROIDERY is the art of using stitches as a decorative feature in their own right. It is very versatile, does not require ponderous equipment like weaving and, unlike weaving where the patterns are perforce linear, curvilinear work is easy to achieve.

TYPES OF STITCHES

THERE are countless stitches in use by embroiderers all over the world, though they are all variations of three basic kinds – flat, knotted, and linked and looped. Flat stitches, such as running, satin and cross stitch lie on the surface of the fabric. Knotted stitches such as French and Pekin knot leave a raised or studded pattern on the surface. The classic example of a linked or looped stitch is chain stitch where the first stitch is held in place by the subsequent stitch.

Above: A peasant girl, from the Czech Republic, wearing festive costume, which includes ribbons, lace, a printed shawl and considerable quantities of floral embroidery.

SEVEN

Right: A Meghwal woman, from Gujarat, India, embroidering a blouse front. In North-West India a large part of a girl's dowry consists of items embroidered by her and her family.

Left: *In the home embroidery is usually done by women, but professionals, like this man from Pont l'Abbé in Brittany, France, have often been male.*

Right: *A Dutch girl, from Leiden, embroidering with a wooden hoop to keep the work taut.*

CHOICE OF STITCHES

STITCHES can be used in several ways to create different effects. They can be used to reinforce and decorate an edge (e.g., buttonhole stitch, blanket stitch and eyelet stitch), to outline a shape (e.g., running stitch, chain stitch or couched threads), to fill an area (e.g., satin stitch or leaf stitch), and finally, they can be used to create texture as is the case with French or Pekin knots.

SEVEN

Above: *Uighur women selling embroidered hats. Embroidered skull caps are worn, on their own or with a turban wrapped around them.*

Above, right: *An Ahir woman, from Gujarat, India, drawing out embroidery patterns.*

MATERIALS

EMBROIDERY can be adapted to an enormous range of materials, but fine work requires smooth, consistent thread and a base with a balanced weave suitable for counting threads. The very finest embroidery is sewn on linen with cotton or silk thread.

RUNNING STITCH

To sew running stitch, the most basic of all the stitches, a threaded needle is quite simply passed in and out, in and out, through the ground fabric, giving the appearance of a broken line. It is a quick, easy stitch and in this form is used to tack two pieces of cloth together temporarily, to quilt layers of fabric together permanently, or to sew linear patterns. Running stitch is used for the decorative elements in the quilted *kanthas* of Bangladesh and Eastern India, and the background is often echo quilted in white on white, in running stitch.

Below: *A detail of the border embroidered around the back of an Akha woman's indigo-dyed cotton jacket from North-East Myanmar (Burma). The simple geometric patterns have been sewn mainly in running stitch, with small amounts of cross stitch.*

Variations

There are many possible variations on running stitch, but it is most often used to make a line, sometimes solid, sometimes broken.

To sew Holbein stitch, a row of evenly spaced running stitch is worked in one direction. The direction of the needle is then reversed and a second row of stitches is worked to fill the gaps in the first row. Holbein stitch is used for embroidering geometric patterns, often in combination with cross stitch, and is the major stitch used in blackwork, an embroidery style employing black thread on a white ground

Opposite, above, left: *A kantha from Faridpur, Bangladesh. A variety of stitches are employed on* kanthas, *but the background is always densely quilted with patterns of running stitch.*

Above: *A cotton coverlet, from Yunnan, China, sewn with white stitches on an indigo background in a crude imitation of Japanese sashiko embroidery.*

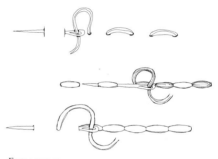

From top to bottom: Running, Holbein, back and darning stitch.

that was at its most popular in England in the 16th and 17th centuries.

Back stitch produces the appearance of a solid line on the surface of the fabric. This is achieved by taking short, 'backward' stitches on the surface and longer, overlapping stitches on the back. Two steps forward, one step back.

Darning stitch (not to be confused with the mending technique) is worked in rows of long stitches with tiny spaces between and is often used as a filler with subsequent rows worked in parallel, staggered like brickwork.

Left and above, right: *Wedding scarves, or* bukhani, *from Gujarat, India, worn by a Hindu bridegroom over his turban. The stylized images of elephants, parrots, flowers and gods are executed using coloured thread, in widely spaced running stitch on a lightly coloured background. Many of the motifs are intended to bring luck and protection to the wearer.*

SATIN STITCH

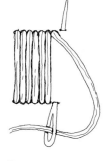

SEWING SATIN
STITCH.

S ATIN stitch is used to sew some of the most beautiful embroideries as it produces a precise, shiny, silken effect, which is replicated on the reverse. Though simple in conception, the stitch requires much patient skill to keep the design even with a well-defined edge. The stitches must also be worked very close together to give the required satiny look. If a padded effect is wanted, the satin stitches can be worked over a base of tightly packed running or chain stitches or even over pieces of ready-shaped card. Satin stitch can be worked horizontally or diagonally.

SEVEN

Above: *Miao woman's jacket from Guizhou, South-West China. The panels of silk and the satin-stitch embroidery sewn onto the shoulders and sleeves identify this jacket as being from the east of the province.*

Above, right: *A curtain, from Rabat in Morocco, with the raised stitching typical of much satin-stitch embroidery.*

Right: *A eunuch, from Shanghai, China, before the 1911 revolution, wearing robes embroidered in satin stitch.*

Technique

THE needle is brought up on the left-hand side of the motif to be embroidered and the thread is carried across the design. The needle is then inserted in the right-hand guideline of the motif and taken under the fabric to emerge just below the beginning of the first stitch. The stitch is then repeated, making sure the stitches lie flat and parallel, touching each other.

Distribution

SATIN stitch is very characteristic of Chinese embroidery, although large areas to be covered or shaded are often worked in long and short stitch, a variant of satin stitch. It is in widespread use, being common in India, the Middle East, Europe, North Africa and Latin America.

Right: *A tensifa,* harem or mirror curtain, *from Tétouan, Morocco. It is made of silk decorated with floral, silk embroidery worked in satin stitch. Silk thread is often used with satin stitch to imitate the smooth sheen of the petals of flowers.*

Below and below, right: *Sleeve panels from Miao women's jackets from Shidong in Guizhou, South-West China. Images of auspicious creatures are worked on these panels using satin stitch in a colour scheme that is predominately either red or blue. Embroiderers buy thin tissue paper templates of the motifs from local women specialists.*

SURFACE SATIN STITCH

SURFACE satin stitch can be used as a substitute for satin stitch. As it is only worked on the surface of the fabric, it is much more economical than satin stitch and is used to cover greater areas. It is not as smooth in appearance as satin stitch because the stitches cannot be placed so close together. Loosely stitched textiles of this type are very vulnerable to wear and tear and are usually reserved for special occasions.

Below: *Square hanging, or chakla, embroidered in floss silk thread by the Mahajan caste in Saurashtra, Gujarat, India. The long stitches catch easily and so these embroideries are often damaged.*

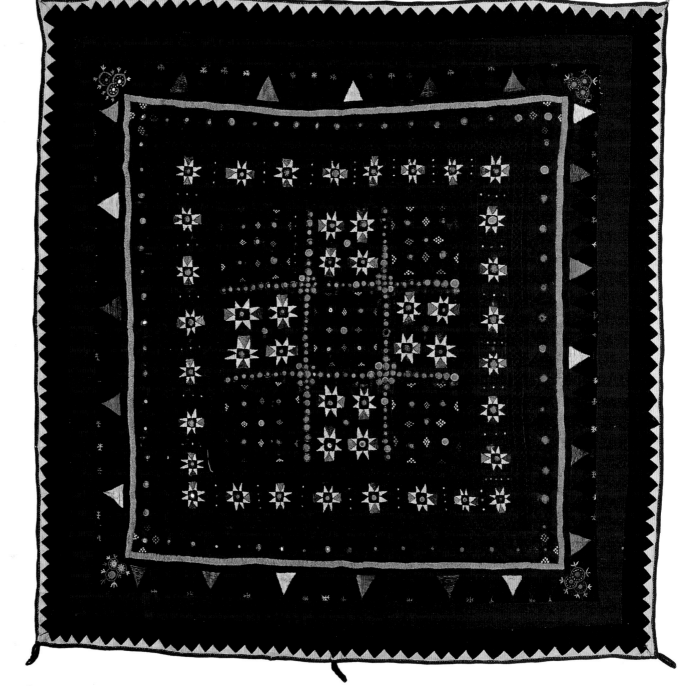

Technique

Fɪʀsᴛ the needle is brought up on the right-hand side of the design outline, the thread is carried across the motif and the needle inserted at the opposite design line. A very small amount of material is picked up, so that the needle emerges just below its entry point. Then the thread is passed over to the opposite side of the motif and another tiny stitch is inserted. This process is repeated until the motif is filled in.

LEFT: SURFACE SATIN STITCH HAS A FLAT APPEARANCE, SINCE IT IS ONLY WORKED ON ONE FACE.

Above: Torans, *decorated with flowers, animals and gods, are made to hang over the windows and doors in North-West India. Elephant-headed Ganesh often appears in the centre. The outlines to be embroidered are frequently printed on with a stamp, but the Kanbi of Saurashtra prefer freehand designs.*

Opposite, far left: *Detail of a* bagh *from the Punjab, Pakistan.*

Right: *A woman's black cotton shawl embroidered with the red silk thread typical of the mountainous region of Hazara in Northern Pakistan.*

Below: *A silk* phulkari *shawl from the Punjab, India. It has embroidery covering so much of the ground that it is called a* bagh, *meaning garden. Yellow and gold are the colours most often used.*

Uses

Oɴᴇ of the most delightful uses of surface satin stitch is in the *phulkari* work of Punjab in the Indian sub-continent. *Phulkari* (lit. flower work) shawls were everyday wear for women in rural Punjab before Partition in 1947. Usually much of the ground cloth was exposed in the border and the field of the shawl, but for festive occasions a special kind of *phulkari*, known as a *bagh*, was made where the whole of the ground was covered with embroidery, so that the base cloth was not visible at all. On the birth of a girl, the maternal grandmother would start to embroider a *bagh*. It would take several years to complete and was embroidered with special care to be used later at the granddaughter's wedding after which it would be kept as a family treasure.

Stitching ran both in horizontal and vertical directions in order to give a variation in texture. It is easy to imagine the effect light, playing upon the smooth sheen of the embroidered surface, would have on these juxtaposed sections of contrasting stitchery.

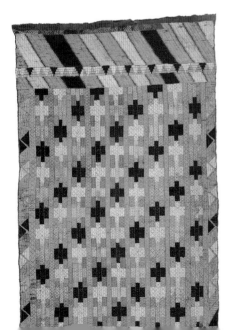

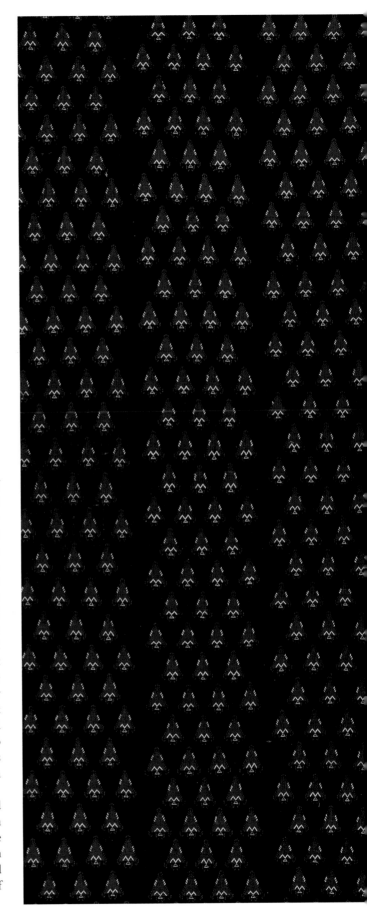

CHAIN STITCH

C HAIN stitch is a very versatile stitch with many variations and is in wide use in many parts of the world. It is often used to define lines or borders and can also be used as a filling and padding when a raised effect is required. It is ideal for linear work, effectively 'drawing in thread', so it is very popular for pictorial work such as the Kashmiri *numdahs* and Persian Resht work.

Chain stitch is one of the most ancient stitches. Examples in silk have been excavated in China and dated to the time of the Warring States period (475–221 BC) and earlier.

Technique

T HE needle is first brought to one side of the material, the thread is held in a loop with the thumb while the needle is inserted and brought up a short space along. The thread is then drawn through the loop, but not pulled tight, and the stitch is repeated by inserting the needle where the thread emerged from the first stitch, thus fixing this first stitch in place. As the stitch is repeated, taking care to ensure that the stitches are even, a chain appears on the surface which will show as backstitch on the underside. Chain stitch can also be worked with a tambour hook or *ari* instead of a needle.

EACH STITCH ANCHORS
THE PREVIOUS STITCH.

Above: *Wodaabe skirt from Niger. This is a superb example of the way in which chain stitch can be used to create flowing, linear designs. Great subtlety can be achieved by embroidering lines rather than solid blocks of colour.*

Uses

B ECAUSE of its ease of stitchery and adaptability, chain stitch is in widespread use, along with its many variants, for the floral, bird and animal representations so beloved in rural communities for clothing and wall hangings.

Variations

O PEN chain is a very common and widely used variation as are double and feathered chain. Detached chain, often called lazy daisy stitch is used for floral motifs. The loops are worked independently and tacked down with a holding stitch. Chain stitch can also be combined with back stitch and when used in conjunction with coral stitch creates a laddered effect.

Above, left: *H'mong embroidery in chain stitch, from Northern Vietnam, using motifs that also appear in the wax-resist textiles of the region.*

Left: *A distinctive Hungarian style of densely worked chain-stitch embroidery known as 'Big Writing'.*

SEVEN

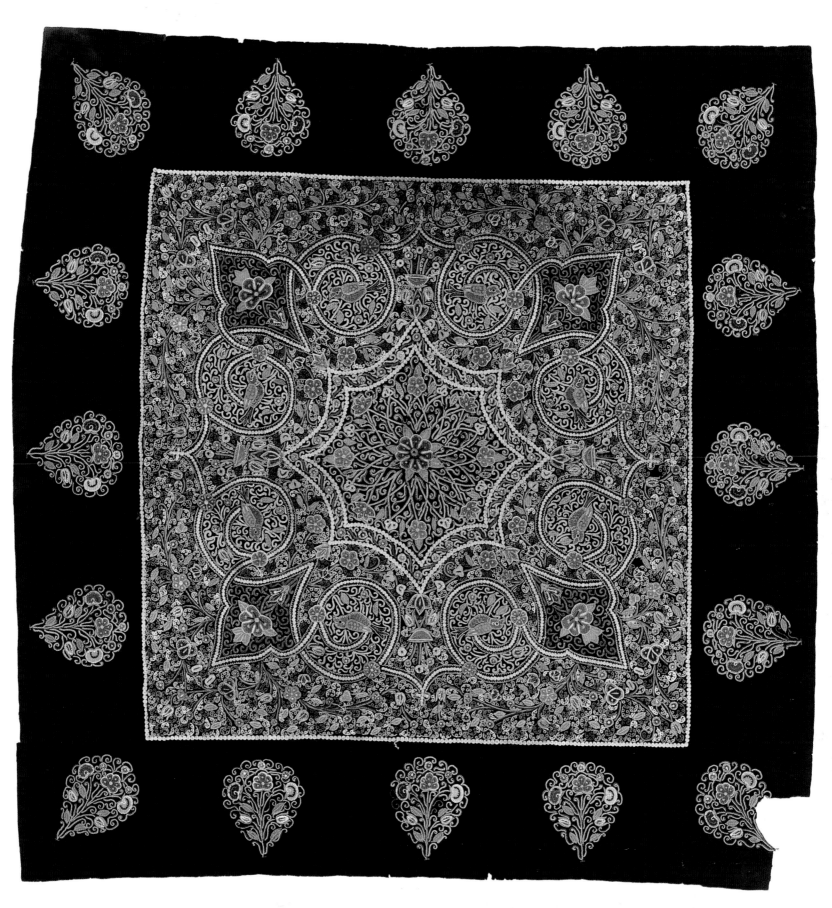

Resht work, from Iran, employing dense chain-stitch embroidery of flowers and arabesques on a ground of felted woollen cloth.

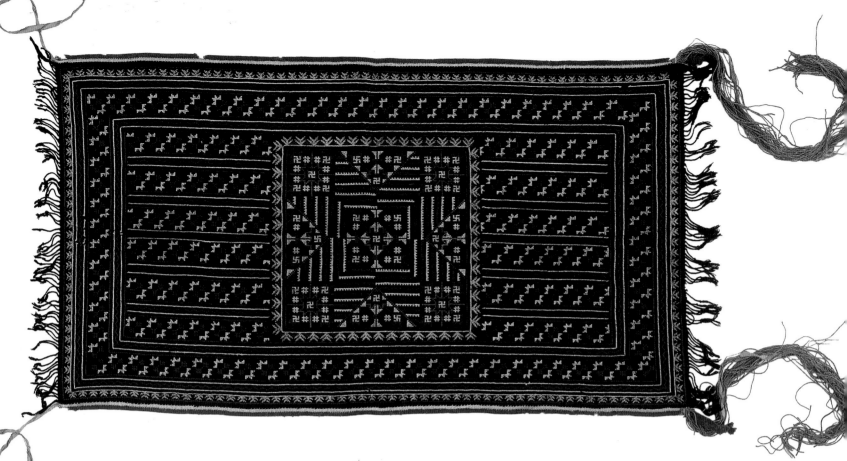

Above: *A head cloth embroidered in cross stitch worn by a Zhao bride from Vietnam. Cross stitch, having a regular, square shape, is used most often for formal and stylized designs or for patterns arranged in rows, as on this head cloth. It is also frequently employed for embroidering patterns that have first been worked out on a grid.*

Right: *Cross stitch is ideal for covering the surface of a piece of cloth as the individual stitches fit so closely together. Here, Sri Nathji, a form of the Hindu god Krishna popular in North-West India, is surrounded by worshippers and a herd of cows on a chakla from Gujarat, India. Cross stitch is a popular medium amongst the Jains of the region.*

Opposite, below, left: *A prize-winning English cross-stitch sampler. In Victorian and Edwardian times, from the middle of the 19th century to the beginning of the 20th, all young ladies were expected to learn embroidery.*

Opposite, above, right: *A Syrian woman's wedding dress, from Saraqeb, decorated with intense embroidery in cross stitch. Almost identical garments are found in Jordan, Israel, Palestine and Sinai, the main identifying feature is which part of the garment is embroidered.*

Opposite, below, right: *A wedding coat, from es-Suchne in Syria, embroidered with patterns of stylized carnation flowers.*

SEVEN

CROSS STITCH

Cross stitch is one of the oldest and most popular forms of embroidery. Amongst the treasures of the Victoria and Albert Museum in London are a set of delightfully naive panels of wild animals stitched in the 16th century by Mary Queen of Scots and her ladies-in-waiting in half cross or tent stitch.

Counted thread work

Many stitches, like cross stitch, are at their best when precise and regular. To achieve this they are often worked on a fabric with an even, balanced weave, such as canvas or linen, so that the threads can be counted and the needle inserted at exact intervals. Counted thread stitches are ideal for needlepoint or canvaswork.

Distribution

Cross stitch is probably the most widely used stitch of all. Ideal for neatly filling large areas with little risk of snagging, it is popular for embroidering clothing and can be found on the dresses of Bedouin women in Syria, Palestine, Israel and Jordan, the shirts and blouses of Balkan peasants and the samplers worked by young English ladies during Victorian times in the 19th century. In the Middle East cross stitch was formerly worked directly onto hand-woven cloth, but today sateen fabric is preferred which necessitates working the cross stitch over a canvas mesh. The threads of the mesh are withdrawn after the stitching is complete.

Different styles

Berlin work, popular in 19th-century England and France, is embroidered on canvas with brightly coloured German wool. Assisi, an Italian form of embroidery, uses red or blue stitches on a linen ground to cover the background and leave the pattern in negative.

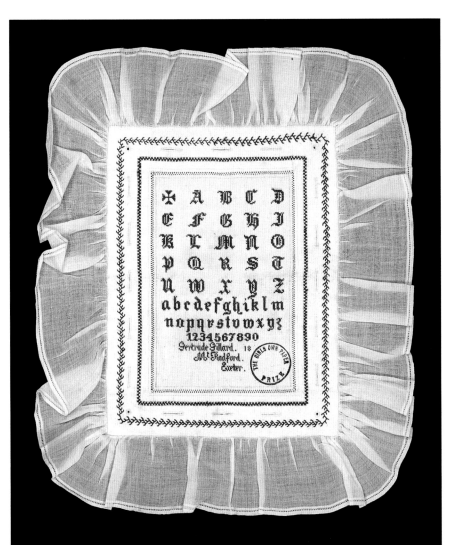

Left: Cross stitch in a neat row of abutting stitches.

HERRINGBONE STITCH

HERRINGBONE stitch, sometimes known as catch stitch or Russian stitch, is a very common variant of cross stitch, and has many variations.

Above: *A chakla,* from Gujarat, India, depicting Hanuman, the heroic monkey god, carrying a mountain in his right hand and a club in his left. The areas of solid colour have been embroidered in fishbone stitch.

Technique

HERRINGBONE stitch has a similar appearance to cross stitch except that the crossing over is not central, but alternates between high and low to give a trellised look. To achieve this, sewing proceeds diagonally up and down, as in cross stitch, but the needle is brought back slightly behind the previous stitch each time so that it will cross over it.

Distribution

HERRINGBONE stitch and its variations are in widespread use. They are amongst the stitches used most frequently by the Bedouin women of Jordan, Syria, Palestine and Israel and by women living in the oases of Western Egypt, both of whom embroider patterns in red floss on their black dresses. Variants of herringbone stitch are very popular for embroidering hangings and skirts in Gujarat, North-West India. Closed herringbone stitch is used in the Hazarajat region of Afghanistan for working bands and borders.

Variations

CLOSED herringbone stitch is built up by densely overlapping the individual stitches and completely covering the background which makes it good for blocking in a band of colour.

Fishbone stitch is usually employed as a filling stitch in leaf or petal motifs where the area to be covered is too wide for satin stitch. It is worked with the cross over in the middle of the motif like a spine. In raised fishbone, each stitch crosses from one edge to the other to give a raised, padded appearance. In open fishbone, the stitches only just cross the spine.

Flat stitch is worked in exactly the same way as open fishbone stitch, but with flatter diagonals.

Above: *An okbash made by the Lakai of North Afghanistan to protect the roof struts of their tents during transportation by pack animals. These bags are most often made from felt or felted woollen cloth with distinctive hooked motifs embroidered in buttonhole or chain stitch which is sometimes outlined, as in this case, with bands worked in closed herringbone stitch.*

Opposite, above: *Embroidered skirt worn by women of the Ahir herding caste of Gujarat, India. The Ahir draw on a treasury of motifs, like the flowers and stylized parrots on this skirt, filling in many of the shapes with large herringbone stitches. The more skilful and patient the embroideress, the more solid the stitches will appear.*

Opposite, below: *The border of a bridegroom's smock, from Ghazni, Afghanistan, embroidered with horizontal bands of closed herringbone stitch. The bands are sewn densely enough to rise above the rest of the embroidery. Red, green or white stitching on a white ground is typical of this area.*

SEVEN

RIGHT: FISHBONE AND RAISED FISHBONE STITCH.

RIGHT: HERRINGBONE AND CLOSED HERRINGBONE STITCH.

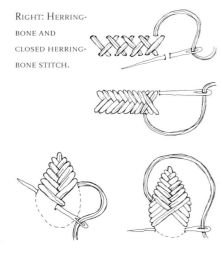

Left: *Red velvet dress, from Kabul, Afghanistan, decorated with military-style metal-thread work.*

Below: *Montenegrin chieftain wearing apparel elaborately couched with gold thread. Montenegro became part of Yugoslavia in 1918.*

184

COUCHING

WHEN threads or cords are laid on a piece of fabric and stitched onto the surface this is known as couching. It is a widely used method of giving emphasis to lines and borders and is often executed with metal thread which is too abrasive for stitching in the normal fashion.

Technique

A CORD or group of threads is first laid in position on the base fabric. A needle that has been threaded with a matching or contrasting thread is then used to tack down the cord at intervals with a series of tiny stitches. The more the design curves, the more frequent the couching stitches will need to be. Sometimes the couching stitches may be worked in a more elaborate stitch, such as blanket stitch or chain stitch, for extra impact.

ABOVE: LAID THREADS ARE HELD IN PLACE WITH STITCHES.

Uses and distribution

As couching is an extremely popular way of decorating clothing, examples can be discovered on jackets, dresses and waistcoats in most parts of the world. The grandeur suggested by couched metal threads has lead to the adoption of the technique for the embellishment of ecclesiastical robes and military uniforms. The couched metal cords of the frogging on soldiers' uniforms was rapidly absorbed into the repertoire of embroiderers from Canada to Afghanistan as a result of the incursion of European imperialists in the 18th and 19th centuries.

Top: *Man's waistcoat, from Pakistan's North-West Frontier Province, with appliqué panels and couched metal-thread braids.*

Above, centre: *A jacket, from Southern Syria, with stylized floral patterns worked in couched threads.*

Near right: *A wide-sleeved dress, from the Red Sea coast of Yemen, with dense couching around the neck and on the central panel.*

Far right: *Palestinian dress panel, from Bethlehem, couched in cotton and metal threads.*

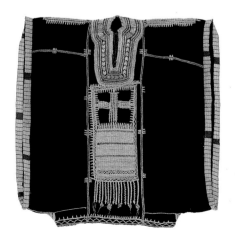

SEVEN

BOKHARA COUCHING

ABOVE: A SOLAR MOTIF IN BOKHARA COUCHING.

IN Central Asia, the walls of the palaces and hovels alike have for centuries been hung with spectacular embroidered hangings known as *suzanis* (from the Persian for needle). *Suzanis* are used to adorn the wedding hall, providing an awning for the bride and groom, and to cover the bridal bed. The main filling stitch for the leaf and petal motifs that predominate in *suzani* work is known as Bokhara couching.

Technique

ACONTINUOUS thread produces the couching effect in this diagonally worked stitch. First the needle is brought up on the left-hand side of the motif to be embroidered and then the thread is carried diagonally over to the right-hand side. The needle is inserted and the thread is drawn through a little to the left and brought up to make a small securing stitch over the long stitch and then brought back to the left of the motif to begin the next stitch. The design is built up by repeating the process, blocking in the whole motif with the successive securing stitches touching and appearing diagonally below each other.

Similar stitches

ROMANIAN couching is similar to Bokhara couching except the couching stitches do not join up to form a diagonal, but are normally placed to form a regular pattern. This stitch forms a good filling for large areas and is employed, for example, on the large panels of embroidered Hausa robes.

Above: *Detail of a very large* suzani *from Samarkand, Uzbekistan. An expert would draw out the design for a suzani on several strips of cloth which were then embroidered independently by different women.*

Opposite: *A suzani, from Uratube in Tajikistan, embroidered in chain stitch and Bokhara couching. Carnations and pomegranate flowers, symbols of fertility, worked in red on white, are frequently the dominant images on suzanis from this area.*

Opposite, inset: *An Uzbek woman standing in front of an Urgut suzani. It has been suggested that the swirling tendril patterns were inspired by Chinese bat's wing motifs, symbols of happiness.*

Above: *A coverlet, from Tajikistan, with stars and flowers worked in Bokhara couching.*

SEVEN

LEFT: THE COUCHING STITCHES FORM A DIAGONAL ACROSS THE LAID THREADS.

Left: *An Uzbek horse blanket, from Afghanistan, with motifs, typical of the region, which appear to be a composite of ram's horns, flowers and sun-wheels. Bokhara couching creates blocks of very solid colour.*

Right: *A densely couched Urgut* fandalik, *from Uzbekistan, for covering the brazier that heats a room.*

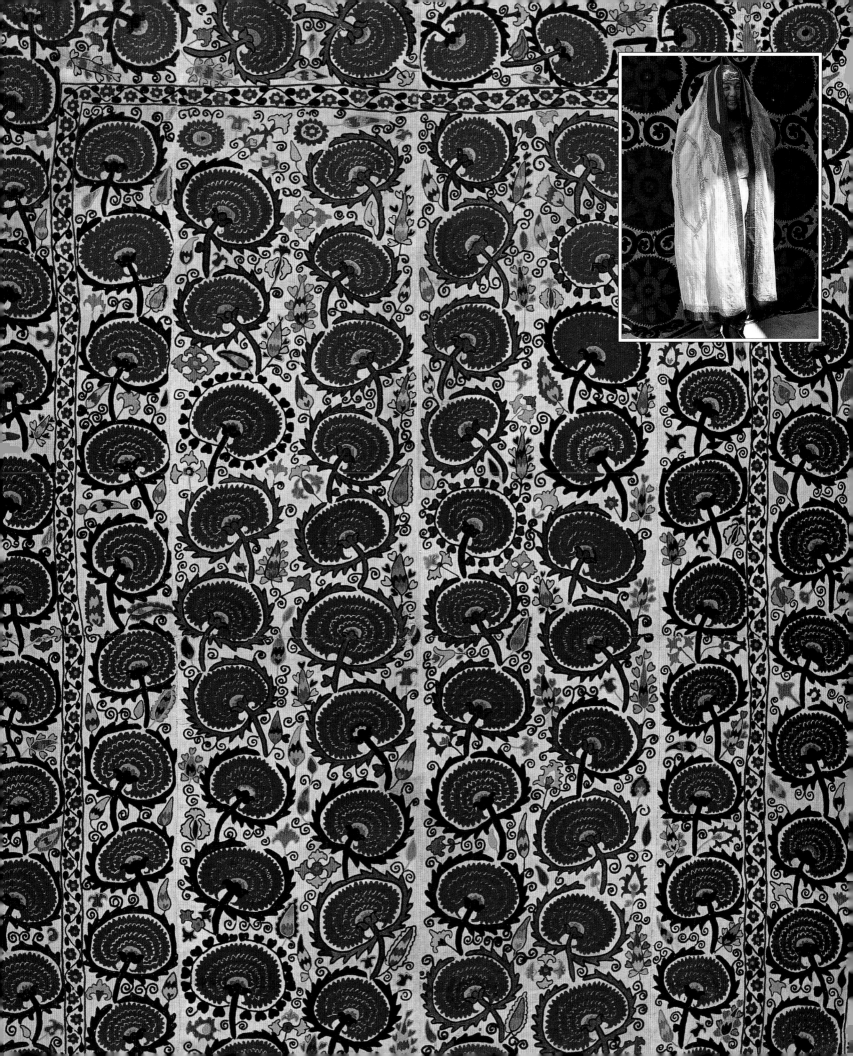

Below: *A Kuba raphia skirt from the Congo (formerly Zaire). The rectangular patchwork panels are decorated with embroidered lozenges punctuated with circles worked in eyelet stitch. Kuba textiles frequently employ a number of different techniques. As well as embroidery and patchwork, this skirt also has patterns in the borders created by stitched dye-resist.*

Above: *An embroidered panel from an aska takwas, or 'eight knives', shirt, from Nigeria, worked largely in buttonhole stitch. The triangular shapes at the top represent five of the knives, the other three are embroidered at the side of the neck opening.*

Left: *Abigah, the son of the King of Lokoja, wearing an 'eight knives' shirt.*

BLANKET, BUTTONHOLE AND EYELET STITCH

BLANKET, buttonhole and eyelet stitch were all originally developed to reinforce edges and holes, but are now often exploited for their decorative value.

Blanket stitch

BLANKET stitch *(below)* is still in common use for strengthening the edges of woollen blankets. A series of stitches are made around the raw edge of the cloth, with each stitch linking through the previous one so that a line of thread is built up that will help prevent the fabric fraying. Blanket stitch is worked, often in wool, with spaces between the stitches. When used as a decorative feature it may be sewn in parallel rows or with stitches alternating between long and short.

Buttonhole stitch

BUTTONHOLE stitch is worked in exactly the same way as blanket stitch except that for greater strength the stitches are packed tightly together, giving it a much more solid appearance. The hole itself is cut after the stitching has been completed. Decoratively, buttonhole stitch can be sewn to make bars, scallops and even floral motifs. Much of the fine, linear embroidery from the Hazarajat region of Afghanistan is worked in dense buttonhole stitch. Detached buttonhole stitch, which is made by working a row of stitches onto a previous row, independently of the fabric, is used for needlelace, raised elements of stump work and the neck decoration of Hausa robes.

Eyelet stitch

ALTHOUGH it is similar in appearance to buttonhole stitch, eyelet stitch *(below)* is used to pull open a hole between the threads of a fabric. In effect, a circle of stitches is worked, but between each stitch the thread is drawn from the circumference through the centre of the circle and back to the circumference to build up a sunburst effect. Algerian eye stitch is worked in radiating stitches with no ring. Eyelet stitches are common in Western Europe, North Africa and the Middle East.

Above: *A Tekke woman's* chyrpy, *from Turkmenistan. The hook and tulip motifs are embroidered in* kesdi, *a variant of buttonhole stitch.*

Below, left: Abocchnai, *or wedding shawl, embroidered in buttonhole stitch with silk thread. Abocchnai are made by or for women of merchant and landowning castes in the Thar Parkar, Sind, Pakistan.*

Below, right: *Panel of a man's shirt, from Ghazni, Afghanistan, embroidered in white silk on white cotton and featuring herringbone and buttonhole stitches.*

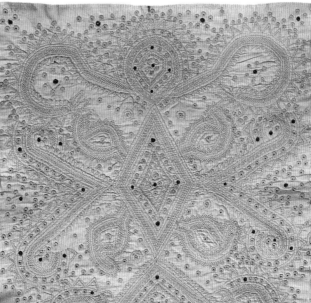

SEVEN

FRENCH AND PEKIN KNOTS

BOTH French and Pekin, or Chinese, knots are raised stitches employed when a textured effect is required. The size of the knot depends on the thickness of the thread and the number of times it is twisted around the needle. The embroiderer must ensure that a needle is chosen that will easily slip through the tightly coiled thread.

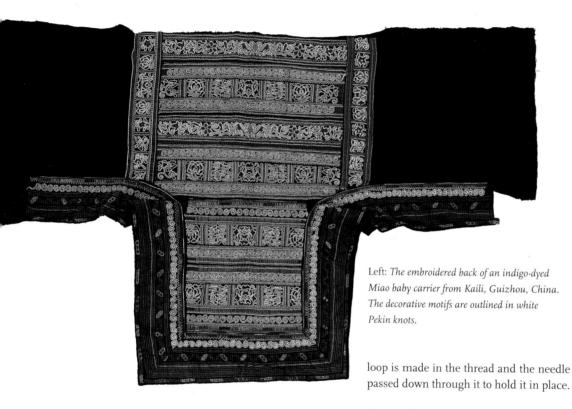

Left: *The embroidered back of an indigo-dyed Miao baby carrier from Kaili, Guizhou, China. The decorative motifs are outlined in white Pekin knots.*

loop is made in the thread and the needle passed down through it to hold it in place.

Technique

To form a French knot, the needle is first brought up through the base fabric and one or two turns of thread are taken around it before it is pulled down tightly once more into the base. Pekin knots have a neater appearance and lie flatter than French knots. Instead of wrapping the thread around the needle, a small

LEFT: FRENCH KNOT.

RIGHT: PEKIN KNOT.

Uses and distribution

FRENCH and Pekin knots are used as filling stitches for relatively small areas such as the petals of a flower, or they can be used singly to provide emphasis, or where a dot is needed in the design, such as for the eye of a bird. Pekin knots are particularly used in South-West China for working linear patterns and outlines, often in white thread, on panels that will later be sewn onto clothing. The designs usually depict flowers, birds, butterflies and mythological creatures such as the phoenix. French knots are more common in Europe, for example in Sweden where knots in woollen yarn are sometimes sewn on hangings and cushions.

Other knotted stitches include bullion, coral and colonial knots.

Above: *A pair of silk-embroidered Chinese cuffs.*

Opposite: *A Miao woman's jacket from Guizhou, China. The bands of pattern, with Pekin-knot outlines, are embroidered on strips of cloth that are sewn onto the garment after completion. Baby carriers are also made in this way.*

SEVEN

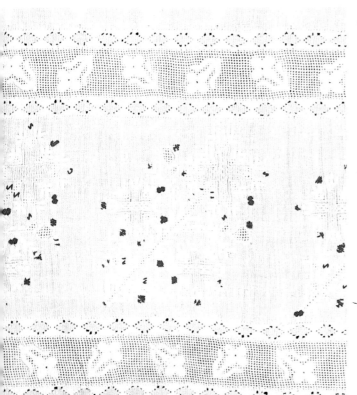

DRAWN-THREAD AND PULLED-THREAD WORK

DRAWN thread and pulled thread are two techniques whereby the structure of the fabric is changed by creating holes. Both techniques are worked on relatively loose woven fabric where threads can be counted accurately. A blunt needle must be used that will not snag on the background threads and the sewing thread must be fine enough not to show, but strong enough to hold the threads of the fabric with no danger of breaking.

Right: A white cotton kerchief, from South Syria, with a border of multi-coloured drawn-thread work. Drawn threads are most often used to decorative effect in borders.

Drawn-thread work

IN drawn-thread work threads of the ground fabric are actually pulled right out. The threads remaining are then pulled tightly together with stitches to create an open, lace-like effect. As this leaves the fabric weakened, the technique is most often used to work margins and borders on decorative items.

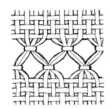

DRAWN THREADS.

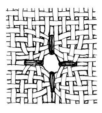

PULLED THREADS.

Pulled-thread work

THIS technique results in a much more durable fabric as no threads are removed. Instead, groups of counted threads are pulled together out of their original alignment by gathering them with stitches, thus creating small holes.

Distribution

TEXTILES worked with drawn and pulled threads are to be found in the repertoire of embroiderers in Europe, Latin America and many parts of Asia.

Opposite, above: A drawn-thread sampler, from Mexico, showing the range of patterns that can be worked in this technique with the introduction of colour.

Opposite, below, left: The end of a Greek towel on which the rectangular border shows the netted effect typical of drawn-thread work.

Opposite, below, right: A Russian pulled-thread towel-end in which ties of red thread have been employed to create a pattern of horsemen.

Left: A textile made in Cyprus in about 1850 in which pulled-thread work has been used to create a geometric pattern of openwork shapes. Some of the solid areas have been high-lighted with satin-stitch embroidery.

SEVEN

NEEDLEWEAVING

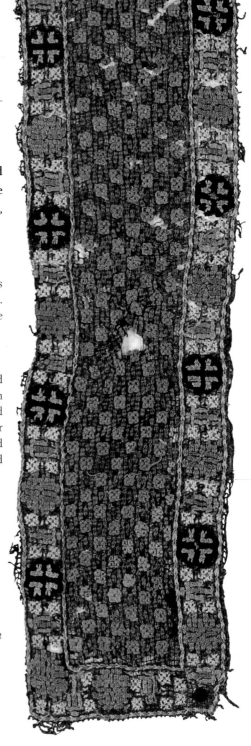

EEDLEWEAVING, sometimes called Swedish weaving, is a variant of drawn-thread work and is used most often to make decorative bands or borders around the edges of linen or cotton cloth. Sometimes, to increase the range of effects possible, the weaving is carried out with thread of a contrasting colour.

Technique

THREADS lying lengthways along the section of cloth in which the border is to be worked must first be cut and drawn. Then the exposed edges are hemstitched which reinforces them and also divides the remaining threads into groups.

Using a blunt needle, or the wrong end of a needle, the top section is worked, weaving two groups of threads together at a time, passing the needle back and forth, over and under.

When all the groups of threads in the top section have been woven in pairs, the work moves down to the next section, and proceeds in the same way, only this time staggering the groups to be woven together.

When working on a large area it is possible to build up openwork designs. With the introduction of colour, quite complex patterns can be produced.

Distribution

NEEDLEWEAVING has been used to decorate shawls and table linen in many parts of Eastern Europe and Russia, most often worked in one colour only. Multi-coloured work can be found in the Middle East, Sumatra, China and even Mexico.

Right: *A decorative border from a Russian cotton towel featuring a checkered field and stylized floral border executed in coloured needleweaving. Needleweaving was also a feature of traditional Russian peasant costume.*

Below: *A cotton border made in England in about 1910. A variety of techniques have been used, including cutwork, pulled threads, drawn threads and needleweaving. The cruciform motifs that appear in diagonal lines at intervals along the textile were worked in needleweaving.*

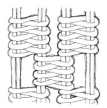

ABOVE: NEEDLEWEAVING.

SEVEN

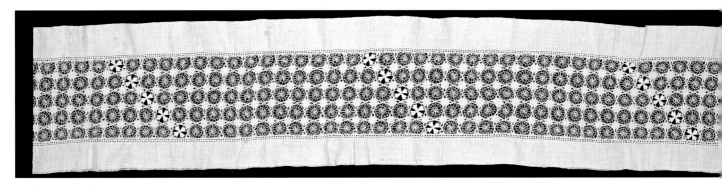

Above: *The end section of a Russian cotton towel. As needleweaving is worked around the warps and wefts of a textile's ground structure, which form a grid, it has often been employed to decorate the ends and borders of textiles with simple geometric patterns of lattices and crosses.*

Right: *A Chinese kerchief from West Sumatra. The ground cloth is an Indian tabby-weave plaid woven in Chennai (Madras) which has been embellished by drawing threads from the border and needleweaving a multi-coloured, abstract pattern of stars.*

WHITEWORK

WHITEWORK is a general term covering a myriad of techniques. The unifying factor is that, independently or in combination, the techniques can all be worked on white fabric with white thread. Whitework may be carried out on an opaque surface, such as linen or cotton, or, for particularly fine work, on sheer fabrics, such as muslin or net.

Above: *A man's embroidered smock front, from Ghazni, central Afghanistan, decorated with an exquisite combination of mirrors and subtle white-on-white stitches.*

Techniques

THERE are three main techniques used in whitework.

Openwork relies on drawn or pulled threads to create holes that will appear dark in contrast to the white ground.

In cutwork, shapes are actually cut into the ground and then hemmed with buttonhole stitch to prevent fraying. Stitches of needlelace are often used to fill the spaces left by cutwork.

Classic whitework employs white stitchery to create heavy or padded shapes which cast grey shadows.

Opposite: A whitework panel from a christening robe sewn in Ayrshire, Scotland, utilizing embroidery and pulled threads.

Opposite, inset above: French women, from Valence, wearing whitework aprons.

Opposite, inset below: A Kabyle girl from Algeria. Whitework creates interest through the use of texture.

Above and below: Two examples of chikan *work from Lucknow, Uttar Pradesh, India. Chikan is a form of whitework using predominately floral patterns on a net of loosely woven cotton muslin. A raised effect is achieved by executing the patterns in a variety of techniques including appliqué, pulled- and drawn-thread work and embroidery.*

Styles of whitework

WHITEWORK has been produced for hundreds of years all over the world and has developed many distinctive styles using different combinations of techniques. Hardanger is a Norwegian style using satin stitch and blocks of drawn threads or cutwork. Cutwork styles range from the dainty holes of broderie anglaise to the floating shapes of Italian reticella in which the amounts of background that are cut away are so large it can often be mistaken at first glance for lace. Styles of whitework sewn on net or gauze include the Scottish Ayrshire, Irish Carrickmacross, Dresden from Germany and *chikan* from the Indian city of Lucknow.

SEVEN

Uses

WHITEWORK has long been popular for decorating cuffs, collars and bonnets. In Europe, the finest work has been reserved for ecclesiastical vestments, bridal wear and christening robes.

NEEDLEPOINT

NEEDLEPOINT, or canvaswork, is very ancient in origin. Sometimes called needlework tapestry because of its similarity to woven tapestry, it is used to embroider figurative designs in counted-thread embroidery stitches that completely cover the fabric on which it is worked.

FROM TOP TO BOTTOM: TENT STITCH OR PETIT POINT, GOBELIN OR GROS POINT, AND CROSS STITCH.

The basic stitches of many embroideries are the diagonal tent stitch, sometimes referred to as petit point, and the longer gobelin stitch, also called gros point. Longer still is the Byzantine stitch which resembles a diagonal satin stitch and is used to cover large areas quickly. Cross stitch is the best known of all needlepoint stitches and many books of patterns fill the shelves of European and American bookshops. The other major stitches are those worked vertically. These include the straight gobelin stitch and the longer Florentine or Irish stitch.

Types of needlepoint

MANY styles of needlepoint exist, among them are Berlin work, which employs tent and cross stitch and wool yarn (the best used to come from Berlin), and Bargello work which uses vertical stitches in patterns of subtly coloured zigzags.

Far left: *English 19th-century upholstery fabric with a textured finish produced by embroidering in a combination of gobelin and tent stitch.*

Near left: *English Bargello work. Bargello, sometimes called flame work or Florentine work, has distinctive patterns of zigzags worked in long or short vertical stitches.*

Above: *Afghan sai goshas embroidered in cross stitch and used for decorating rolled-up bedding during the day.*

Below: *An English Berlin-work bag. In the 19th century the most colourful yarn was dyed in Germany.*

Opposite: *A dress panel, from Hazarajat, Afghanistan, embroidered with silk thread in a densely worked brick stitch. The lozenge patterns and bright colours are diagnostic of the embroideries of this region.*

Materials

FOR centuries the preferred base for needlepoint was linen, but now the most popular base is canvas, a fabric woven mainly from hemp (the Italian for hemp is *canavaccio*). In the West, two different kinds of fabric are used as a base – one, a canvas woven of single threads, the other, Penelope canvas, is made up of double threads. Both come in a variety of fine and coarse grades. Historically, the threads used most often were wool and silk, but cotton has long been in vogue.

Needlepoint stitches

NEEDLEPOINT stitches resemble those used in other embroidery, but they are worked densely and must, therefore, be regular. Canvas is the ideal base for this sort of work as the threads can be counted easily to ensure that the entry and exit points of the needle are precisely spaced.

SMOCKING

SMOCKING is a term originally applied to the technique used in the construction of the linen smock-frocks worn by agricultural workers in parts of England and Wales in the 19th century. These were loose-fitting garments gathered to fit around the chest by means of smocking stitches. The layers of cloth and heavy embroidery on vulnerable places were not only decorative, but also made the smock very hard-wearing. The patterns of stitches employed have often been interpreted as identifying a man's place of origin and trade. Such a garment, frequently made by specialists, could cost as much as a week's wages. Smocks were normally white, although they were sometimes blue, brown or olive green. The stitching was usually the same colour as the base cloth.

Technique

HORIZONTAL rows of dots must first be marked out on a piece of cloth three times the required width. A needle and thread is passed in and out of these dots and pulled tight so that the fabric is drawn into small, vertical pleats (these threads are later removed). A variety of stitches that are either decorative in their own right or pull the pleats out of alignment to form raised patterns of waves, diamonds or honeycombs are then sewn.

Uses

TODAY, in Britain, smocking is most often used on clothing for children as it is not only attractive, but also flexible. Clothing for special occasions, such as Christening robes and party frocks, has often been lovingly sewn for small children by doting mothers.

The use of smocking is also widespread in Europe and the Americas.

Smock-like garments

SMOCK-LIKE garments are found in many cultures. In Nuristan, Eastern Afghanistan, men wear loose, white, cotton shirts embroidered with black thread. The stitches create an amazingly diverse array of vertical bands of pattern between ridges caused by tight stitching.

Above: *A narrow-necked bag from Portugal. Although the embroidery on the bag and handle is comparatively crude, the join between them is beautifully worked with tightly gathered smocking.*

Opposite: *A fragment of a smock, from Gloucestershire, England, with chain- and feather-stitch embroidery on the collar and shoulder and a panel of tight smocking on the chest.*

Opposite, inset: *The last man in Worcestershire, England, to wear a traditional smock, once the distinctive costume of many English and Welsh agricultural labourers.*

SMOCKING IN DIAMOND STITCH.

SEVEN

Left: *A man's smock from the Hindu Kush, Afghanistan. The vertical bands of delicate black stitching pull the fabric into long ridges. Usually the neckline alone is embroidered with pink thread.*

TAMBOUR WORK

TAMBOUR work was developed in the East as a quick method of producing embroidery in a style resembling chain stitch. In the late 19th century it became popular in the West for sewing beads onto fabric.

Tambour beadwork

WHEN the tambour is used for beadwork, the fabric is mounted with the reverse side up. Beads or sequins are threaded on and one by one are pulled up tight to the fabric as each loop is hooked up in the usual way.

Uses

As it is so quick and versatile, tambour-work embroidery continues to be a commonly used method of working linear designs on clothing and decorative textiles.

The Mochi cobbler caste of Kutch and Saurasthra in Northern India, who have been credited with the invention of this technique, use the tambour frame and the *ari* to embroider skirts, blouses and hangings in silk thread on satin. The designs are of parrots, peacocks, flowers and human figures.

In the region around Bokhara, in Uzbekistan, fine, white, cotton textiles, called *suzanis*, are embroidered, often using the tambour, as part of a girl's dowry. These exquisite hangings and coverlets are adorned with subtly coloured trellises of carnations and pomegranate blossoms.

Left: *A section of a silk* choli, *or blouse, embroidered in silk thread with a tambour and hook, by Mochi embroiderers in Kutch, North-West India.*

Below: *A large tambour-work* suzani *made as part of a bride's dowry in the Bokhara area of Uzbekistan.*

Opposite: *Detail of a skirt embroidered by Mochi embroiderers in Kutch, North-West India. It is the men of the Mochi cobbler caste who are professional embroiderers.*

Technique

TAMBOUR comes from the French word for a drum – in this form of embroidery fabric has to be stretched over a drum-like frame. Instead of a needle, a special hook or *ari*, rather like a fine crochet hook, is used to pull loops of thread through the fabric. As one loop lies on the surface, another loop is hooked through it. By repeating this process a chain of stitches is built up which can be made to meander around the fabric according to the desires of the embroiderer. This simple, but ingenious, technique led ultimately to the invention of the sewing machine.

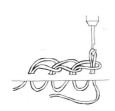

LEFT: LOOPING STITCHES TOGETHER WITH AN *ARI* HOOK.

FAR LEFT: *OYA* BORDERS FROM THE AEGEAN COAST OF TURKEY.

ABOVE: A SHAWL FROM NAGALAND, EASTERN INDIA, WITH METAL AND COWRIE SHELL DECORATION.

LEFT: A *CHAKLA* FROM SAURASHTRA, INDIA, EMBELLISHED WITH MIRRORS AND EMBROIDERY.

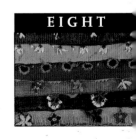

EMBELLISHMENT

EMBELLISHMENT

THE coveting of shells, beads and shiny objects with which to adorn clothing and the body for reasons of superstition or vanity has led to the setting up of trade routes and the establishment of diplomatic relations between many different countries and cultures. Beads and trinkets were the essential luggage of the traveller or explorer for centuries.

SOCIAL IDENTITY

DIFFERENT styles of clothing are often worn as uniforms and are frequently enhanced with signs of rank, whether military, clerical or occupational. Metal thread is very popular for this purpose as it is opulent and eye-catching. Buttons, beads and medallions that glitter and sparkle similarly set the wearer above the common herd suggesting importance, wealth or power.

On a less formal level, humbler objects may be used to identify the allegiance or achievements of an individual – for instance, the scallop shell worn by medieval pilgrims, the white cockade worn by Jacobites in their bonnets or the eagle feathers, awarded for bravery, worn by the Native Americans of North America.

Left: *A Kiowa woman from the southern Plains of North America. Her finery has been embellished with wool and buckskin fringes, tassels, metal concha discs and bead embroidery. On her blouse are seven rows of elk teeth.*

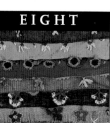

Above: *Chief Ben Charles, a Blackfoot Indian, in North America, wearing a costume featuring a feathered war bonnet and bead embroidery.*

Left: *A Meghwal woman, from the Rann of Kutch, North-West India, wearing a choli decorated with rickrack braid, embroidery and mirrors.*

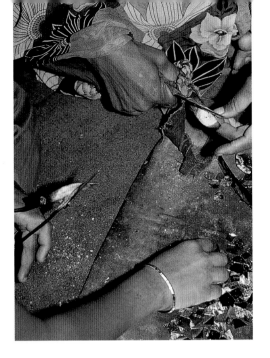

Left: *Using scissors to cut a sheet of mirrored glass into pieces suitable for* shisha *work at Limbdi, Gujarat, India. Shisha or* abla *mirrors are now made at several sites in Gujarat.*

Right: *An Indian beadworker in Rajkot, Gujarat. In India interlooping rows of threaded beads is the most common way of making a beaded structure.*

MAGIC AND SUPERSTITION

MANY objects believed to have magic powers may be attached to clothing to protect the wearer from evil spirits or to ensure fertility. Shiny items such as coins are commonly sewn on to avert the evil eye, while objects with shapes suggesting genitalia are considered to promote fertility and potency. In Central Asia amulets resembling ram's horns are widely used because of their association with vitality and power.

Right: *Detail of the bottom of a cap, from Samokov in Bulgaria. Many materials and techniques have been used to embellish this cap, including fringes, beads, coins, metal chains, shells and buttons. Bits and pieces are often attached to clothing, particularly the hats of children, to give magical protection.*

Far right: *An inhabitant of Mangareva, the largest islet of the Gambier group in the South Pacific. In the South Pacific shells are readily available in many colours and are used in the construction of a wide range of beautifully patterned adornments.*

VANITY

THE desire to attract the admiration of others is as common to every part of the globe as the need to feel beautiful or important. In the cause of vanity enormous amounts of time and effort are expended, cost becomes a minor consideration, anything goes. The search for new and different items with which to adorn oneself has led to amazing invention and creativity – not always with the greatest subtlety.

METAL THREAD

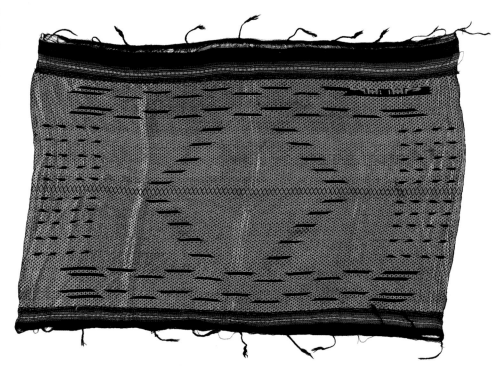

IN many cultures precious metals have a long history of being used to adorn prestigious textiles. Whether for court or religious use, or merely for ostentation, the use of gold and silver threads is used to show wealth and importance on ceremonial occasions.

Above: *Couched metal-thread panel on the back of a jacket from Guizhou, China. The metal thread used here is a long flat strip which means that only angular and not curved patterns are possible. The tassels are also made of metal-wrapped thread.*

Below: *Hama brocade shawl from Syria. A striking effect has been achieved by enhancing the black woven ground with supplementary gold-wrapped threads.*

Opposite, above, left: *The front panel of an embroidered wedding blouse, or guj, from Sind, Pakistan, decorated with spiralling floral patterns of couched, flat metal thread.*

Metal-thread manufacture

TRADITIONALLY, gold or silver is drawn through a series of dies until very fine thread is obtained. This can be hammered flat and either used to embroider as it is, or in ribbon form, in purl, or else wound round a silken core to make thread. Nowadays, in most cases very thin ribbons of shiny base metal or copper-wire silver gilded by electrolysis are wrapped around cotton thread. Plastic may even be substituted for metal.

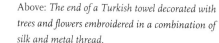

Above: *The end of a Turkish towel decorated with trees and flowers embroidered in a combination of silk and metal thread.*

Metal-thread embroidery

WHATEVER the origin of the metal thread the techniques of embroidery remain the same. Most professional metal-thread work is done by men who, by and large, sew in workshops using a frame as this keeps the fabric taut and leaves the embroiderer with both hands free. Women use metal thread for folk embroidery extensively in the Balkans, the Islamic world, in India and South-East Asia and mainly embroider without using a frame.

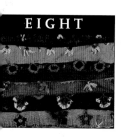

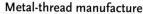

EIGHT

Right: *A tulle scarf made from beaten silver tinsel yarn on a net base, with patterns of lozenges, plants and dancing figures, from Baalbek, Lebanon.*

Right, inset: *A Palestinian woman from Bethlehem wearing a bodice and jacket embroidered with silk and couched metal threads.*

Metal threads are laid on a background and couched down with stitches in a matching or contrasting colour. To add bulk, the metal threads may be laid over a base of cotton threads or even wrapped around a cardboard shape before sewing down. Purl, a very fine, long coil of metal, cut into sections and stitched on like a flexible bead, is often used for borders.

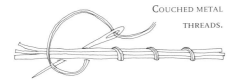

COUCHED METAL
THREADS.

Distribution

METAL-THREAD embroidery worked on costly materials such as velvet, silk and satin is used for vestments and hangings in churches, mosques and temples, and for court costume and furnishings for ceremonial umbrellas and banners and for animal trappings. It is also used in moderation to embellish the dress of the rich and wealthy.

Certain styles originating in the Islamic world have spread to India and South-East Asia and have their counterparts in Christian Europe and Africa. China has its own style of metal-thread work, which has spread to South-East Asia. The New World had no indigenous tradition of metal-thread work, until the Spanish introduced it for church and court use.

Above, inset: *A Rabari shepherdess, from Morvi District, Gujarat, India, wearing a mirrorwork marriage shawl.*

Above: *Meghwal girl's embroidered wedding choli from Sind, Pakistan.*

Right: *A mirrored Rajput toran for decorating a doorway from Kutch, North-West India.*

210

MIRRORS

Mirrorwork embroidery seems to have originated in the Indian subcontinent. The heartland of the technique is the Indian states of Gujarat and Rajasthan and the adjoining province of Sind in Pakistan. All are arid desert areas where water is consequently scarce. The profusion of mirrors, known as *shisha*, used to embellish marriage and festival costume brings to mind the delight the people of this area feel at the sight of light on water. Although the abundant use of mirrors is a result of past trade with Europe (trading ships used shards of mirrored glass as ballast), the original reflective material used in embroidery was pieces of mica which can be found in the Sind desert.

Technique

The mirrored glass made in great spheres at Kavadganj in Gujarat is shattered into hand-sized pieces and distributed to the small market towns of Kutch and Saurashtra. There, women of the peasant and pastoral communities take it home and cut it up with scissors into small, roughly square, circular or triangular shapes.

As the mirrors have no holes through which they can be tacked to the background cloth, they are normally first held in place with two vertical and two horizontal threads. The object is then to hold the mirror firmly and decoratively in place by the surrounding threads. The tension of these base stitches is important as they get pulled towards the edges of the mirror by the top stitching – if they are too loose or if the holding stitches are too close to the edge, the mirror will fall out. The top stitching can be of the *shisha* stitch, buttonhole, herringbone or cretan stitch, but there are numerous variations.

Distribution

Apart from in the north-west of the Indian subcontinent, the technique of mirrorwork is found in a number of other locations, most notably amongst the Banjara people of the Indian Deccan plateau, in Afghanistan and amongst the Melayu people of Eastern Sumatra, disseminated no doubt by trade and migration.

Top: *A mirrored skirt worn by a woman of the Ahir herding caste from Kutch, North-West India.*

Above: *The leg of a pair of drawstring trousers,* salwar, *from Kutch, India, embroidered with mirrors and motifs of peacocks, parrots and flowers.*

Below: *The bodice of an Afghan dress decorated with couched metal threads and mirrorwork.*

DECORATIVE FINISHING STITCHES.

TACKING DOWN MIRRORS.

Above: *A Banjara* galla, *or neck decoration, from South India, decorated with mirrors, embroidery and a cowrie-shell border. The Banjara normally use a muted range of colours in their embroidery.*

Right: *An intensely mirrored* toran *embroidered by the Rabari shepherd caste, from Kutch, North-West India, decorated with stylized flowers, parrots and trees.*

COINS AND SEQUINS

Coins

SINCE money was invented by the ancient peoples of Anatolia coins have been worn as jewelry and sewn onto clothing as a form of decoration. Not only is this a convenient way for valuables to be safeguarded, but it is also a way of displaying one's wealth. Young brides and small children are still often bedecked with coins as in many cultures the sparkling and flashing is believed to confuse and avert the 'evil eye'.

Sequins

THE sequin was a small, gold, Venetian coin in use from the early 17th century. During the 19th century the name was given to small spangles used to decorate dresses. Made of very thin metal or plastic, lighter than coins and more resilient than glass, sequins are an inexpensive way of making a costume or textile eye-catching and glamorous, although, used in excess, the effect can be cheap and tawdry.

Uses and distribution

SEQUINS are normally round with a hole either in the middle or near the edge which makes it possible to sew them onto fabric. Coins, with a few exceptions, need to have a hole drilled in them or to be welded onto a metal loop. Sequins and coins are sometimes sewn on independently, as around the edges of Syrian headscarves, but they are frequently applied like miniature chainmail in overlapping rows. Some of the most common images depicted on the *kalagas* of Myanmar (Burma) are horses and

Above: *A chakla, from Gujarat, India, decorated with plain and coloured sequins.*

Left: *One of a pair of Chinese panels, from Sumatra, which is so densely encrusted with gold thread and gold sequins that it gives a three-dimensional effect.*

Below: *A child's tunic, from Turkmenistan, decorated with talismans to avert evil and misfortune. These include discs, bells, beads, cowrie shells, amulet cases, containing texts from the* Koran, *and two rows of coins.*

EIGHT

Above: *An apron, from Guizhou, China, with densely sewn, multi-coloured sequins.*

Far left: *A woman's cap, from Hungary, adorned with embroidery, tubular beads and sequins.*

Left: *Knitted money pouch, or monedero, from Bolivia, with attached coins.*

elephants which appear metallic due to the way in which they are encrusted with sequins.

One of the most outrageous uses of sequins is on hangings worked in the Karachi region in Pakistan which sparkle as if spangled with whole constellations of stars.

Right: *Spangled wedding hanging, from Karachi, Pakistan, with a base of cotton cloth worked in reverse appliqué.*

Top: *A Balouch juval for storing and transporting a family's belongings. The yarn of the tassels has been threaded through blue beads and seashells.*

Left: *A dress from the Siwa oasis in Egypt. Although Siwa is isolated and a long way from the sea, shells are still a common costume accessory.*

Right: *A Kailash woman's headdress, from Chitral, Pakistan, decorated with cowrie shells.*

214

SHELLS

Since prehistoric times shells have been used for jewelry and the embellishment of clothing. Whether whole, as beads or cut into discs, they have been employed for decoration in virtually every corner of the globe and have sometimes travelled vast distances from their places of origin as trade items. Many different shells have been used, but a few are worthy of special comment.

Cowrie shells

The shell of the cowrie, *Cypraea moneta*, which is abundant in the Indian Ocean, has been used in parts of Africa and Southern Asia as a form of currency for 4,000 years, partly because of its intrinsic beauty and convenient size, but mainly for magical reasons. The aperture of the cowrie is considered to resemble a woman's sexual parts and therefore, according to the theory of sympathetic magic, the carrying or wearing of the shells should ensure fertility. The shape of the shell has also been interpreted as resembling an eye and eye-shaped beads and talismans are considered capable of averting the force known as the evil eye. Cowries are in use on textiles as far from the ocean as Tibet.

Mother-of-pearl

The innermost layer of a shell, the nacreous layer, is made up of many thin coats of crystals. The softly reflective nacre of three shells in particular is so beautiful that it is known as mother-of-pearl. These three shells are the pearl-oyster, *Pinctada margaritifera*, and two univalve shells, *Trochus niloticus* and *Turbo marmoratus*.

Mother-of-pearl is surprisingly tough and can be cut, ground, polished or drilled. Many artefacts have been decorated with it, but its most common use is in the form of pearl buttons which are not only used as fastenings, but are also sewn onto textiles purely as decoration in many countries. They have been employed by such diverse groups as the Pearly Kings of London and the hill peoples of Kohistan in Pakistan.

Wampum

Wampum beads were used by the indigenous peoples of North America as currency four hundred years ago, if not before. Belts woven with different arrangements of wampum were also used to keep records and send messages. The most commonly used shells were the Quahog clam, *Mercenaria mercenaria*, prized for its purple colour, whelks and, in California, the iridescent abalone, *Haliotis*. With the coming of settlers and traders from Europe, wampum were gradually superseded by glass 'pony' beads.

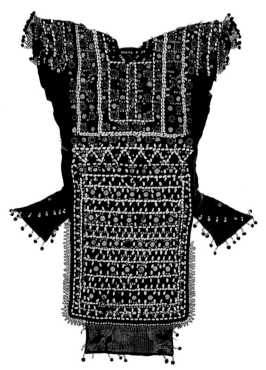

Left: A choli *made by the Chauhan caste of carters from Sind, Pakistan, embellished with mirrors and hundreds of tiny shells.*

Top: A Bilaan blouse from Mindanao in the Philippines. The patterns are made up from hundreds of pearly sequins cut and ground from the lustrous nacreous layer of seashells.

Above: A Banjara chakla, *from South India, embroidered with eye-dazzling zigzag patterns. Banjara textiles frequently make use of cowrie shells in fringes and tassels or sometimes sewn down to form a row or, as on this* chakla, *a rosette.*

EIGHT

215

BEAD EMBROIDERY

BEADS made of stone and animal teeth found at La Quina in France have been dated back to 38,000 BC. The use of beads is found in every inhabited place on earth and every conceivable material has been used in their manufacture including glass, metal, wood, shell, plastic, seeds, clay and resin. Beads are most commonly used for making jewelry, but are frequently used in embroidery or even woven into a form of fabric on a loom.

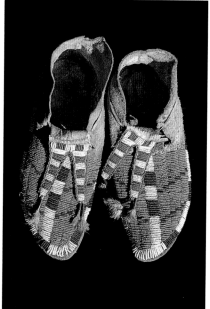

Far left: *A Zulu bead belt, from Southern Africa.*

Near left: *Sioux moccasins made in about 1890. After the arrival of white traders in North America, European glass beads quickly replaced porcupine quills and shell beads as decoration on the clothing of Plains Indians.*

Right: *The beaded cap and waistcoat of a Sarakat shepherd boy from the Macedonian region of Greece.*

Technique

THERE are three main ways to embroider with beads. Firstly, each bead may be sewn on individually by passing a threaded needle through it and then through the backing. The second method is to use lazy stitch which involves passing the needle through several beads before passing a stitch through the backing. Finally, a couching stitch may be used to tack down a thread onto which a number of beads have already been strung.

Densely sewn, bead-encrusted textiles are common in Africa south of the Sahara, Indonesia and Polynesia.

Distribution

GLOBAL disparity in the availability of materials, the development of diverse techniques in different regions and the

BACK STITCH.

LAZY STITCH.

COUCHING STITCH.

vagaries of local taste have meant that beads have been one of the most widely traded commodities of all time. Gold and ivory from Africa, precious stones from India, amber from the Baltic, glass from Venice, jade from the East, lapis lazuli from Afghanistan and many other prized substances have travelled thousands of miles and influenced the rise and fall of empires. Manhattan island, the site of New York City, was acquired from the Mohawk Indians for a handful of trade goods which included Venetian glass beads.

Magic

IN many places the embellishment of a textile with beads is considered to be auspicious. Blue beads in particular are considered good protection against the evil eye and are commonly used as edgings in the Middle East and in Central Asia. Red is the colour of life and red beads are therefore widely used to ensure fertility and vitality.

Opposite: *A panel of embroidered glass beadwork, from Hardanger, worn on the bodice of the Norwegian national costume as shown in the inset.*

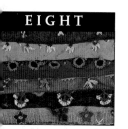

A Bilaan *jacket, from Mindanao in the Philippines, decorated with white beads.*

BEAD WEAVING

A N alternative to sewing beads onto a backing is to weave with them. This
decorative technique is a popular method of working decorative belts and bands
in East Africa, particularly amongst the Kikuyu and the Masai who work mainly with
white and red. This is also how wampum and decorative beadwork was constructed
by the indigenous peoples of North America. It is possible to construct a beaded
fabric purely with a needle and thread, but to facilitate the task a bead or bow loom
can be employed.

The bead loom

A NUMBER of warp threads are strung
on the loom according to the width
required. The frame of the loom is bent
like a bow to keep the warps taut. The
weft is threaded with beads and passed
underneath so that one bead lies between
each pair of warps. Using a needle, the
weft is then passed back through the
beads, but this time above the warps. This
process is repeated, back and forth,
varying the sequence of the beads to build

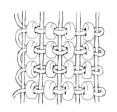

LEFT: LOOM-WOVEN
BEADS.

Above, left: *Mahajan beadwork from Gujarat,
India.*

Above, right: *Woven beadwork bag from Timor.*

Right: *A beadwork sash of about 1900, possibly
Apache, woven in New Mexico on a loom.*

Below, left: *Mahajan beaded* ganeshtapan *from
Gujarat, India.*

Below: *Bohemian knitted beadwork purse.*

up the pattern. Although the structure dictates a geometric arrangement, an astounding variety of representational and symbolic designs can be found.

Other techniques

ONCE beads have been threaded up, it is actually possible to employ a large number of techniques to construct a fabric incorporating them. The ground structure can be woven, netted, crocheted, knitted, looped or knotted.

Above, right: *A Basuto girl in the beaded costume once worn by Basuto and Zulu women in Southern Africa.*

Above, far right: *Two Zulu or Xhosa woven bead aprons from South Africa. Part of the courtship ritual of the Zulus was the weaving of beaded 'love letters' by teenage girls which were given to young men. The arrangement and colouring of the beads was used to convey an allegorical message.*

Below: *Beadwork* bidang *skirts and shellwork jackets worn by Taman women from Putussibau, Upper Kapuas River, Kalimantan, Indonesia.*

Right: *A Kenyah Dyak bag, from Sarawak, Malaysia, beaded with the convoluted monster motifs that appear on weavings, carvings and paintings of the region.*

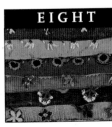

EIGHT

219

FEATHERS

Apart from skins, hides and wool, many parts of animals are used in the construction and decoration of textiles – bones, teeth, claws, hair, beetles' wing cases and feathers. Featherwork is widespread and although it is at its most colourful in the tropical and equatorial regions of the world, such as New Guinea and the Amazon rain forest, where the plumage of birds is most brilliant, the technique is at its most refined in New Zealand and North America. Even in the British Isles, feathers have often been in great demand as a fashion item and in Victorian times in the 19th century the popularity of feather muffs brought about the virtual extinction of the bittern. Today, the threat to bird life continues, for instance, in New Guinea where birds of paradise are endangered because of their beautiful plumage.

Techniques

Large and distinctive feathers have often been used in the construction of headdresses to show status and achievement – as amongst the Sioux Indians of the North American Plains or the Ayoreode of Bolivia, but the more subtle techniques developed by the Native Americans of California include gluing, stitching, appliqué and weaving. The Hupa and Yurok used whole woodpecker skins and glued them to deerskin to make headbands, while in central California individual feathers were sewn together in strips to form bands. The Pomo Indians also made baskets and even blankets in which feathers were incorporated into the structure by twining or weaving.

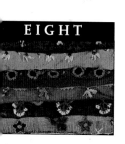
Maori feather cloaks

For centuries the Maoris of New Zealand have woven rain capes from the leaves of *Phormium tenax*, New Zealand flax, which are similar to those made by the Japanese from rice straw. Cloaks incorporating feathers into the borders were sometimes made, but it was not until the late 19th century that they began to weave cloaks entirely covered in the feathers of kiwis and other indigenous birds. These garments are called *Kaha Hururhuru* by the Maori.

Weaving is a secretive process amongst the Maoris and has not only survived the deprivations of colonization, but has also been enjoying a revival along with other traditions including wood carving and the Maori language. A foundation cord is stretched between two wooden pegs and warps are suspended from it. The wefts are then twined from left to right around the warps in a variety of ways, using the fingers. The quills of feathers are twined in as weaving progresses and secured by bending the ends over and twining that in too. An average feather cloak may take a year to make.

Above: A Sioux chief, from North America, and his wife in full regalia, including an impressive, eagle-feather war bonnet.

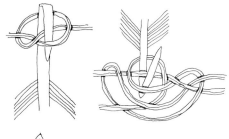

Methods of attaching feathers in Peru (ABOVE, LEFT), New Guinea (ABOVE, RIGHT) AND New Zealand (LEFT).

Above, left: *A Plains Indian eagle-feather head decoration from about 1850, of a type favoured by the Apache.*

Opposite: Kaha Hururhuru, *a Maori feather cloak from New Zealand. The ground structure of this cloak is a weft-twined fabric of* Phormium tenax *fibres.*

Opposite, inset above: *'Te Kawau and his nephew Orokai', by George French Angas, published in 'New Zealanders Illustrated', 1847.*

Opposite, inset below: *Two Maori girls wearing feather cloaks.*

PORCUPINE QUILLS

BEFORE the introduction of glass beads by white traders and settlers porcupine quills were one of the major decorative accessories of the indigenous North American peoples, particularly on the Plains and in the woodlands of the north-east, where the American porcupine lives. The quills, which are usually about two or three inches long, may be dyed before use as decoration for clothing, footwear, pouches or animal trappings.

Techniques

OCCASIONALLY porcupine quills may be woven together, but more often they are stitched onto brain-tanned leather, plaited or wrapped around a rawhide thong. The two latter techniques are normally used for decorating objects and utensils rather than textiles. Traditionally, immediately prior to use, the quills are softened in the mouth before being flattened by pulling between the teeth.

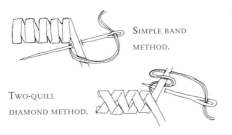

SIMPLE BAND METHOD.

TWO-QUILL DIAMOND METHOD.

Embroidery

THE basic technique used in porcupine-quill embroidery is to sew down the quill and then fold it back to hide the stitch. The quill is bent back and forth and sewn down at each fold. This will produce a texture of bands or zigzags depending on whether the quill is folded back over or under itself. By introducing different-coloured quills at strategic intervals, a geometric pattern can be built up.

Right: A Sioux breast ornament of bone 'hair-pipe' beads, once made from the centre of conch shells. The fringe is made of rawhide strips wrapped in dyed porcupine quills.

Below: The quill-wrapped rawhide fringe of a Teton Sioux pipe bag.

Opposite: Teton Sioux porcupine-quill embroidery on buckskin couched in the simple band method using sinew for thread, North America.

Opposite, inset above: An old Stoney Indian couple from Banff, Canada. They are dressed in buckskin embellished with porcupine quills and ermine tails.

Opposite, inset below, left: A Blackfoot Indian from the reservation in Montana, North America, with quillwork panels and roundel on his shirt.

Opposite, inset below, right: The hood of a Sioux baby carrier, from North America, made in 1860 and decorated with linear patterns of quillwork.

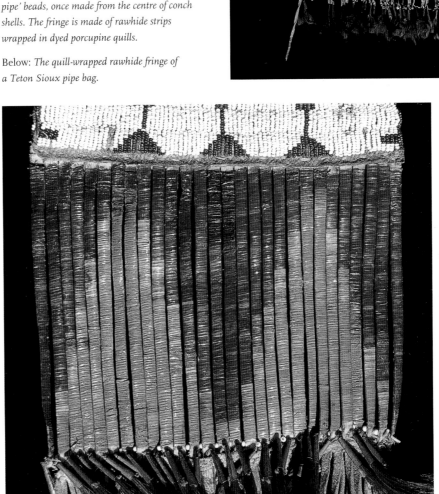

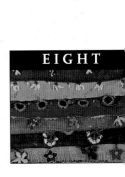

EIGHT

EPHEMERA

WE take many objects for granted, viewing them from a familiar, functional standpoint. It is only when they are taken out of context that we recognize their intrinsic appeal. Items rejected and thrown away in our consumer-based society are often the unconsidered trifles snapped up eagerly in the Third World. The teeth of dismembered zips are considered an attractive edging by the occupants of the Hindu Kush as are British naval buttons and plastic beads, while flattened Coca-Cola cans and bottle tops are much sought after in New Guinea for the decoration of personal attire.

Natural objects

SINCE time immemorial people have bedecked themselves with flowers. Worn in the hair, tucked into a hat or pinned to a jacket, flowers add a touch of passing beauty, and also convey messages of love, availability or, as in the case of Scottish Highlanders before the adoption of specific clan tartans, affiliation to a social group.

Many other natural objects have been exploited for adornment. Some, like seeds such as Job's Tears, may last for years, but others, like the iridescent wing cases of beetles, are fragile and last only a short time.

Above, left: *Scalp, North America, 1850. The Plains Indians used enemy scalps to decorate clothing, weapons and horse trappings.*

Above, right: *Ch'in apron, from Myanmar (Burma), with tassels made from sardine tins.*

Right: *A Siberian shaman, his shirt decorated with metal objects such as bells, coins and nails.*

Below, left: *Woman's* jumlo, *from Kohistan, Pakistan, decorated with embroidery, beads and buttons.*

Magical protection

THE most fruitful hunting ground for incongruous ephemera is on clothing for children, notably in the mountainous valleys of Kohistan in Pakistan. In the attempt to protect the young and vulnerable from evil forces, all manner of talismans may be attached to hats, dresses or shirts and any shiny object, glass, coin or button, may be used to reflect and avert the evil eye. Even the metal medallions from bottles of Brut aftershave have been found sewn on children's clothes.

Right: *A girl's hat, from Yemen, ornamented with beads and metal objects.*

Below: *Islanders, from Nauru in the South Pacific, adorned for the Fish Dance.*

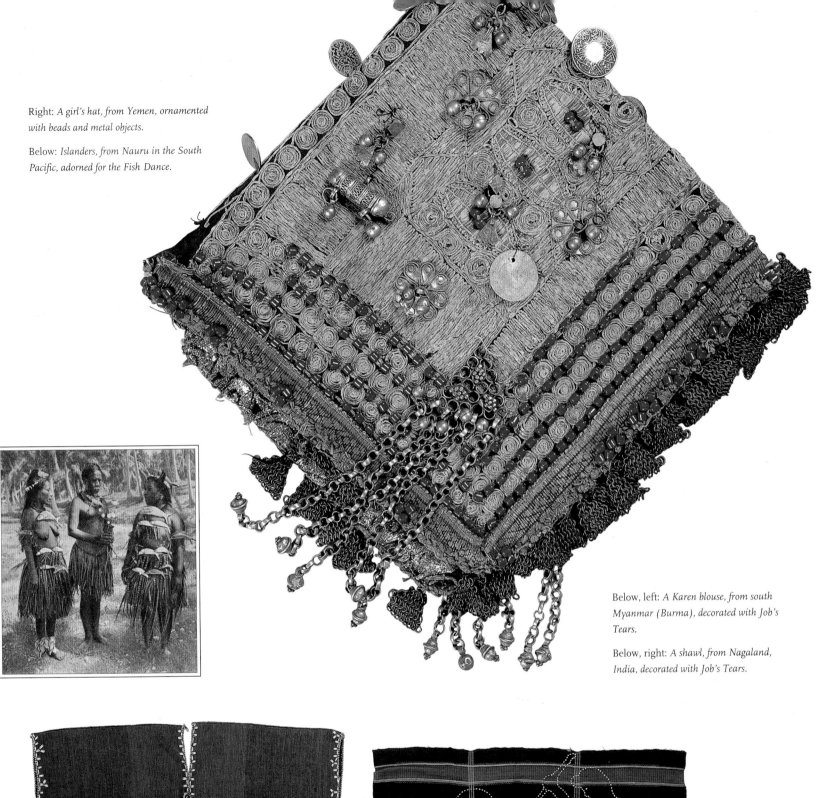

Below, left: *A Karen blouse, from south Myanmar (Burma), decorated with Job's Tears.*

Below, right: *A shawl, from Nagaland, India, decorated with Job's Tears.*

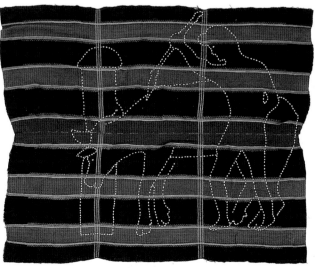

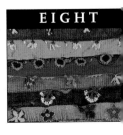

EIGHT

FRINGES

FRINGES have been in popular use for thousands of years and appear in the Babylonian stone carvings of the 8th century BC. In Java they are so popular that the effect is often simulated on the batik shawl, or *selendang*, worn by all Javanese women.

Techniques

WHEN any woven textile is taken from the loom, a fringe of warp strands that have not been bound in by the weft remains. This can be quite attractive, but the weft is vulnerable to unravelling with wear and so more elaborate ways of securing the ends of textiles have evolved. The simplest and most common method is to tie groups of warps into knots and trim the loose ends to the same length, thus creating a row of tassels.

A more sophisticated method is to divide the loose end of each tassel and tie one half to the adjoining half of its neighbour on the left and the other half to half its neighbour on the right. This can be repeated ad infinitum to create a net-like

effect. In Central Asia a more elaborate technique is employed in which the groups of warps are not finished in a knot, but in a braid which is either plaited or worked in sinnet as in macramé. Sometimes these braids are interlaced with each other obliquely and can be extended downwards indefinitely to form a net. In fact, this technique has often been used in its own right to construct bags for carrying spoons and purely as decoration for dwellings and animal trappings.

On occasion, a fringe is considered so desirable that extra threads are added to the ends or sides of textiles and garments specifically for the construction of fancy fringes.

Above, right: *A Montangard loincloth, from Vietnam, with a simple, loose, unknotted fringe anchored by a supplementary weft border.*

Below: *A hanging, from Kirghizia, for the inside of a nomad's yurt with an added fringe of oblique interlacing terminating in tassels.*

BELOW, RIGHT: AN 8TH-CENTURY BC BAS-RELIEF CARVING IN STONE, FROM THE PALACE OF SARGON, DEPICTING AN ASSYRO-BABYLONIAN GENIE IN HEAVILY FRINGED ROBES.

Opposite, above, left: *A nomad's spoon bag from Afghanistan. The whole bag is an open netted structure of interlaced braids with a fringe of cords ending in tassels.*

Opposite, below, left: *This Balouch bag is, in effect, one large fringe with a bag sewn inside.*

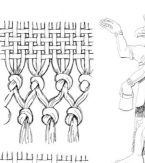

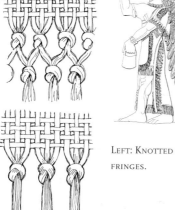

LEFT: KNOTTED FRINGES.

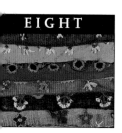

EIGHT

226

Above: *An Uzbek yurt hanging. Suspended from a piece of warp-faced weaving is a loosely netted structure embellished with tassels.*

Right: *A Native American woman wearing a buckskin dress and skirt. Fringes were often cut directly into the bottom of garments.*

EIGHT

TASSELS

THE ultimate extension of a fringe is a tassel – an ending becomes a flourish. A tassel adds a third dimension to a textile. Its swish and sway give the excitement of movement, making it a popular feature of costume and animal trappings.

Techniques

THE simplest form of tassel is made by tying a bunch of warps in an overhand knot.

A more elaborate tassel can be made by knotting a bundle of threads, twice the required length, in the middle, folding both ends down and then tying the two bunches together. The head of the tassel is sometimes enlarged by wrapping it over a piece of cloth or wood.

The pom-pom is a spherical tassel made from yarn. To make a pom-pom two rings of card are placed back to back and yarn is wrapped around both passing through the hole in the middle. When the hole is choked and it is impossible to thread any more yarn through, a cut is made around the circumference so a knot can be tied tightly between the two rings. The card is then pulled off, allowing the yarn to spring out into a fluffy ball. Tassels are often further embellished with beads, knots, embroidery or wrapped cords.

EIGHT

Far left: *Three silk and mother-of-pearl tassels from China.*

Left, centre: *A Bolivian festival bag, from Lake Titicaca, embellished with dangling multi-coloured pom-poms.*

Near left: *Peruvian hair ties, from Cuzco, made from narrow, tightly woven bands with fringes formed from unwoven warps strung with beads.*

Opposite, below, left: *Red Zhao girls, from Sapa in Vietnam, wearing headdresses of woollen tassels.*

Opposite, right, from left to right: *Afghan tassels with wrapped cords and Josephine knots; tassels, from Sinai, with wrapping and beads; Afghan wrapped tassels worn in the hair.*

Opposite, above, right: *An itinerant musician wearing a tasselled leather satchel made by Hausa craftsmen in Nigeria.*

Distribution

TASSELS are used wherever textiles are made, not only to provide a secure hem for a textile, but also as a decorative feature. They are used all around the world on rugs, clothing, bags, domestic decorations and animal trappings. One imposing tassel on its own is sometimes considered sufficient, but frequently a whole mass are used to emphasize the swish and sway of clothing or beasts of burden.

Elaborate tassels are made in many countries, but the most sophisticated are probably those made in China and Japan.

Above: *Three French tassels for embellishing curtains and drapes. The heads of two of them have been exaggerated by tying the cords over a piece of turned wood and building up stitched decoration over the top.*

aba A tunic-shaped dress worn over trousers by Muslim women.

abocchnai Embroidered wedding shawl made by merchant castes in Thar Parkar, Sind, Pakistan, and also Banni Kutch, India.

abr (Persian for cloud) Fabric dyed in Central Asia using the ikat technique.

adinkra **cloth** Fabric from Ghana covered in symbolic designs printed using stamps carved from calabash shell.

adire Yoruba for resist-dyeing in indigo.

adire alabere A West African tie and dye technique in which the dye is resisted using stitching.

adire eleko A West African method of dyeing in indigo in which a resist paste is painted or stencilled onto the fabric.

adjective dye A dyestuff that has to have a mordant to make it permanent.

ajrakh Cloth from North-West India which is printed with mordants and resist paste before dyeing.

aniline dyes Chemical or synthetic dyes derived originally from coal tar.

ari A small notched awl or hook used in tambour work.

babouche Leather slippers worn in Morocco.

back-strap loom A loom that is tensioned by the weaver leaning back against a strap or backrest.

bagh A special kind of Punjabi shawl, *phulkari*, densely covered with silk embroidery.

bandhani Gujarati for tie and dye.

bast Fibre obtained from the stems of certain herbaceous plants.

batik The Javanese method of resist-dyeing using wax.

bidang Tubular skirt worn by the Dyak tribes of Borneo.

billum A bag from New Guinea with a structure of interconnected looping.

binding system The method used to interweave the elements of a loom-woven textile – can be tabby, twill or satin weave.

blackwork Embroidery worked in black thread on a white ground, once popular in England.

bogolanfini Black and off-white 'mud' cloth from Mali.

bolim posh Canopy held over a bride and groom in Central Asia.

bukhani Scarf or sash worn by a bridegroom in Kutch and Saurashtra, North-West India, and Sind, Pakistan.

cable A raised area on a knitted fabric bearing a resemblance to rope.

canting An instrument for drawing batik patterns with a reservoir for containing hot wax.

cap A copper block for printing wax onto cloth during the batik process.

carding The separation and cleansing of wool fibres by stroking them between two blocks covered with bent wire teeth.

cetak The application of chemical dyestuff directly onto sections of yarn as a short cut in the ikat technique.

chakla A square hanging from North-West India.

chikan An Indian form of whitework consisting of white floral embroidery on a net ground.

chintz Printed and painted cloths produced in South India for export.

choli A backless blouse worn by women in Rajasthan and Gujarat, Western India.

chullo A knitted hat from the Andes.

chumpi A woven belt worn in the Andes.

chyrpy An embroidered coat with vestigial sleeves worn by Turkoman women.

'cisele' velvet Velvet on which a pattern is created by the contrast in texture between areas of cut and uncut pile.

combing Method of separating long wool strands for weaving fine worsted cloth.

complementary warp or weft Extra structural elements incorporated into a woven textile to create patterns.

dhoti A length of cloth tied around the waist by Hindu men to form loose trousers.

drawloom A hand loom capable of raising individual warps and therefore suitable for weaving complicated patterns.

dye A colouring agent that soaks into the fibres of cloth or yarn.

end An individual warp thread.

float Where the warp or weft is not woven into the ground weave, but floats across the surface.

galla Embroidered cloth worn over the back of the neck by Banjara women from South India.

ganeshtapan Indian pentagonal embroidered hanging depicting the Hindu god Ganesh.

ger Mongolian nomad dwelling with collapsible trellis walls covered in felt, known in Central Asia as a yurt.

geringsing Double-ikat cloth woven in Bali.

ghudjeri An Uzbek horse blanket made from narrow woven strips sewn together.

gin A mangle used to remove seeds and impurities from cotton.

goncha Woollen robe worn by men and women in Tibet and the Himalayas.

guj An embroidered wedding blouse or dress from Kutch, North-West India, and Sind, Pakistan.

happi Japanese short, cotton coat.

heddle A device for lifting a group of warp ends to open a shed.

hinggi A man's ikat-woven mantle from the Indonesian island of Sumba.

huilpil Short poncho worn by women in Central America.

Jacquard loom An automated system of raising heddles in a programmed order using punched cards.

jamawar A Kashmiri tapestry-weave shawl.

juval A woven bag used for storing and transporting belongings in Central Asia.

kaha hururhuru A Maori cloak covered with feathers.

kain A rectangle of cloth wrapped around the body in Indonesia.

kalaga Padded temple hanging from Myanmar (Burma) decorated with glass, couched cords and sequins.

kalam A pen with a reservoir of felt or wool to hold dye, used in South India to draw the outline of *kalamkari*.

kalamkari A textile, from South India, usually decorated with religious images. The lines are drawn with a pen, or *kalam*, made from a stick with an absorbent wad of cotton bound to the tip.

kanduri Appliquéd cloths given as offerings by pilgrims at the shrine of Salar Masud in the state of Uttar Pradesh in India.

kantha Quilted and embroidered cloths made from recycled fabric in Bihar, West Bengal and Bangladesh.

kasuri The Japanese ikat technique.

katazome Japanese for dyeing with a stencil.

kente cloth Stripweave cloth from Ghana.

khes Double-weave cloth from India and Pakistan.

kilim/kelim A rug constructed in tapestry weave.

kinkhab Silk and metal brocade woven in India.

ladao The copper-tipped 'Chinese knife' used to apply wax-resist in South-West China.

mashru Satin-weave fabric with silk warp and cotton weft.

mechita A Colombian bag made of string.

monedero A knitted purse used in the Andes to carry coins.

mordant A metallic salt which combines chemically with the dyestuff to fix the dye permanently.

nariyal A decorated coconut carried at Hindu weddings.

numdah A Central Asian felt rug.

odhni A shawl worn by women in North-West India and Pakistan.

okbash A bag used by Central Asian nomads for protecting the ends of a yurt's roof poles during transportation.

par A painted hanging depicting the adventures of Pabuji, a Rajasthani folk hero.

patola Double-ikat textile woven in Gujarat, Western India.

phulkari Punjabi wedding shawl decorated in surface satin stitch or darning stitch.

pick A single passage of the weft from one selvedge to the other.

picot A decorative loop on the edge of a piece of tatting, macramé or embroidery.

pigment A colouring agent, usually mineral in origin, that adheres to the surface of a fabric.

pis A cotton kerchief from the Philippines.

plangi (Indonesian for rainbow) The name for tie and dye in Indonesia.

ply The number of spun threads twisted together to make yarn, i.e., two threads twisted together are called two ply.

pojagi A Korean wrapping cloth.

ralli A North Indian or Pakistani quilt.

rawhide Tough, untanned animal skin.

Resht work Chain-stitch embroidered textiles named after the Iranian city of Resht.

retting Soaking plant stems to soften them in the preparation of bast fibres.

rolag Roll or bundle of wool or cotton from which the fibres are drawn out during spinning.

rumal An Indian kerchief or square cloth.

sai gosha Chevron-shaped embroidered textiles used in Uzbekistan to cover bedding when stacked away.

sari A length of cloth worn by Indian women wrapped around the waist and over the shoulder.

sarong An untailored rectangle of cloth wrapped around the waist in Indonesia.

sashiko Japanese textiles quilted with running stitch (also a technique).

selendang A long, narrow, multi-purpose cloth used by women in Indonesia as a shawl, for carrying babies, wrapping shopping and so on.

selvedge The edge of a woven fabric where the weft begins its return run.

serape Central American shawl.

shed An opening between the warps through which the weft can be passed whilst weaving.

shibori Japanese for tie and dye.

shigra Bag, made of interlooped plant fibre, used in the Andes.

shisha Mirrored glass used in Indian embroidery.

sinnet/sennet Macramé cord created by tying reef knots or granny knots around a core of twine.

songket Indonesian brocade woven with silk or metal thread.

soumak A method of weft wrapping used in the manufacture of bags and rugs.

substantive dye A dye that does not require the use of a mordant to make it permanent.

suspension loom A loom where the warps have weights attached to them to maintain the tension.

suzani (Persian for needle) A large embroidered cover or hanging from Central Asia.

tambour A drum-shaped frame used for holding fabric taut whilst embroidering with a tambour hook or *ari*.

tanning Soaking skins in acidic substances to make them supple and prevent decay.

tapa Polynesian barkcloth made from the paper mulberry tree.

tapis Sarong worn by women in Sumatra.

tensifa An embroidered Moroccan curtain.

toran A embroidered door hanging from Gujarat, India.

tritik Indonesian for stitched resist.

tsutsugaki The Japanese technique of applying starch-resist paste through a bamboo tube.

tulis Javanese batik in which the wax-resist has been drawn on by hand using a *canting*.

vertical loom Loom on which the warps are stretched vertically rather than horizontally.

wampum Shell beads made by Native Americans from the North Atlantic coast.

warp The fixed longitudinal elements stretching the length of a woven fabric.

weft The transverse elements of a woven fabric.

weft inlay The process of weaving a supplementary weft in with the ground weft.

whitework A combination of sewing and embroidery techniques using white thread on a white ground.

worsted Fine-quality fabric in which long, combed wool fibres are used.

yurt The circular dwelling of many Central Asian nomads which consists of a wooden lattice and strut frame covered in felt.

FURTHER READING

All of the books listed were published in London or New York unless otherwise stated.

Materials

Baines, P., *Linen Hand Spinning and Weaving*, 1989
Balfour-Paul, Jenny, *Indigo*, 1998
———, *Indigo in the Arab World*, 1992, 1997
Burkett, M. E., *The Art of the Felt Maker*, Kendal, 1979
Burnard, Joyce, *Chintz and Cotton*, 1994
Dixon, M., *The Wool Book*, 1979
Feltwell, John, *The Story of Silk*, Stroud, 1990
Gibson, Thomas, *Feather Masterpieces of the Ancient Andean World*, exhibition catalogue, Thomas Gibson Fine Art, London, 1990
Sandberg, Gösta, *Indigo Textiles*, 1989
———, *The Red Dyes, Cochineal, Madder and Murex Purple: A World Tour of Textile Techniques*, Asheville, North Carolina, 1997
Saul, M., *Shells*, 1974
Scott, Philippa, *The Book of Silk*, 1993

Techniques

Bühler, A., and Fischer, E., *Clamp Resist Dyeing of Fabrics*, Ahmedabad, 1977
Burnham, D. K., *A Textile Terminology: Warp and Weft*, 1981
Cave, O., and Hodges, J., *Smocking: Traditional and Modern Approaches*, 1984
Clabburn, Pamela, *Beadwork*, Aylesbury, 1980
Clark, Hazel, *Textile Printing*, Aylesbury, 1985
Collingwood, P., *The Techniques of Ply-split Braiding*, 1998
———, *The Techniques of Sprang*, 1974
———, *The Techniques of Tablet Weaving*, 1982
———, *Textile and Weaving Structures: A Source Book for Makers and Designers*, 1987
Dyrenforth, Noel, *The Technique of Batik*, 1988
Embroiderers Guild Practical Study Group, *Needlework School*, 1984
Emery, I., *The Primary Structure of Fabrics, An Illustrated Classification*, Washington, D.C., and London, 1980, reprinted 1994
Farrell, Jeremy, *Socks and Stockings*, 1992
Fuhrmann, B., *Bobbin Lace*, 1985
Hecht, A., *The Art of the Loom*, 1989
Heinbuch, J., *A Quillwork Companion*, Liberty, Utah, 1990
Hooper, Luther, *Hand-Loom Weaving: Plain and Ornamental*, 1979
Larsen, Jack, Bühler, Alfred, and Solyom, Garret, *The Dyers Art*, 1976
Leadbeater, Eliza, *Spinning and Spinning Wheels*, Princes Risborough, 1979, reprinted 1985
Morrell, Anne, *The Techniques of Indian Embroidery*, 1994
Nicholls, E., *Tatting: Technique and History*, Toronto, 1962
Oelsner, G. H., *A Handbook of Weaves*, 1975
Puls, H., *The Art of Cutwork and Appliqué, Historic, Modern and Kuna Indian*, 1978
Reigate, E., *An Illustrated Guide to Lace*, Woodbridge, 1986
Ryan, M. G., *The Complete Encyclopaedia of Stitchcraft*, 1981

Seward, L., *The Country Quilter's Companion*, 1994
Stillwell, Alexandra, *Cassell Illustrated Dictionary of Lacemaking*, 1996
Storey, J., *The Thames and Hudson Manual of Textile Printing*, 1974
Swain, Margaret, *Ayrshire and Other Whitework*, Princes Risborough, 1982
Thurstan, T., *Dye Plants and Dyeing, A Handbook*, 1973
———, *The Use of Vegetable Dyes*, Leicester, 1975

History

Anton, F., *Ancient Andean Textiles*, 1987
Clabburn, Pamela, *Samplers*, Princes Risborough, 1977
Coe, R. T., *Sacred Circles: Two Thousand Years of North American Indian Art*, exhibition catalogue, Arts Council of Great Britain, 1976
D'Harcourt, Raoul, *Textiles of Ancient Peru, and their Techniques*, 1962
Geijer, Agnes, *A History of Textile Art*, 1979
Hall, Rosalind, *Egyptian Textiles*, Aylesbury, 1986
Harris, Jennifer, *5000 Years of Textiles*, 1993
Humphrey, C., *Samplers*, Cambridge, 1997
Stone-Miller, Rebecca, *To Weave for the Sun, Ancient Andean Textiles in the Museum of Fine Arts, Boston*, 1994
Thurman, C. C. M., *Textiles in the Art Institute of Chicago*, Chicago, 1992
Volbach, Fritz, *Early Decorative Textiles*, 1969

North America

Amsden, Charles, *Navaho Weaving, Its Technic and History*, 1991
Crews, Patricia Cox, and Naugle, Ronald C., *Nebraska Quilts and Quiltmakers*, 1991
Dockstader, Frederick, *Weaving Arts of the North American Indian*, 1993
Feest, Christian F., *Native Arts of North America*, 1980, rev. ed. 1992
Horse Capture, George P., *Robes of Splendor*, 1993
Hughes, Robert, *Amish, The Art of the Quilt*, 1990, 1994
Oakes, Jill, and Riewe, Rick, *Our Boots, An Inuit Women's Art*, 1996
Smith, Monte, *The Technique of North American Beadwork*, 1983
Whiteford, A. H., *North American Indian Arts*, Wisconsin, 1970
Wien, C. A., *The Log Cabin Quilt Book, Complete Patterns and Instructions for Making All Types of Log Cabin Quilts*, 1984
Wildschut, William, and Ewers, John, *Crow Indian Beadwork*, 1959

Central America

Cordy, Donald and Dorothy, *Mexican Indian Costume*, 1968
Deuss, Krystyna, *Indian Costumes from Guatemala*, 1981
Kapp, Kit, *Mola Art*, 1972
Parker, A., and Neal, A., *Molas Folk Art of the Cuna Indians*, 1977
Pettersen, Carmen L., *Maya of Guatemala, Their Life and Dress*, Seattle, 1976
Puls, H., *Textiles of the Kuna Indians of Panama*, Princes Risborough, 1988
Sayer, Chlöe, *Mexican Textile Techniques*, Aylesbury, 1988
———, *Mexican Textiles*, 1990
Schevill, Margot Blum, *Evolution in Textile Design from the Highlands of Guatemala*, 1985
Start, Laura, *The McDougall Collection of Indian Textiles from Guatemala and Mexico*, Pitt Rivers Museum, Oxford, occasional paper, 1980

South America

Davies, Lucy, and Fini, Mo, *Arts and Crafts of South America*, 1994
D'Harcourt, Raoul, *Textiles of Ancient Peru and their Techniques*, 1962
Feltham, Jane, *Peruvian Textiles*, Aylesbury, 1989
Frame, Mary, *Andean Four-Cornered Hats*, exhibition catalogue, Metropolitan Museum of Art, New York, 1990
Meisch, L. A. (ed.), *Traditional Textiles of the Andes: Life and Cloth in the Highlands*, The Jeffrey Appleby Collection of Andean Textiles, exhibition catalogue, Fine Arts Museums of San Francisco, 1997
Stone-Miller, Rebecca, *To Weave for the Sun, Ancient Andean Textiles in the Museum of Fine Arts, Boston*, 1994
Villegas, Liliana and Benjamin, *Artefactos, Colombian Crafts from the Andes to the Amazon*, 1992

Europe

Bossert, H., *Peasant Art in Europe*, 1927
Cheape, H., *Tartan, the Highland Habit*, Edinburgh, 1995
Johnstone, Pauline, *A Guide to Greek Island Embroidery*, 1972
Kasparian, Alice, *Armenian Needlelace and Embroidery*, McLean, Virginia, 1983
Morris, B., *Victorian Embroidery*, 1962
Proctor, M., *Victorian Canvas Work, Berlin Wool Work*, 1972
Taylor, Roderick, *Embroidery of the Greek Islands and Epirus*, 1998
Wardle, P., *A Guide to English Embroidery*, 1970
Yefimova, L., and Belogorskaya, R., *Russian Embroidery and Lace*, 1987

Africa

Adler, Peter, and Barnard, Nicholas, *African Majesty, The Textile Art of the Ashanti and Ewe*, 1992
———, *Asafo! African Flags of the Fante*, 1992
Carey, Margaret, *Beads and Beadwork of East and South Africa*, Princes Risborough, 1986
Clarke, Duncan, *The Art of African Textiles*, San Diego, 1997
Eicher, Joanne, *Nigerian Handcrafted Textiles*, Ife, 1976
Fagg, William, *Yoruba Beadwork, Art of Nigeria*, 1980
Jereb, James, *Arts and Crafts of Morocco*, 1995
Lamb, Venice and Alastair, *Au Cameroun, Weaving, Tissage*, 1981
———, *Sierra Leone Weaving*, 1984
Lamb, Venice, *West African Weaving*, 1975
———, and Holmes, Judy, *Nigerian Weaving*, 1980
Mack, John, *Malagasy Textiles*, Princes Risborough, 1989
Picton, John, *The Art of African Textiles, Technology, Tradition and Lurex*, 1995
———, and Mack, John, *African Textiles*, 1979, 2nd ed. 1989
Reswick, Imtraud, *Traditional Textiles of Tunisia and Related North African Weavings*, Los Angeles, 1985
Spring, Christopher, *African Textiles*, 1989
———, and Hudson, Julie, *North African Textiles*, 1995
Stone, Caroline, *The Embroideries of North Africa*, 1985

The Middle East

Baker, Patricia, *Islamic Textiles*, 1995
Johnstone, Pauline, *Turkish Embroidery*, 1985
Kalter, Johannes, Pavaloi, Margareta, and Zerrwicke, Maria, *The Arts and Crafts of Syria*, 1992
Rajab, Jehan, *Palestinian Costume*, 1989
Stillman, Yedida Kalfon, *Palestinian Costume and Jewelry*, 1979
Taylor, Roderick, *Ottoman Embroidery*, 1995
Weir, Shelagh, *Palestinian Costume*, 1989
———, and Shahid, Serene, *Palestinian Embroidery, Cross-stitch Patterns from the Traditional Costumes of the Village Women of Palestine*, 1988

Central Asia

Ferrier, R. W., *The Arts of Persia*, London and New Haven, 1989
Fitzgibbon, Kate, and Hale, Andy, *Ikat, Silks of Central Asia, The Guido Goldman Collection*, 1997
———, *Ikats, Woven Silks from Central Asia, The Rau Collection*, 1988
Harvey, Janet, *Traditional Textiles of Central Asia*, 1996
Hull, Alastair, and Barnard, Nicholas, *Living with Kilims*, 1988
Kalter, Johannes, *The Arts and Crafts of Turkestan*, 1984
———, and Pavaloi, Margareta, *Uzbekistan, Heirs to the Silk Road*, 1997
Phillips, E. D., *The Royal Hordes, Nomad Peoples of the Steppes*, 1965
Wulff, Hans, *The Traditional Crafts of Persia, their Development, Technology, and Influence on Eastern and Western Civilizations*, London and Cambridge, Massachusetts, 1966

South Asia

Adams, Barbara, *Traditional Bhutanese Textiles*, Bangkok, 1984
Askari, Nasreen, and Crill, Rosemary, *Colours of the Indus, Costume and Textiles of Pakistan*, exhibition catalogue, Victoria and Albert Museum, London, 1997
Barnard, Nicholas, *Arts and Crafts of India*, 1993
Bühler, Alfred, Fischer, Eberhard, and Nabholz, Marie-Louise, *Indian Tie-dyed Fabrics*, Ahmedabad, 1980
Cooper, Ilay, Gillow, John, and Dawson, Barry, *Arts and Crafts of India*, 1996
Crill, Rosemary, *Indian Ikat Textiles*, 1998
Fisher, Nora (ed.), *Mud, Mirror and Thread: Folk Traditions of Rural India*, Ahmedabad and Middletown, New Jersey, 1993
Gillow, John, and Barnard, Nicholas, *Traditional Indian Textiles*, 1991
Gittinger, Mattiebelle, *Master Dyers to the World: Technique and Trade in Early Indian Dyed Cotton Textiles*, Washington, D.C., 1982
Guy, John, *Woven Cargoes, Indian Trade Textiles in the East*, 1998
Hitkari, S. S., *Phulkari, The Folk Art of Punjab*, New Delhi, 1980
Irwin, John, *The Kashmir Shawl*, 1973
———, and Hall, Margaret, *Indian Embroideries*, 1973
———, *Indian Painted and Printed Fabrics*, 1971
Jacobs, Julian, *The Nagas: Hill Peoples of Northeast India, Society, Culture and the Colonial Encounter*, 1990
Konieczny, M. G., *Textiles of Balouchistan*, 1979
Krishna, Rai, Anand and Vijay, *Banaras Brocades*, 1966
Levi-Strauss, Monique, *The Cashmere Shawl*, 1987
Lynton, Linda, *The Sari*, 1995
Mohanty, B. C., *Brocaded Fabrics of India*, 1984
Murphy, Veronica, and Crill, Rosemary, *Tie-Dyed Textiles of India: Tradition and Trade*, 1991

Nabholz-Kartaschoff, Marie-Louise, *Golden Sprays and Scarlet Flowers, Traditional Indian Textiles from the Museum of Ethnography* [Basel, Switzerland], Kyoto, 1986

Sarabhai, Mrinalini, and Dhamija, Jasleen, *Patolas and Resist-Dyed Fabrics of India*, 1988

Stockley, Beth (ed.), *Woven Air*, exhibition catalogue (of Bangladeshi textiles), Whitechapel Art Gallery, London, 1988

Talwar, Kay, and Krishna, Kalyan, *Indian Pigment Paintings on Cloth*, Ahmedabad, 1979

Zaman, Niaz, *The Art of Kantha Embroidery*, Dhaka, 1993

South-East Asia

Campbell, Margaret, *From the Hands of the Hills*, Hong Kong, 1978

Connors, Mary, *Lao Textiles and Tradition*, 1996

Conway, Susan, *Thai Textiles*, 1992

Fraser-Lu, Sylvia, *Handwoven Textiles of South-East Asia*, Oxford and Singapore, 1988

Gavin, Traude, *The Women's Warpath, Iban Ritual Fabrics from Borneo*, 1996

Gillow, John, and Dawson, Barry, *Traditional Indonesian Textiles*, 1992

Gittinger, Mattiebelle, *Splendid Symbols, Textiles and Tradition in Indonesia*, 1979, 1984

———, and Lefferts, Leedom, *Textiles and the Thai Experience in Southeast Asia*, Washington, D.C., 1992

Haddon, A. C., and Start, L. E., *Iban or Sea Dayak Fabrics and their Patterns, a Descriptive Catalogue of the Iban Fabrics in the Museum of Archaeology and Ethnology, Cambridge*, 2nd ed., 1982

Hauser-Schaublin, B., Nabholz-Kartaschoff, Marie-Louise, and Ramseyer, Urs, *Balinese Textiles*, 1991

Hitchcock, Michael, *Indonesian Textiles*, 1991

Lewis, Paul and Elaine, *Peoples of the Golden Triangle, Six Tribes in Thailand*, 1984

Mallinson, J., Donelly, N., and Hang Ly, *H'mong Batik*, Chiang Mai, 1988

Maxwell, Robyn, *Textiles of South-East Asia, Tradition, Trade and Transformation*, Oxford and Melbourne, 1990

Pastor-Roces, Marian, *Sinaunang Habi, Philippine Ancestral Weave*, 1991

Selvanayagam, Grace Inpam, *Songket, Malaysia's Woven Treasure*, Oxford and Singapore, 1990

Veldhuisen, Harmen, *Batik Belanda, Dutch Influence in Batik from Java*, 1993

Warming, Wanda, and Gaworski, Michael, *The World of Indonesian Textiles*, Tokyo, 1981, 1991

Warren, William, and Invernizzi Tettoni, Luca, *Arts and Crafts of Thailand*, 1994

The Far East

Benjamin, Betsy, *The World of Rozome, Wax-Resist Textiles of Japan*, London and Tokyo, 1996

Faulkner, R., *Japanese Stencils*, Exeter, 1988

Gao, Hanyu, *Chinese Textile Designs*, 1992

Garrett, Valery, *Chinese Clothing: An Illustrated Guide*, Oxford and Hong Kong, 1994

Kennedy, Alan, *Japanese Costume, History and Tradition*, Paris, 1990

Middleton, Sheila Hoey, *Traditional Korean Wrapping Cloths*, Seoul, 1990

Minick, Scott, and Ping, Jiao, *Arts and Crafts of China*, 1996

O'Connor, D., *Miao Costumes from Guizhou Province, South West China*, exhibition catalogue, James Hockney Gallery, W.S.C.A.D., Farnham, 1994

Rathbun, W. J., *Beyond the Tanabata Bridge: Traditional Japanese Textiles*, exhibition catalogue, The Art Institute of Seattle, Washington, 1993

Tsultem, N., *Mongolian Arts and Crafts*, 1987

Wada, Yoshiko, Kellogg Rice, Mary, and Barton, Jane, *Shibori, The Inventive Art of Japanese Shaped Resist Dyeing, Tradition, Techniques, Innovation*, Tokyo, 1983

Wang, Loretta, *The Chinese Purse*, 1991

Wilson, Verity, *Chinese Dress*, 1986, 1990

The Pacific

Clunie, Fergus, *Yalo i Viti, a Fiji Museum Catalogue*, Suva, 1986

Hemming, Steve, and Jones, Philip, *Ngurunderi, An Aboriginal Dreaming*, exhibition catalogue, South Australian Museum, Adelaide, 1989

Kooijman, Simon, *Polynesian Barkcloth*, Princes Risborough, 1988

———, *Tapa on Moce Island, Fiji, a Traditional Handicraft in a Changing Society*, Leiden, 1977

Ling Roth, H., *The Maori Mantle*, Bedford, 1979

Neich, R., and Pendergrast, M., *Traditional Tapa Textiles of the Pacific*, 1997

Pendergrast, M., *Kakahu, Maori Cloaks*, Auckland, 1997

———, *Te Aho Tapu, The Sacred Thread*, Auckland, 1987

General

Faegre, T., *Tents, Architecture of the Nomads*, 1979

Hull, Alastair, Barnard, Nicholas, and Luczyc-Wyhowska, José, *Kilim, The Complete Guide*, 1993

Paine, Sheila, *Embroidered Textiles, Traditional Patterns from Five Continents with a Worldwide Guide to Identification*, 1990, paperback 1995

Thompson, Jon, *Carpets from the Tents, Cottages and Workshops of Asia*, rev. ed. 1988

COLLECTIONS

AUSTRALIA
Adelaide
National Textile Museum of
Australia
Urrbrae House
Fullarton Road
Urrbrae
Adelaide
South Australia (5064)
Collections: Worldwide textiles

South Australian Museum
North Terrace
Adelaide
South Australia (5000)
*Collections: Aboriginal, Oceanic
and South-East Asian textiles*

Canberra
Australian National Gallery
Lake Burley Griffin
Canberra City
A.C.T. (2600)
*Collections: South-East Asian
textiles*

AUSTRIA
Vienna
Museum für Völkerkunde
Neue Hofburg
Heldenplatz
A-1014 Vienna
*Collections: African and
Oceanic textiles*

BANGLADESH
Dhaka
National Museum
Junction of New Elephant
Road and Mymensingh Road
Dhaka
Collections: Kantha quilting

BELGIUM
Antwerp
Ethnology Museum
International Zeemanshuis
Falconrui 2
2000 Antwerp
*Collections: African, South
Asian and South-East Asian
textiles*

Brussels
Musée du Costume et de la
Dentelle
6 rue de la Violette
1000 Brussels
Collections: Lace

Musées Royaux d'Art et
d'Histoire
10 Parc du Cinquantenaire
1040 Brussels
*Collections: European, American
and Far Eastern textiles*

Tervuren
Musée de l'Afrique Centrale
Royal
13 Steenweg op Leuven
3080 Tervuren, Brabant
Collections: Congolese textiles

BOLIVIA
La Paz
Museo Nacional
Calle Tihuanacu 93
La Paz
Collections: Bolivian costume

National Museum of Folklore
Calle Ingani 942
La Paz
Collections: Bolivian costume

BRAZIL
Rio de Janeiro
Museu do Indio
Rua Mata Machado 127
20000 Rio de Janeiro
*Collections: Brazilian Indian
costume*

São Paulo
Folklore Museum
Pavilhao Garcez
Parque Ibirapuera
01000 São Paulo
*Collections: Brazilian folk
costume*

BRITISH ISLES
Bath
Museum of Costume
Assembly Rooms
Bennett Street
Bath BA1 2QH
*Collections: English period
costume*

Bradford
Cartwright Hall Art Gallery
Lister Park
Manningham
Bradford BD9 4NS
*Collections: Indian and
Pakistani textiles*

Bristol
City Museum and Art Gallery
Queens Road
Bristol BS8 1RL
*Collections: Asian, African and
North American textiles*

Cambridge
University Museum of
Archaeology and
Anthropology
Downing St
Cambridge CB2 3DZ
*Collections: Worldwide
ethnographic textiles, including
major holdings of Iban and
Naga tribal textiles*

Durham
Oriental Museum
University of Durham
Elvet Hill, Durham DH1 3TH
Collections: Asian textiles

East Molesey
Embroiderers' Guild
Collection
Apartment 41
Hampton Court Palace
East Molesey
Surrey KT8 9AU
*Collections: Worldwide
embroidery*

Edinburgh
Royal Museum of Scotland
Chambers Street
Edinburgh EH1 1JF
*Collections: European and
Asian textiles*

Halifax
Bankfield Museum
Boothtown Road
Halifax HX3 6HG
*Collections: Worldwide
ethnographic textiles*

Honiton
Allhallows Museum
High Street
Honiton, Devon EX14 8PE
Collections: English lace

Horsted Keynes
The Forge North American
Indian Museum
Horsted
West Sussex RH17 7AT
*Collections: Native American
textiles*

Leicester
Leicestershire Museum and
Art Gallery
New Walk, Leicester LE2 0JJ
*Collections: Indian and
Pakistani textiles*

London
British Museum
Great Russell St
London WC1B 3DG
*Collections: Worldwide
ethnographic textiles*

Horniman Museum
100 London Road
Forest Hill, London SE23 3PQ
*Collections: Worldwide
ethnographic textiles*

Victoria and Albert Museum
Cromwell Road
London SW7 2RL
*Collections: The most extensive
holdings from Europe and Asia*

Manchester
Gallery of English Costume
Platt Hall, Rusholme
Manchester M14 5LL
*Collections: British, Indian and
Pakistani textiles*

Whitworth Art Gallery
University of Manchester
Oxford Road
Manchester M15 6ER
*Collections: Worldwide
ethnographic textiles*

Nottingham
Lace Centre
Severns Buildings, Castle
Road, Nottingham NG1 6AA
*Collections: Costume,
embroidery and lace*

Museum of Costume and
Textiles
43–51 Castle Gate
Nottingham NG1 6AF
*Collections: European and
Asian textiles*

Oxford
Ashmolean Museum of Art
and Archaeology
Beaumont Street
Oxford OX1 2PH
*Collections: European and
Asian textiles*

Pitt Rivers Museum
University of Oxford, South
Parks Road, Oxford OX1 3PP
*Collections: Worldwide
ethnographic textiles*

BRUNEI
Begawan
Brunei Museum
Kota Batu, Banda Seri
2018 Begawan
*Collections: South-East Asian
textiles*

BULGARIA
Sofia
Etnografski institut s muzej
kam Balgarska akademija
na naukite (National
Ethnographic Museum
of the Bulgarian Academy
of Sciences)
ul Moskovska 6a, 1000 Sofia
*Collections: Bulgarian folk
costume*

CAMEROON
Yaounde
National Museum
Direction des Affaires
Culturelles, Yaounde
*Collections: Cameroon folk
textiles*

CANADA
Ottawa
National Museum of Natural
Sciences
MacLeod and Metcalfe Sts
Ottawa, Ontario KIA OM8
*Collections: Worldwide
ethnographic textiles*

Toronto
Canadian Museum of Carpets
and Textiles
585 Bloor St West
Toronto, Ontario M6G 1KT
*Collections: Central Asian and
Canadian textiles*

Royal Ontario Museum
100 Queen's Park
Toronto, Ontario M5S 2C6
*Collections: European and
Asian textiles*

CHINA
Beijing
Museum of the Cultural
Palace of National Minorities
Changan Street
100 000 Beijing
*Collections: Hill-tribe textiles,
embroidery, batik and weaving*

Giuyang
Guizhou Provincial Museum
Beijing Rd
Guiyang
550 000 Guizhou
*Collections: Miao, Dong and
Shwe tribal textiles*

Kunming
Yunnan Provincial Museum
2 May Day Road
Dongfeng St
Yuantong Shan Hill
Kunming
650 000 Yunnan
Collections: Hill-tribe costume

COLOMBIA
Bogotá
Museo Etnografico de
Colombia
Calle 34, No 6–61 piso 30
Apdo. Aéreo 10511
Bogotá
Collections: Colombian costume

THE CONGO (formerly ZAIRE)
Kinshasa
Museum of Ethnology and
Archaeology
Université National du Congo
B.P. 127
Kinshasa
Collections: Congolese textiles

CYPRUS
Nicosia
Folk Art Museum
Archbishop Kyprianos Square
PO Box 1436
Nicosia
Collections: Cypriot folk costume

CZECH REPUBLIC
Prague
Náprstkoro Muzeum
asijskych, africkych a
americkych kultur
(Náprstkoro Museum of
Asian, African and American
Culture)
Betlemské nám 1
11000 Prague
Collections: Asian, African and American textiles

DENMARK
Copenhagen
National Museum of
Denmark
Ny Vestergade 10
Copenhagen
Collections: Greenland, North American, African, Indonesian and Oceanic textiles

EGYPT
Cairo
Arabic Museum
Midal Babel-Hkalk
Cairo
Collections: Islamic costume

Cotton Museum
Egyptian Agricultural Society
Khediv Ismael St
PO Box 63
Cairo
Collections: History of cotton growing in Egypt

FIJI
Suva
Fiji Museum
Thurston Gardens
PO Box 2023
Suva
Collections: Fijian tapa (bark cloth)

FRANCE
Lyon
Musée des Tissus et des Arts
Décoratifs
30–34 rue de Charité
69002 Lyon
Collections: Historical European and Middle Eastern textiles

Mulhouse
Musée de l'Impression sur
Etoffes
3 rue des Bonnes-Gens
68100 Mulhouse
Collections: European and Asian block-printed textiles

Paris
Musée de l'Homme
17 place du Trocadéro
75016 Paris
Collections: Worldwide ethnographic textiles

Musée National des Arts
Asiatiques Guimet
19 avenue d'Iéna
75116 Paris
Collections: Asian textiles

Musée National des Arts
d'Afrique et d'Océanie
293 avenue Daumesnil
75012 Paris
Collections: African and Oceanic textiles

GERMANY
Berlin
Museum für Indische Kunst
Staatliche Museen zu Berlin –
Preußischer Kulturbesitz
Lansstrasse 8
14195 Berlin
Collections: Indian textiles

Museum für Völkerkunde
Staatliche Museen zu Berlin –
Preußischer Kulturbesitz
Lansstrasse 8
14195 Berlin
Collections: Worldwide ethnographic textiles

Pergamonmuseum Staatliche
Museen zu Berlin –
Preußischer Kulturbesitz
Bodestrasse 1–3
Museumsinsel
10178 Berlin
Collections: Worldwide ethnographic textiles

Cologne
Rautenstrauch-Joest-Museum
für Völkerkunde der Stadt
Köln
Ubierring 45
50678 Cologne
Nordrhein-Westfalen
Collections: Asian, American and African textiles

Dresden
Staatliches Museum für
Völkerkunde Dresden
Japanisches Palais, Palaisplatz
01097 Dresden
Collections: Indian and South-East Asian textiles

Frankfurt am Main
Museum für Völkerkunde
Schaumainkai 29
60594 Frankfurt am Main
Collections: Worldwide ethnographic textiles

Krefeld
Deutsches Textilmuseum
Krefeld
Andreas-markt 8
47809 Krefeld
Nordrhein-Westfalen
Collections: European textiles

Stuttgart
Linden-Museum Stuttgart-
Staatliche Museum für
Völkerkunde
Hegelplatz 1
70174 Stuttgart
Collections: Central Asian and Oceanic textiles

GHANA
Accra
Ghana National Museum
Barnes Rd
PO Box 3343, Accra
Collections: Ghanaian kente cloth

GREECE
Athens
Museum of the Greek
Folklore Society
12 Didotou St, Athens

National History Museum
13 Stadiou St, Athens
Collections: Greek folk costume

GUATEMALA
Ciudad de Guatemala
Museo Nacional de Artes
e Industria Populares
Avenida 10 No. 10–70
Zona 1 Ciudad de Guatemala
Collections: Guatemalan folk costume

HUNGARY
Budapest
Magyar Nemzeti Múzeum
(Hungarian National
Museum)
Múzeum Körút 14–16
1088 Budapest
Collections: Hungarian folk costume

Néprajzi Múzeum
(Ethnographic Museum)
Kossuth Lajos tér 12
1055 Budapest
Collections: Hungarian folk costume

INDIA
Ahmedabad
Calico Museum of Textiles
Retreat, Shahi Bagh
380004 Ahmedabad, Gujarat
Collections: The most important holding of Indian textiles in India

Bhuj
Madansinghji Museum
The Palace, Bhuj
Collections: Kutchi embroidery

Calcutta
Indian Museum
27 Jawaharlal Nehru Rd
700016 Calcutta, West Bengal
Collections: Indian and Myanmarese (Burmese) textiles

New Delhi
Crafts Museum
Pragati Maidan, Bhairon Road
110001 New Delhi
Collections: Indian folk textiles and saris

INDONESIA
Jakarta
Museum Textil
Jl. K. Satsuit Tuban 4, Jakarta
Collections: Batik, ikat and plangi

ISRAEL
Jerusalem
Sir Isaac and Lady Edith
Wolfson Museum
Hechal Shlomo
Rehov Hamelekh George 58
91073 Jerusalem
Collections: Jewish textiles

ITALY
Milan
Museo di Arte Estremo
Orientale e di Etnografia
(Museum of Far Eastern Art
and Ethnography)
Via Mosé Bianchi 94
20149 Milan
Collections: Chinese, Indian and Myanmarese (Burmese) textiles

Rome
Museo Nazionale Preistorico
Etnografico Luigi Pigorini
(Luigi Pigorini Museum of
Prehistory and Ethnography)
Viale Lincoln 3
00144 Rome
Collections: Worldwide ethnographic textiles

JAPAN
Osaka
Kokuritsu Minzokugaku
Hakubutsukan
(National Museum of
Ethnology)
17–23 Yamadaogawa Suita-
Shi, Osaka
Collections: Asian and Oceanic textiles

Museum of Textiles
5–102 Tomobuchi-Cho
1–Chome, Miyakojima-Ku
Osaka
Collections: Worldwide ethnographic textiles

LAOS
Vientiane
National Museum
Saysettha District
PO Box 67, Vientiane
Collections: Laotian weaving

MADAGASCAR
Tananarive
Museum of Folklore
Parc de Tsimbazaza
PO Box 434, Tananarive
Collections: Madagascan textiles

MALAYSIA
Kinabalu
Sabah State Museum
1239 Gaya St
Kota Kinabalu
Collections: Dyak textiles

Kuala Lumpur
Muzium Seni Asia
(Museum of Asian Art)
Universiti Malaya
Kuala Lumpur
Collections: South-East Asian textiles

National Art Gallery
109 Ampang Road
Kuala Lumpur
Collections: South-East Asian textiles

National Museum
Jl. Damansara
Kuala Lumpur
Collections: South-East Asian textiles

Kuching
Sarawak Museum
Jl. Tun Haji Openg
Kuching
Collections: Dyak ikat, bark cloth, bead and shell work

MALI
Bamako
National Museum of Mali
Rue de Général Leclerc
PO Box 159
Bamako
Collections: Mali textiles

MEXICO
Mexico City
Museo Nacional de Historia
Castillo de Chapultepec
11580 Mexico City
Collections: Mexican and European textiles

NETHERLANDS
Amsterdam
Tropenmuseum
Mauritskade 63
1092 AD Amsterdam
Collections: Indonesian and South-East Asian textiles

Delft
Nusan Tara Ethnographical Museum
Agatha Plein 4
2611 HR Delft
Collections: Indonesian and South-East Asian textiles

Leiden
Rijksmuseum voor Volkenkunde (National Museum of Ethnography)
Steenstraat 1
2300 AE Leiden
Collections: Indonesian and South-East Asian textiles

Rotterdam
Museum voor Volkenkunde (Museum of Geography and Ethnology)
Willemskade 25
3016 DM Rotterdam
Collections: Indonesian and South-East Asian textiles

NEW ZEALAND
Auckland
Auckland Institute and Museum
The Domain
Auckland
Collections: New Zealand and Oceanic textiles

Wellington
Museum of New Zealand
PO Box 467, Wellington
Collections: New Zealand, Hawaiian and Oceanic textiles

NIGERIA
Lagos
Nigerian Museum
PO Box 12556, Lagos
Collections: Nigerian textiles

PAKISTAN
Karachi
National Museum of Pakistan
Burns Garden, Karachi
Collections: Pakistani folk textiles

PAPUA NEW GUINEA
Port Moresby
National Museum and Art Gallery
Waigini, Port Moresby
Collections: Papua New Guinea costume

PERU
Lima
Museo Amano
Calle del Retiro 160
Miraflores, Lima
Collections: Pre-Columbian weaves

Museo Nacional de Antropologia y Arqueologia
Plaza Bolivia s/n
Pueblo Libre, Lima
Collections: Peruvian folk and historic costume

PHILIPPINES
Manila
National Museum of the Philippines
P. Burgos St, Rizal Park
1000 Manila
Collections: Philippine folk and tribal costume

POLAND
Warsaw
Muzeum Azji i Pacyfiku (Asia and Pacific Museum)
ul. Solec 24
(00–467) Warsaw
Collections: Asian and Oceanic textiles

PORTUGAL
Lisbon
Museu Etnográfico
Rua Portas de Santo Antao
100 Lisbon
Collections: Asian, African and South American textiles

ROMANIA
Bucharest
Muzeul national de istorie al Romaniei (Museum of Popular Art)
Calea Victoriei nr. 12
79740 Bucharest
Collections: Romanian folk costume

RUSSIA
Moscow
Museum of Oriental Art
ul. Obucha 16, Moscow
Collections: Asian textiles

St Petersburg
Peter the Great Museum of Anthropology and Ethnology
nab Universitetskaja 3
St Petersburg
Collections: Asian textiles

Staatliche Eremitage (Hermitage Museum)
Dworzowaja Nabereshnaja 34–36, St Petersburg
Collections: Russian and historical textiles

State Museum of Ethnography
ul. Inzenernaya, 4–1
St Petersburg
Collections: European and Asian textiles

SINGAPORE
National Museum
93 Stamford Road
0617 Singapore
Collections: South-East Asian textiles

SOUTH AFRICA
Cape Town
South African Cultural History Museum
49 Adderley St, PO Box 645
Cape Town
Collections: African, Asian and European textiles

SPAIN
Barcelona
Museu Etnològic
Parque de Montjuic
08038 Barcelona
Collections: Worldwide ethnographic textiles

Madrid
Museo Nacional de Etnologia
Alfonso XII, 68
28014 Madrid
Collections: Worldwide ethnographic textiles

SWEDEN
Gothenburg
Etnografiska Museet
Norra Hamngatan 12
41114 Gothenburg
Collections: African, South American, South-East Asian and Lappish textiles

Stockholm
The National Museum of Ethnography
Djurgardsbrunnsvägen 34
10252 Stockholm
Collections: Worldwide ethnographic textiles

SWITZERLAND
Basel
Museum für Völkerkunde und Schweizerisches Museum für Volkskunde Basel
Augustinergasse 2
4001 Basel
Collections: Asian, African and Oceanic textiles

St Gallen
Völkerkundliche Sammlung
Museumstrasse 50
9000 St Gallen
Collections: European textiles

Zürich
Völkerkundemuseum der Universität Zürich
Pelikanstrasse 40
8001 Zürich
Collections: Worldwide ethnographic textiles

TAIWAN
Taipei
Taiwan Museum
2 Siangyang Rd
Taipei
Collections: Chinese court textiles and Taiwanese folk costume

THAILAND
Bangkok
National Museum
Bamlampu
Bangkok
Thai court and folk costume

TURKEY
Istanbul
Topkapi Sarayi Müzesi (Topkapi Palace Museum)
Sultanahmed
Istanbul
Collections: Turkish court costume

UNITED STATES OF AMERICA
Berkeley
Lowie Museum of Anthropology
Kroebber Hall, Bancroft Way
University of California
Berkeley, CA 94720
Collections: Worldwide ethnographic textiles

Boston
Museum of Fine Arts
465 Huntingdon Ave
Boston, MA 02115
Collections: Worldwide historic textiles

Cambridge, Mass.
Peabody Museum of Archaeology and Ethnology
Harvard University
11 Divinity Ave
Cambridge, MA 02138
Collections: Worldwide ethnographic textiles

Chicago
The Art Institute of Chicago
111 S. Michigan Ave at Adams St
Chicago, IL 60603-6110
Collections: Chinese, Greek and Turkish textiles

Field Museum of Natural History
Roosevelt Rd at Lake Shore Drive, Chicago, IL 60605
Collections: Worldwide ethnographic textiles

Cincinnati
Cincinnati Art Museum
Eden Park
Cincinnati, OH 45202-1596
Collections: Asian textiles

Cleveland
The Cleveland Museum of Art
11150 East Boulevard
Cleveland, OH 44106
Collections: European, North American and Asian textiles

Denver
The Denver Art Museum
100 West 14th Ave, Parkway
Denver, CO 80204
Collections: European, North American and Asian textiles

Detroit
The Detroit Institute of Arts
5200 Woodward Ave
Detroit, MI 48202
Collections: European and Asian textiles

Indianapolis
Indianapolis Museum of Art
1200 West 38 St
Indianapolis, IN 46208
Collections: Asian textiles

La Jolla
Mingei International
Museum of Folk Art
4405 La Jolla, CA 92037
*Collections: Worldwide
ethnographic textiles*

Los Angeles
Fowler Museum of Cultural
History
University of California
405 Hilgard Ave
Los Angeles, CA 90024
*Collections: Reserve collection of
worldwide ethnographic textiles*

Los Angeles County Museum
of Art
5905 Wilshire Boulevard
Los Angeles, CA 90036
Collections: Asian textiles

Newark
The Newark Museum
49 Washington St
Newark, NJ 07101-0540
*Collections: Asian and African
textiles*

New York City
American Museum of Natural
History
79th St and Central Park West
New York, NY 10024
*Collections: African and
American textiles*

The Brooklyn Museum
200 Eastern Parkway
New York, NY 11238-6052
*Collections: Worldwide
ethnographic textiles*

Cooper-Hewitt National
Museum of Design
Smithsonian Institution
5th Ave at 91st St
New York, NY 10128
*Collections: Asian and
European textiles*

The Metropolitan Museum
of Art
1000 Fifth Avenue
New York, NY 10028
*Collections: Worldwide
ethnographic textiles*

Philadelphia
Philadelphia Museum of Art
26th St and Benjamin
Franklin Parkway
Philadelphia, PA 19130
*Collections: European and
Asian textiles*

Salem
Peabody Essex Museum
East India Square
Salem, MA 01970
Collections: Asian textiles

San Francisco
The Fine Arts Museums of
San Francisco
M.H. de Young Memorial
Museum
Golden Gate Park
San Francisco, CA 94118
*Collections: Asian and
European textiles*

Santa Fe
Museum of International
Folk Art
706 Camino Lejo
Santa Fe, NM 87505
*Collections: Central American,
South American and Asian
textiles*

Seattle
Historic Costume and Textile
Collections
University of Washington
Seattle, WA 98105
*Collections: Italian and Balkan
textiles*

National Museum of Natural
History
Seattle Art Museum
Volunteer Park
Seattle, WA 98122
*Collections: African and Asian
textiles*

Washington
National Museum of Natural
History
10th St and Constitution Ave,
N.W
Washington, DC 20560
*Collections: Worldwide
ethnographic textiles*

Textile Museum
2320 S Street, N.W
Washington, DC 20008
*Collections: Reserve collection of
worldwide ethnographic textiles*

SOURCES OF ILLUSTRATIONS

The following abbreviations have been used: *a*, above; *b*, below; *c*, centre; *i*, inset; *l*, left; *m*, main picture; *r*, right; *t*, top.

All drawings are by Bryan Sentance

All studio photography is by James Austin unless otherwise stated.

Janet Anderson, 27*ar*, 207*bl*; Elizabeth Andrews 206*bl*; Auckland War Museum, New Zealand, 221*ia*; Jenny Balfour-Paul, 118*bl*; Nicholas Barnard, 43*br*, 102*bl*, 119*cr*; Brian Brake, 221*m*; Ilay Cooper, 210*i*; Sian Davies, 30*b*, 31*al*, 70*l*, 75*l*, 107*a*, 107*b*, 110*br*, 122*br*, 143*ar*, 144*al*, 144*bl*, 162*m*, 177*bl*, 205*ar*, 224*tr*, 225*br*; Barry Dawson, 37*c*, 67*b*, 68*a*, 85*bc*, 85*br*, 108, 112*ar*, 113*b*, 119*tr*, 119*cl*, 119*bl*, 119*br*, 135*br*, 136*ar*, 136*bl*, 166*bl*; Mark Farrell, 120*bl*, 228*bl*; John Gillow, 5, 43*bl*, 68*bl*, 69*b*, 103*a*, 103*c*, 103*bl*, 103*br*, 118*al*, 118*r*, 123*al*, 128*ar*, 131*br*, 141*ib*, 148*cr*, 158*il*, 171*bl*, 187*i*, 219*bl*; Nicky Grist, 22*bl*; Caroline Hart, 102*br*; Iles photo, New Zealand, 221*ib*; India Office Library, 18*bl*; Sheila Paine, 197*c*, 197*bl*; Jennie Parry, 170*r*, 171*br*, 207*al*, 207*ar*; Herta Puls, 148*br*, 155*i*; Bryan Sentance, 59*tr*, 83*al*, 83*ar*, 83*bl*, 83*br*, 91*br*, 104*al*, 106*al*, 122*al*, 137*t*, 147*b*, 167*b*, 216*ac*, 218*br*, 220*l*, 222*m*, 222*ir*, 223*al*, 223*b*, 224*al*; Ron Simpson, 164*tr*; Ian Skelton, 112*l*, 202*al*; South Australia Museum, Adelaide, 21*br*; Roddy Taylor, 167*a*, 193*b*, 204; Andrew Turner, 82*l*, 82*r*; Janet Willoughby, 68*br*.

ACKNOWLEDGMENTS

We should like to thank the following for their kind help, for the loan of textiles and photographs and for their advice: Janet Anderson, Elizabeth Andrews, Tim and Ferelith Ashfield, The Auckland Museum, James Austin, Jenny Balfour-Paul, Nicholas Barnard, Ishwar Singh Batti, Ave and Beryl Behrens and Patrick Watson, Dawn Berry, Virginia Bond, Bungo, Mrs Muriel Cass, Peter and Elizabeth Collingwood, Ilay Cooper, Dennis Cope, Caroline Crabtree, Anna Crutchley, Kate Crisp, Barry Dawson, Marjolien and Tony Dibden and family, Joyce Doel, Eve Eckstein, Dave Edmonds, Mark Farrell, Rosie Feesey, Rosie Ford, Jim and Diane Gaffney, Polly Gillow, Seth Gillow, Nicky Grist, Lindsay Hardingham, Peggy Harper, Caroline Hart, Janet Harvey, Sally Hirons, Molly Hogg, C. J. Howlett-Jones and Emma Hubbard, Hiroko Iwatate, Anthea Jarvis, Jessica King, Heidi Kleinschmidt, Raymond Lau, Sue Leighton-White, Alysn Midgelow-Marsden, Claudia Mills, Anne Morrell, Colleen and Bill Morrow, Lucy Moss, Sein Win Myint, Roger Neich, Deryn O'Connor, Sheila Paine, Jane Page, Michael Pak, Dave and Carolyn Phillips, Herta and Oscar Puls, Benonia Puplampu, Barbie Rich and Toshio Okomura, Clare Rose, Alan and Joan Sentance, Paul and Christine Sentance, Ron Simpson, John Smith, Rupert Smith, South Australia Museum, the late Montse Stanley, Marsha Stanyukovich, Christine Sterne, Caroline Stone, the late Marianne Straub, Karun Thakar and Roy Short, Judy and Andrew Taylor, Roddy Taylor, Goodie Vohra, Peter Wallin, Janet Willoughby, Marina Yedigaroff, Ann-Marie Young and once again Alastair Hull for the use of his photographic facilities and Jennie Parry for so thoroughly investigating the techniques of Chinese braid embroidery upon whose original research that section of this book is based. We are much indebted to them all and to the nameless craftsmen and women from all over the globe who created the wonderful textiles that illustrate this book.

INDEX

239